IMAGES
of America

GULF COUNTY

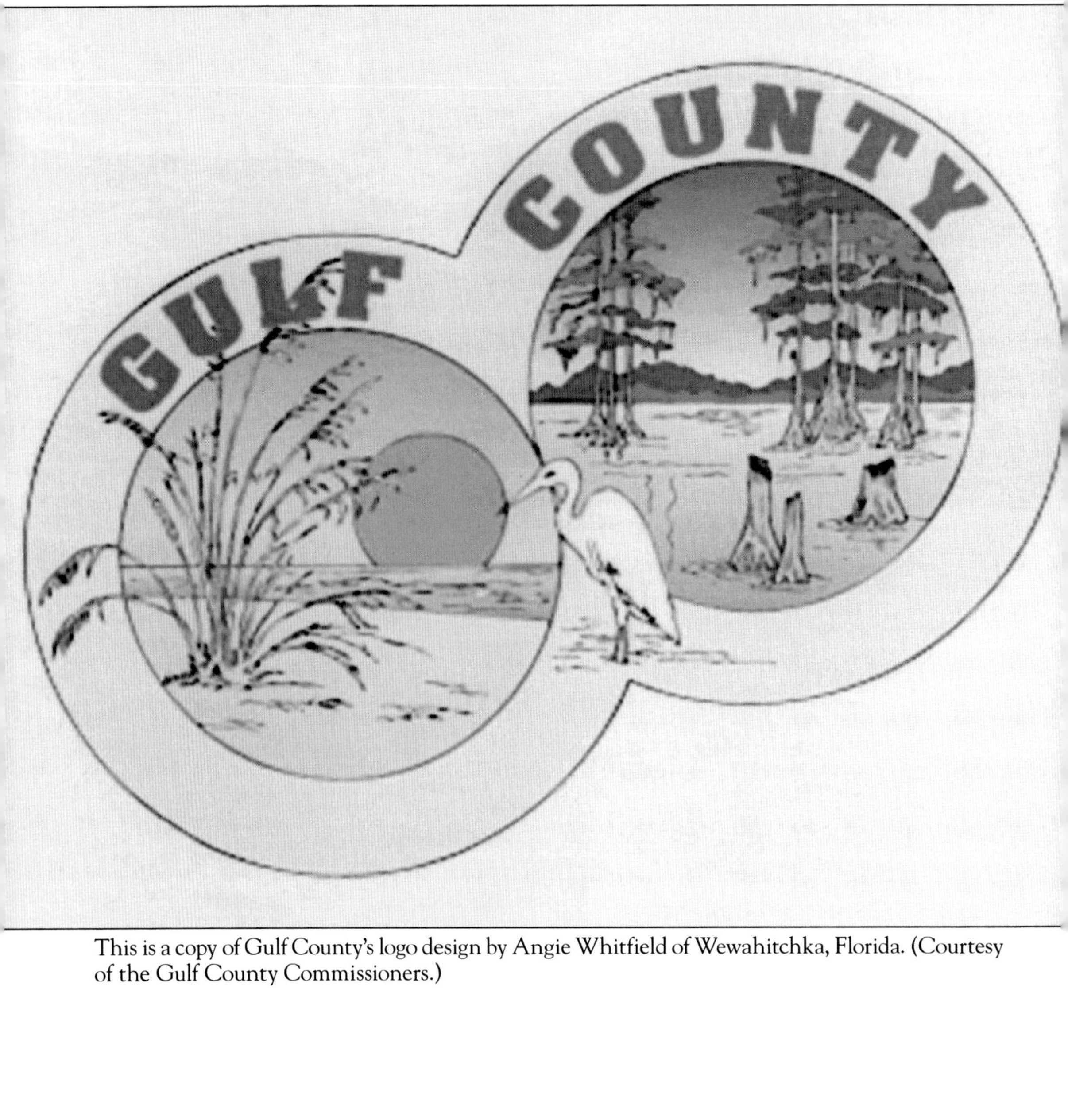

This is a copy of Gulf County's logo design by Angie Whitfield of Wewahitchka, Florida. (Courtesy of the Gulf County Commissioners.)

ON THE COVER: The steamer *Farnham* loads lumber from the old Apalachicola Northern Railroad docks *c.* 1914 at Port St. Joe, Florida. The locomotive at left is Engine No. 101, while Engine No. 123 is alongside the ship. (Billy Howell.)

IMAGES
of America

GULF COUNTY

Beverly Mount-Douds

ARCADIA
PUBLISHING

ISBN 978-0-7385-4396-3

Published by Arcadia Publishing
Charleston, South Carolina

Printed in the United States of America

Library of Congress Control Number: 2006935177

For all general information, please contact Arcadia Publishing:
Telephone 843-853-2070
Fax 843-853-0044
E-mail sales@arcadiapublishing.com
For customer service and orders:
Toll-Free 1-888-313-2665

Visit us on the Internet at www.arcadiapublishing.com

A debt of gratitude is extended to Billy Howell, George Core, Dave Maddox, and Tom Parker for sharing their knowledge of the history and the local pioneers along with their contributions to our city. Special thanks for their guidance and expertise, which ensured a successful project. This book is dedicated to these wonderful men and all the pioneer families of Gulf County.

Contents

ACKNOWLEDGMENTS

I would like to thank the wonderful assistance that my very good friends Pam Lawrence and Sandra Chafin have given me. This would not have been possible without their guidance and caring about completing this work with me. Also thanks for the help of Marlene Womack and others in organizing and assembling the photographs for this book. But most of all, I would like to thank the citizens of Gulf County.

A project like the history of Gulf County, Florida, would have been impossible to complete without the cooperation of the citizens of Port St. Joe and Wewahitchka, who were generous and helpful in sharing their collections of photographs and stories, which appear within these pages.

I want to extend my sincere appreciation to every person who was willing to lend materials and share their knowledge of the early histories of their families and of our county. It would be impossible to name all of the individuals who participated in this project, as most of the photographs came from private family sources.

Some of the best storytellers in the past were D. C. Mahon, Henry A. Drake, Cecil G. Costin Sr., S. H. McPhaul, and Jake Belin. These men were the best; we'll miss their wonderful tales of Old St. Joseph and the early days of the present Port St. Joe and what it was like in the beginning, but as long as we still have with us George Core, Dave Maddox, Billy Howell, and Tom Parker, our little city will never die.

I also want to thank Guy Tucker, Ned Patton, Bobby Bellows, Jake Belin Jr., Charlotte Pierce, Angie and Alfred Whitfield, Linda Shealey, BoBo and Betty Ann Owens, Jean and Damon Peters, the folks at the Port St. Joe Public Library, and Florida State University professors Betsy Purdum and Dean Jue (Institute of Science and Public Affairs). They opened the doors so that I could collect so many wonderful historical stories of our past.

I hope you will enjoy this wonderful collection of photographs and discovering our "Forgotten Coast."

INTRODUCTION

Terrell H. Stone, a pioneer settler of Port St. Joe, moved to the area in 1904 from Iola, near Wewahitchka, and started a turpentine operation with private labor. The location at the time was a wilderness area but now is the heart of the modern city of Port St. Joe. Being without rail transportation during the first few years of the operation, Stone transported his naval stores products to Pensacola in his privately owned boat powered by a marine engine. Meanwhile, he sold his large holdings in the area, acquired from his father, to some St. Louis businessmen who built the Apalachicola Northern Railroad from River Junction, Florida, to Apalachicola in 1907 and extended the line to Port St. Joe in 1909. This opened up an entirely new territory with a heavy growth of longleaf yellow pine timber, suitable for the manufacture of high grades of export lumber and, in addition, heavy production of naval stores. Upon the completion of the 100 miles of railroad in 1909, the owners of the railroad and affiliated companies set about to develop the large area extending from the southern boundaries of Alabama and Georgia along the Apalachicola River valley to St. Joseph Bay, where both domestic and foreign shipping facilities were being provided.

In 1909, work was begun on the 2,500-foot railroad pier into St. Joseph Bay, complete with wharf facilities. By 1911, there were 13 sawmills with a total daily output of some 540,000 board feet operating along the rail line. All were engaged in manufacturing export lumber.

After a town site survey, lots were sold and homes built. The new city of Port St. Joe was incorporated in the year 1913. The new town is located about two miles north of the site of Old St. Joseph. At the outset, the town was provided with schools, churches, macadamized streets, sidewalks, parks, a recreation center, and a 35-room hotel called Port Inn overlooking St. Joseph Bay. The Port Inn burned on October 25, 1944. Railroad shops and general offices were moved from Apalachicola to Port St. Joe. An ice factory, electric plant, and water system that included a 700-foot-deep artesian well all were completed in 1913.

From 1910, the railroad operated regularly scheduled summer Sunday excursions to Port St. Joe, bringing passengers from all intermediate points on the railroad and from points in Alabama and Georgia beyond the River Junction terminal, which is now called Chattahoochee. The first train excursion made three trips from Apalachicola to Port St. Joe on April 30, 1910. In addition to the many fine baseball games usually scheduled, special attractions included boat trips across the bay to Eagle Harbor, Black's Island, and the gulf beach at St. Joseph Point where seashell hunting was a favorite pastime. Also, chartered boats were available for deep-sea fishing, and sailboating in the bay waters was a popular outing. The bathing pier on the bay shore from the Port Inn was a great attraction with its springboards, high chutes, slides, trapeze rings, shower stalls, and concession stands. Adjoining was the hotel park, which included a bandstand, benches, and other amenities amid a setting of palm trees, pines, roses, and flowering shrubs.

In Monument Park stands the marble monument erected by the state in 1922 on the site where the Constitutional Convention Hall stood in 1838. A four-day Centennial Celebration, sponsored jointly by the City of Port St. Joe and the state, was held at the site from December 7 to 10,

1938. The celebration included elaborate fireworks, displays, a spectacular parade of illuminated historical and allegorical floats, band concerts, a free circus carnival, and other entertainment. Thousands attended, and the celebration is considered to have been a very important occasion in Florida history.

The Centennial Building—erected in 1938 and situated in Monument Park at the eastern city limits of Port St. Joe—is on the grounds formerly occupied by the long-dead city of St. Joseph.

The Constitution Convention State Museum at Port St. Joe contains interpretive exhibits of the 1838 historic event as well as contemporary history. Included in the exhibits is a replica of one of the locomotives used on the St. Joseph and Iola Railroad in 1836.

The abundance of wild game, fish, and freshwater attracted the area's first inhabitants—the native Apalachee—whose existence is revealed in middens of shells, fish, and animal remains. These early residents hunted and gathered their food in the summer, following the food supply inland during the cooler months. Today's hunters will still find a good supply of game.

Gulf County's economy is based on the timber industry, wood chemical processing, and commercial fishing. Tupelo honey is the major export of Wewahitchka, also a farming and freshwater fishing community. Port St. Joe boasts tourists, chemical plants, a boat building plant, a commercial fishing and bait processing plant, and several smaller manufacturing concerns.

Whatever brings you to Gulf County—recreation, relocating for a job, or retiring to a new life in the sunshine—you'll find miles of sugar-fine white sandy beaches stretching along the Gulf of Mexico in this relatively undiscovered region of Northwest Florida. You'll find the area is home to friendly people who will undoubtedly make you feel right at home.

Key to Photograph Source Abbreviations

Billy Howell	BH
Dave Maddox	DM
Angie and Alfred Whitfield	AAW
Linda Borders Shealey	LBS
Sue Gaskin Dickens	SGD
Clarence Monette	CM
St. Joseph Historical Society	SJHS
Barbara Eells	BE
Virginia Swatts Harrison	VSH
Marie J. Costin	MJC
Guy Tucker	GT
Ned Patton	NP
Louise Daughtry Ford	LDF
Betsy Purdum	BP
Bobby Bellows	BB
Jake Belin Jr.	JBJ
Janice Player Brownell	JPB
Nathan Peters Jr.	NPJ
City of Port St. Joe	CPSJ
Pam Parker Lawrence	PPL
BoBo and Betty Ann Owens	BBO
Port St. Joe High School	PSJHS
Jean and Damon Peters Jr.	JDP
Mae Clark	MC
Mary Belin	MB
St. Joe Company	St. Joe Co.
Rocky Comforter	RC
Trish T. Warriner	TTW
Eda Ruth Taylor	ERT
St. Joseph Daughters of the American Revolution	DAR
Mel Magidson	MM
George Core	GC
Frann Hannon Smith	FHS
Robert Nedley	RN
Clayton Wooten	CW
Harold Raffield	HR
Gail Alsobrook	GA
Debbie Hooper	DH
Bob Stebel	BS
Joe Sharit III	JSIII

One

Early Pioneers

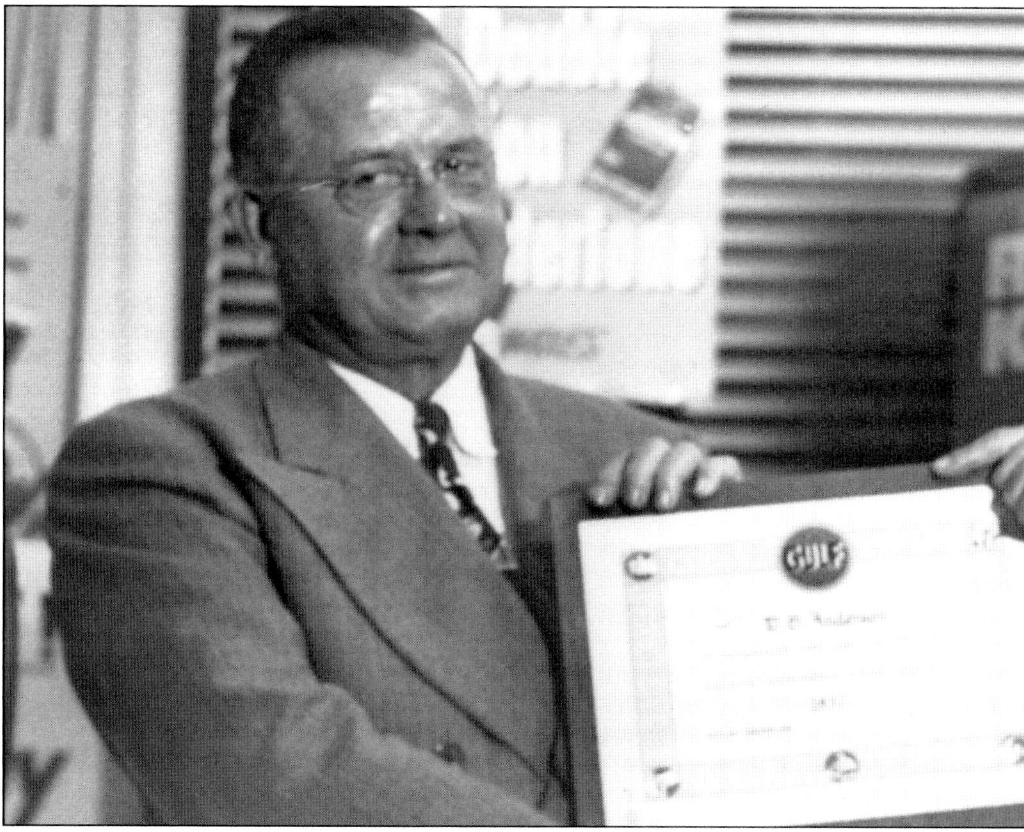

William "Otto" Anderson was born in Franklin County, Florida. He owned and operated the Ford dealership in Apalachicola. Having moved to Port St. Joe in 1938, he opened the Ford Motor Company the following year. He served as an officer and director of the Florida Automobile Dealers Association for many years. Otto and his wife, Emma, raised two daughters, Dorothy and Betty Otto, who both continue to live in Port St. Joe. (FHS.)

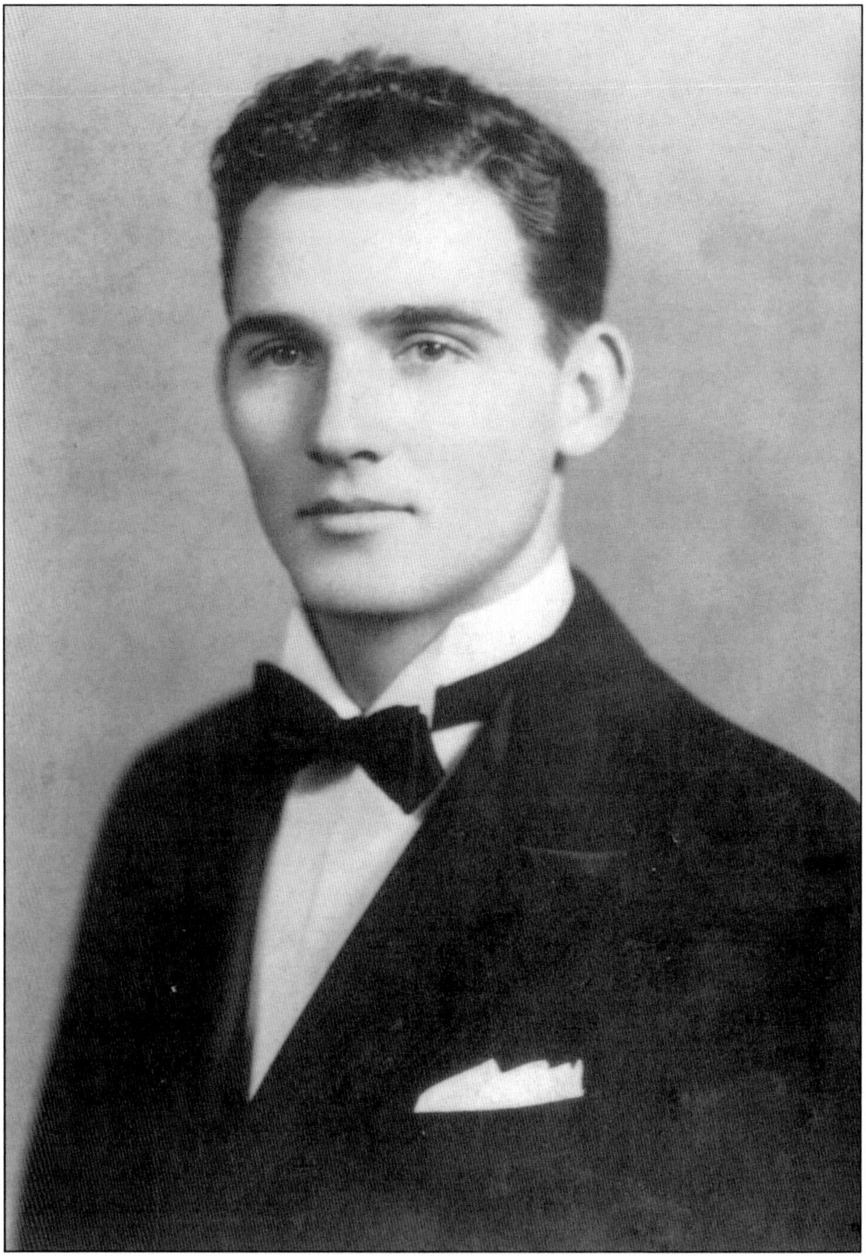

Jacob "Jake" Chapman Belin moved with his family to Port St. Joe in 1924. He worked for the federal government while attending George Washington University. Jake Belin began his professional career with St. Joe Paper Company in 1938. During his lengthy and distinguished career, Belin served as chairman of the Nemours Foundation; trustee of the Alfred I. duPont Testamentary Trust; director of the Alfred I. duPont Foundation; and chairman, director, president, and chief executive officer of the St. Joe Company. Belin was a charter member of Long Avenue Baptist Church. He also served three terms as mayor of Port St. Joe. Additionally, Belin served his community and the state of Florida on numerous voluntary and honorary committees. He was deeply committed to this town of Port St. Joe and its residents and was always concerned about its future. (JBJ.)

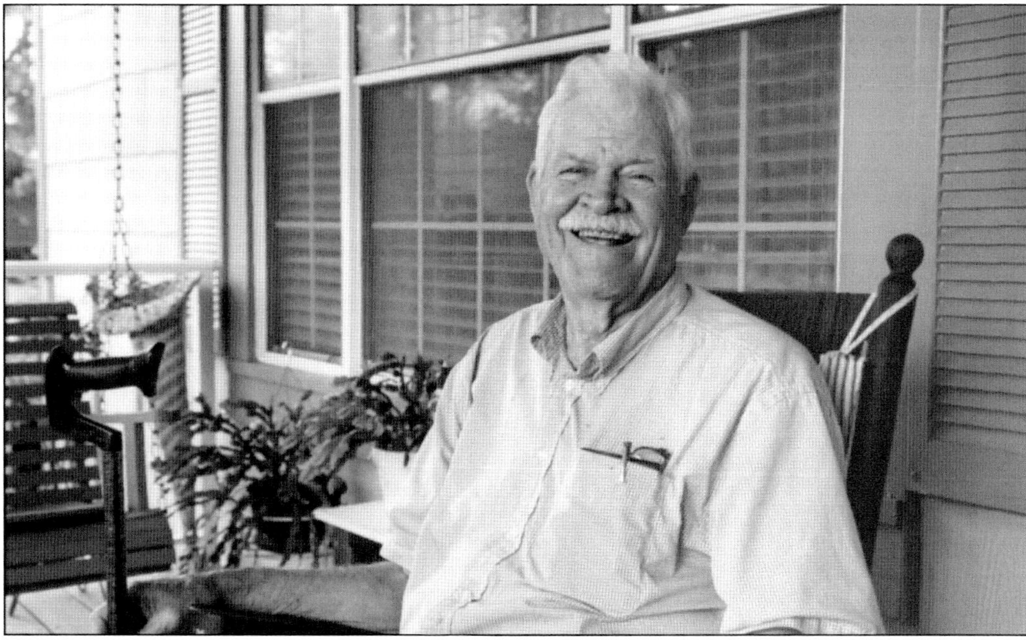

Leonard Belin, Jake's brother, served in World War II, fought in many battles, and was wounded in Normandy. He returned to Port St. Joe and started to work at the paper company's box plant. Leonard played baseball and was the first baseman and star slugger for St. Joe's local baseball team, the Saints, in the 1940s and 1950s. He was dubbed "Big Nose" Belin. Leonard was known as the best hitter in the league. (MB.)

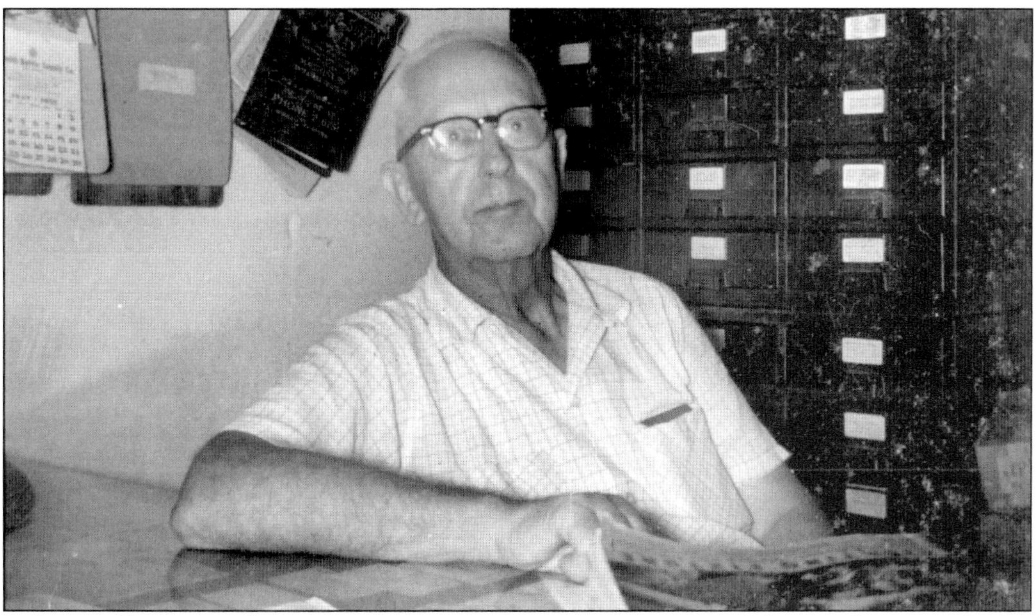

Robert Bellows moved to Port St. Joe in 1923. He was manager of the Southern Menhaden Company, which was owned by one of the Wilmington, Delaware, duPonts. Robert, along with several others, bought the plant in the early 1930s and renamed it the Florida Menhaden Company. In 1935, he and B. W. Eells, J. L. Sharit, and J. A. Smith formed the Gulf Hardware and Supply Company. (BB.)

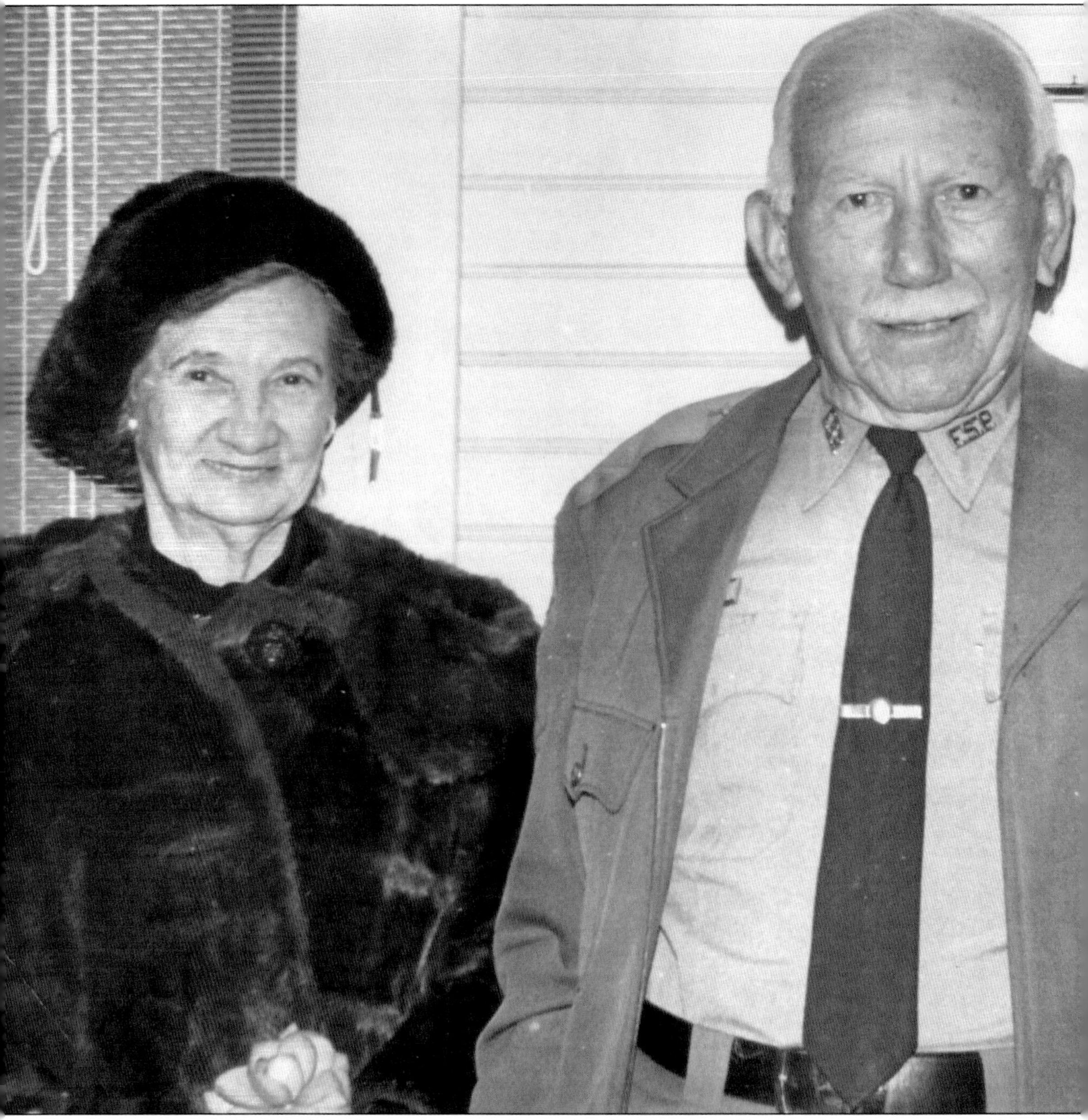

Charles and Ida Ethel (Kilbourn) Brown have the distinction of being the first couple to be married at the St. Joseph Catholic Church in 1929. Ida Ethel was a member of the first Port St. Joe High School graduating class, in 1927. She attended Emory and Henry University in Emory, Virginia, and Florida State College for Women in Tallahassee, Florida. Charles was an outstanding historian. His achievements were noted in newspaper articles, including some in the *London Press*. He was cited for his work by the British Broadcasting Company. He received many other honors as well. Charles was the curator of the Dr. John Gorrie Museum in Apalachicola, Florida. Ida served as the regent for the St. Joseph Bay Chapter of the Daughters of the American Revolution (DAR) in 1980. (DAR.)

Nick Comforter moved to Port St. Joe around 1912. A seafaring man, he served in many important roles here in Port St. Joe. Nick acted as bar pilot—directing ships in and out of the docks—for a number of years. He also owned various properties around town. Folks remember him best as "Capt. Nick." He and his wife, Clara, lived in the house that his nephew Rocky and his family reside in today. (RC.)

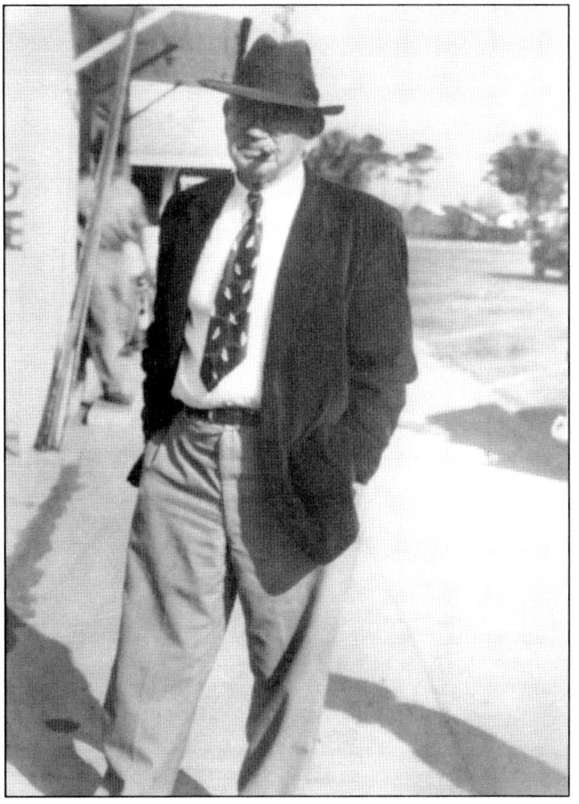

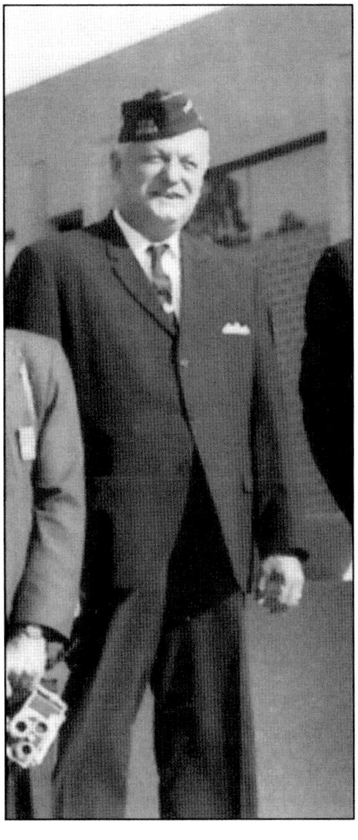

Pete Comforter, Nick's nephew, met Hortense Bobe and won her heart and hand in 1938. At that time, he began his apprenticeship as an embalmer and funeral director in Pensacola, Florida. Hortense was a trained nurse. The couple founded Comforter Funeral Home when they moved to Port St. Joe on October 1, 1946. (RC.)

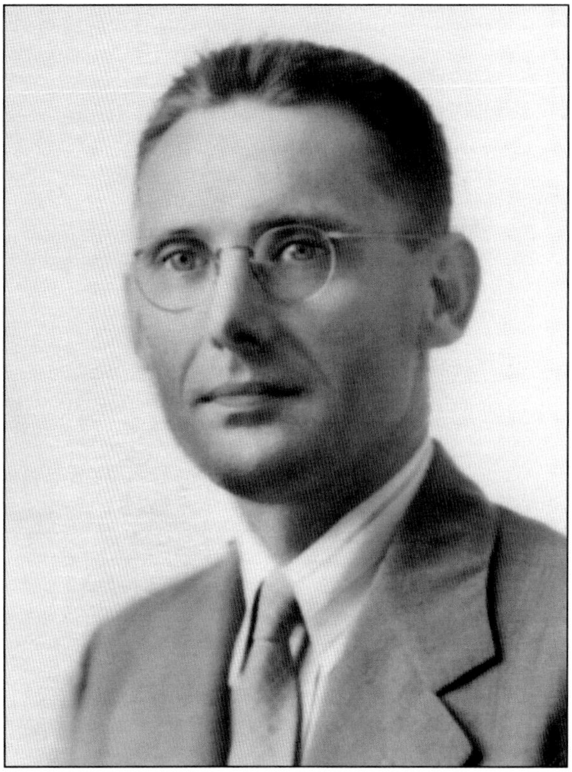

Cecil G. Costin Sr. was one of the leading businessmen and citizens in the community. After school, Cecil ran the department store his family owned, and he later purchased it from his father when his parents moved to Wewahitchka to buy a farm. Cecil and his family were staunch supporters of the First Baptist Church. He was presented the Lifetime Achievement Award at the Chamber of Commerce Annual Meeting and Dinner in 1997. (MM.)

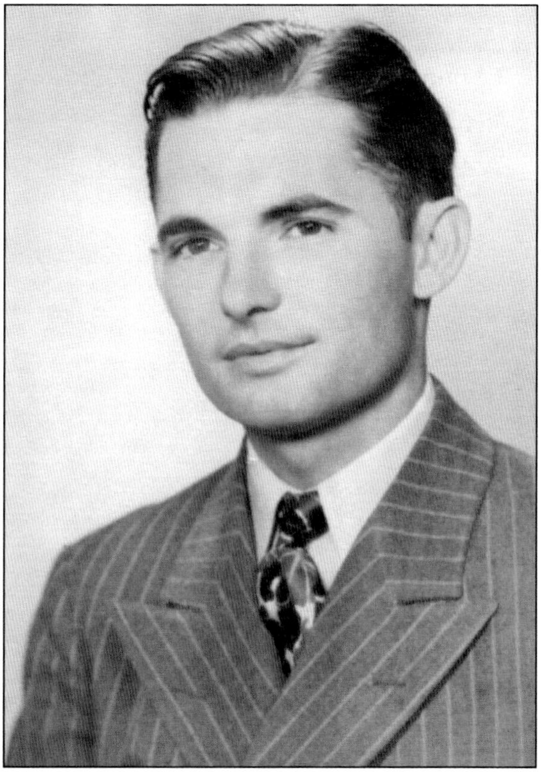

Chauncey L. Costin, Cecil's brother, attended the University of Florida and Georgia Tech. He served two terms as superintendent of public instruction from 1933 to 1941. He has the distinction of being the youngest person in the state to be elected to that office. He served as postmaster in Port St. Joe beginning in 1951 and continued for almost 20 years, during which time he was also active in civic affairs. (MJC.)

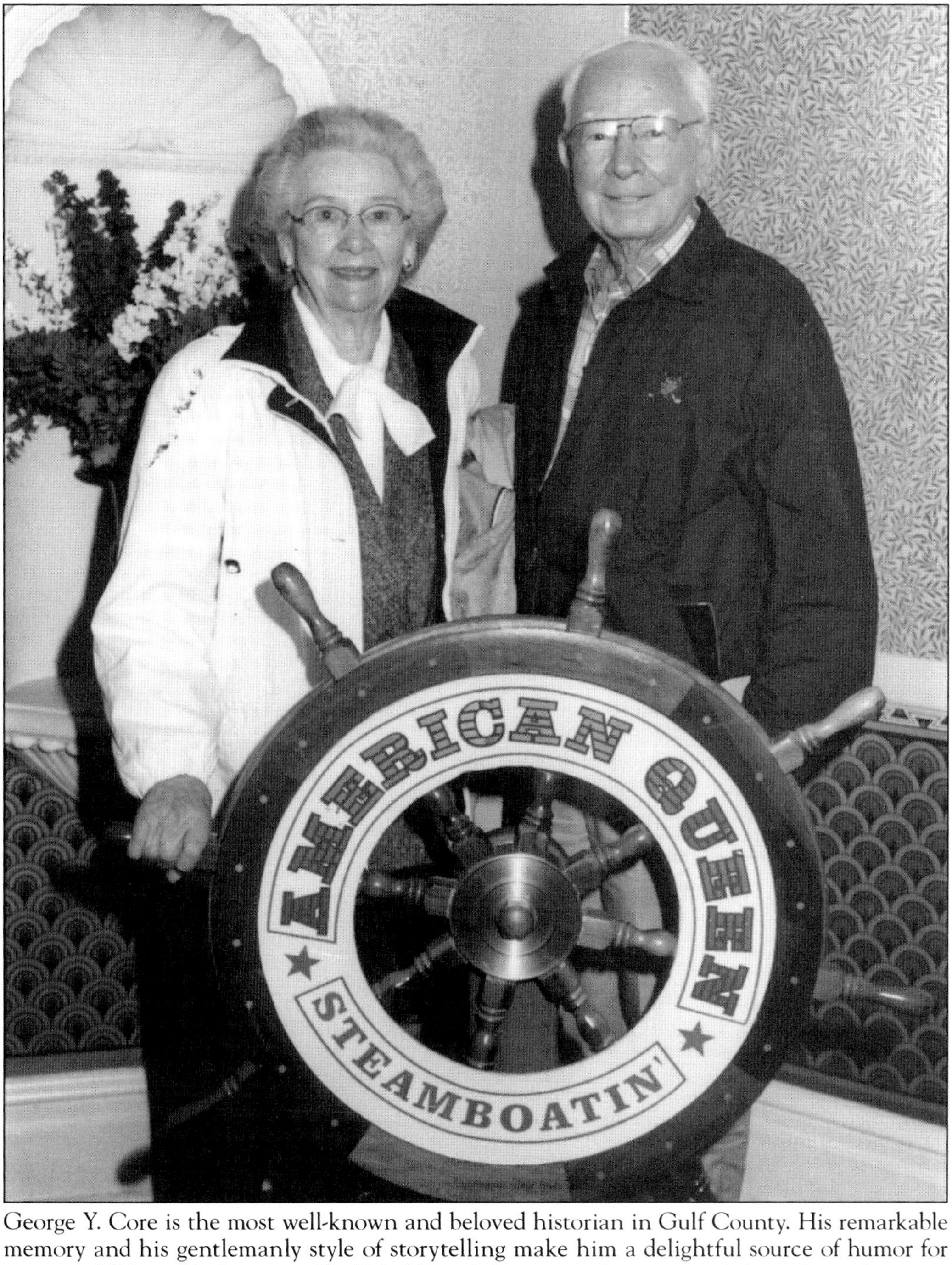

George Y. Core is the most well-known and beloved historian in Gulf County. His remarkable memory and his gentlemanly style of storytelling make him a delightful source of humor for our area folklore. He loves to tell of his life and the events that occurred throughout the years. Core is known as one of the best clerks of the court Gulf County ever had. He will always be remembered for his colorful and humorous stories and his wonderful gift of telling the past. His beloved wife, Alice, passed away in June 2006. She was known as a wonderful Southern lady, always sweet and kind. She will be remembered always for her loving ways and for how well she took care of George. Alice was always willing to help where needed. (GC.)

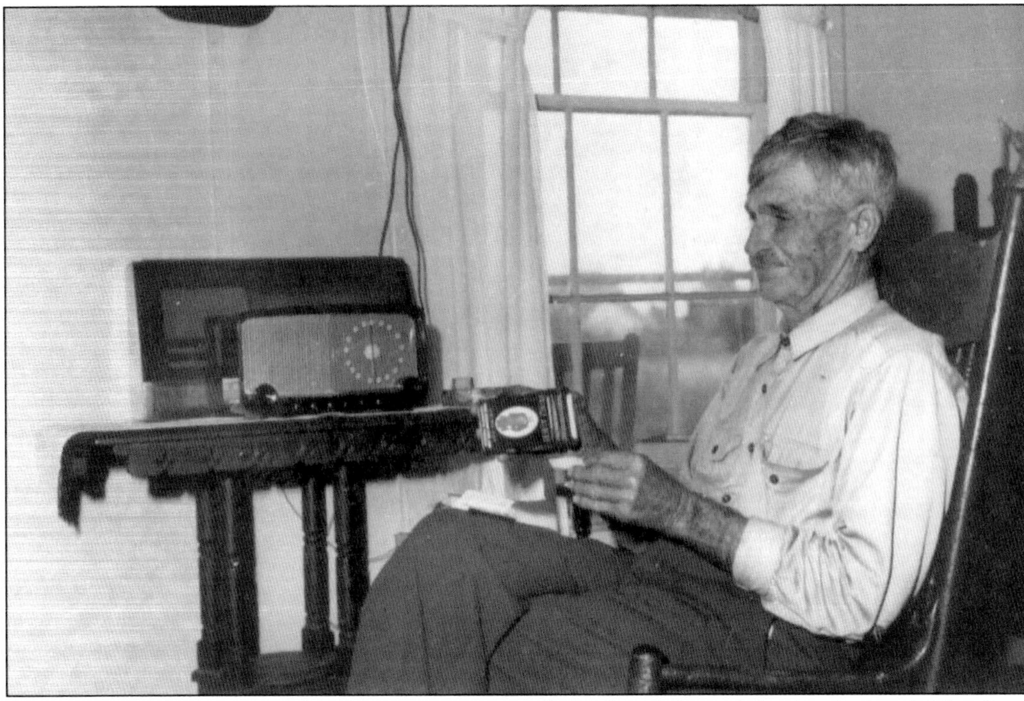

Warren J. Daughtry was a railroad-car carpenter in the railroad shop of the Apalachicola Northern Railroad System for over 35 years. He moved here from Liberty County in 1911. (LDF.)

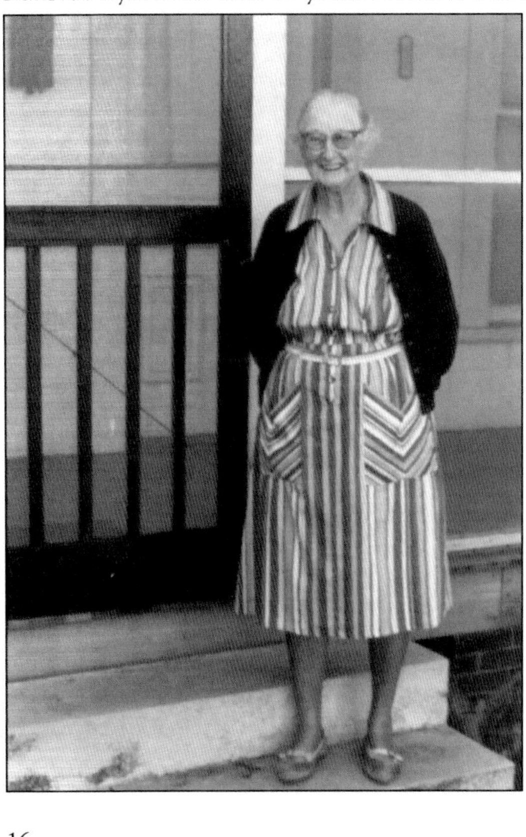

Abby Daughtry, William's wife, taught every generation of boys in Sunday school at the First Baptist Church in Port St. Joe beginning with the foundation of the church until her death in the 1980s. Abby and her famous hat were trademarks in Port St. Joe for many years. (LDF.)

Henry A. Drake was a bank cashier in Georgia at the young age of 16. Drake moved to Port St. Joe in 1914. He took a position in the accounting department of the Apalachicola Northern Railroad. Later he was promoted to chief clerk and in May 1926 was appointed auditor of the railroad company; he served in that capacity for 10 years. He later served as postmaster until his retirement. (GT.)

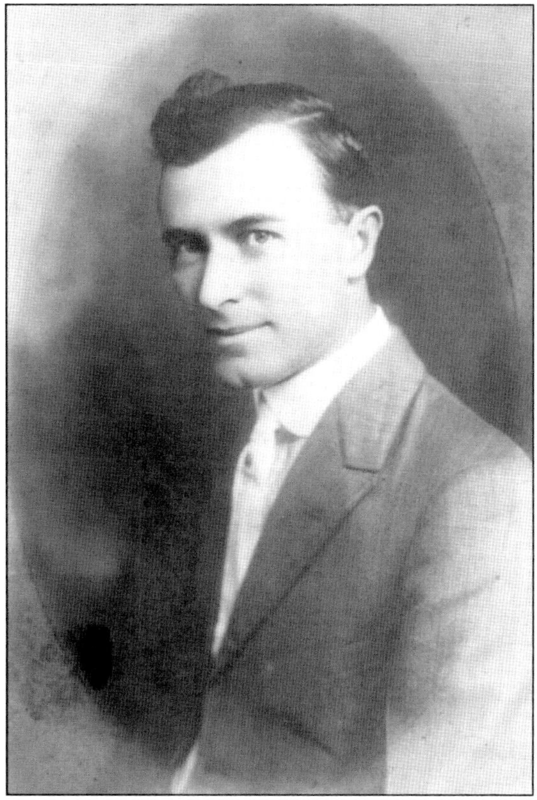

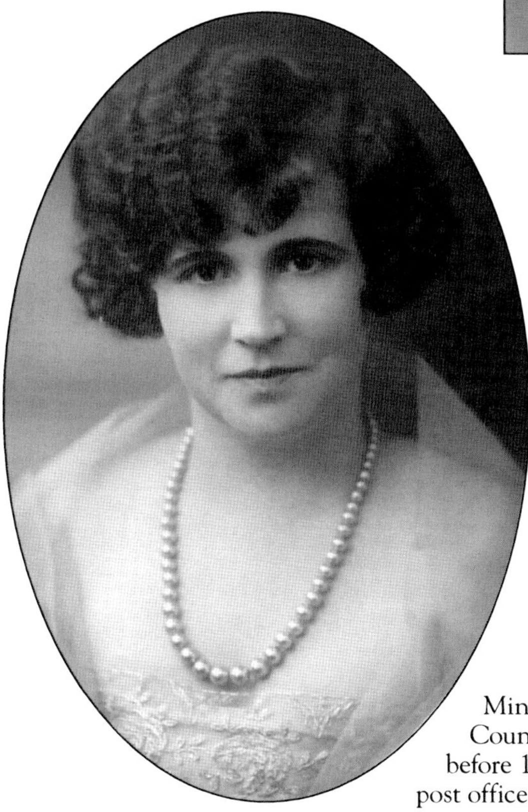

Minnie Ola (Reed) Drake came here from Brooks County, Georgia. She met and married Henry Drake before 1920. She worked alongside her husband in the post office for many years. (GT.)

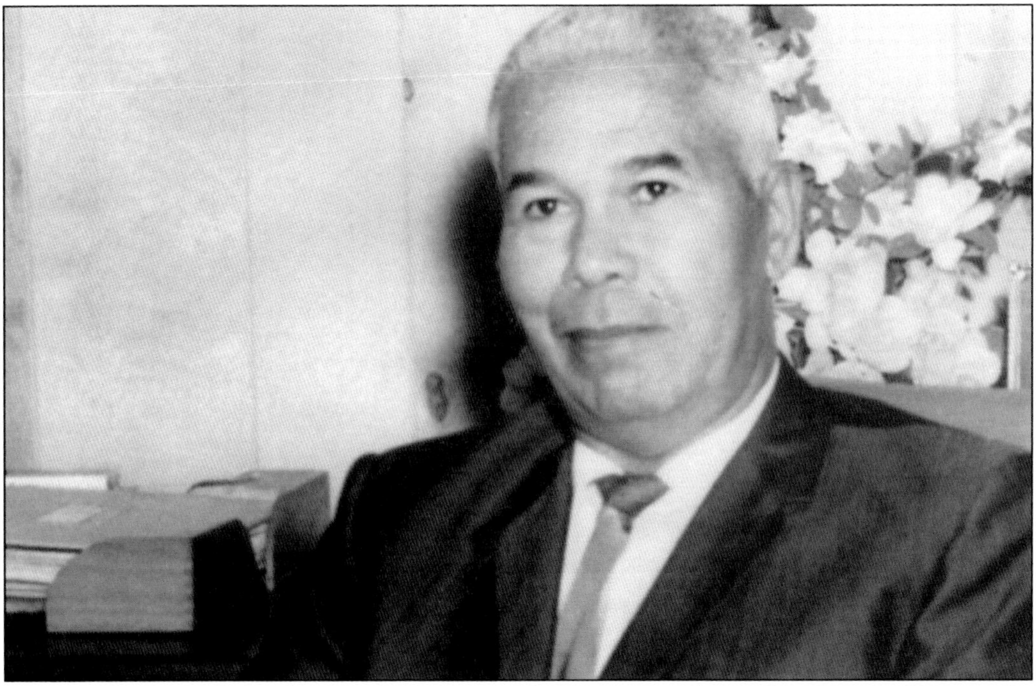

This is the Knights of Pythias Lodge in 1969. The name was changed in honor of Sir Knight Raymond A. Driesbach Sr., pictured, the first grand chancellor of the state of Florida from Port St. Joe. (CM.)

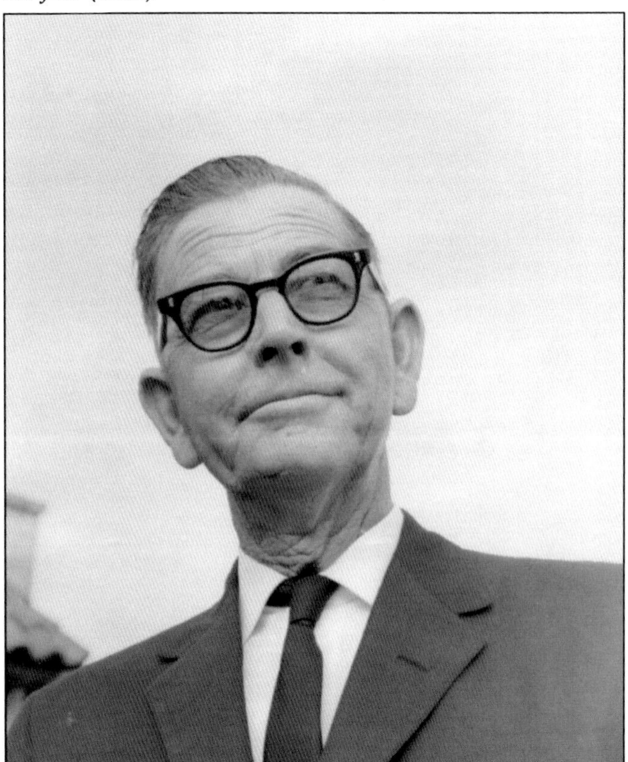

Dave Gaskin, a banker-businessman, was a prominent citizen in Wewahitchka. He nurtured the Wewahitchka State Bank into the community's most prosperous and trusted institution. Gaskin was a successful cattleman and pulpwood businessman. A member of a pioneer northwest turpentine and timber family, Dave was born in Kinard, which is located in neighboring Calhoun County. As a leader in the Florida Bankers Association, he was known throughout the state of Florida. (TTW.)

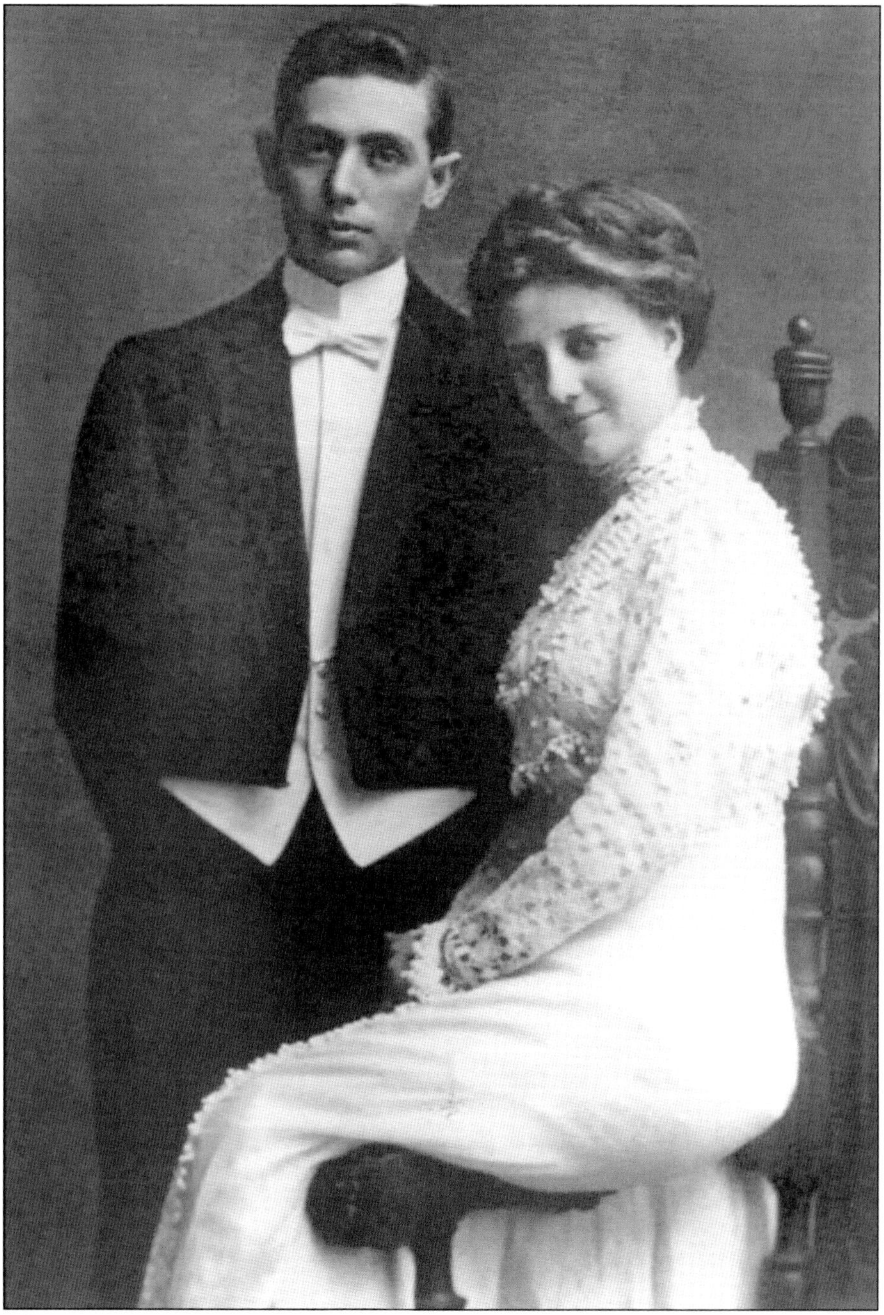

Byron Whetstone Eells Sr. arrived in Port St. Joe about 1914 to assume a position as chief clerk of the Apalachicola Northern Railroad (ANRR). Soon after beginning work, he became an agent in charge of the railroad. In approximately three years, he was promoted to vice president and general manager of the ANRR. He served in that capacity until 1931. His wife, Deloris Eldora Eells, was community minded and, along with other ladies in the small community, helped to start a welfare program for those in need. She served as president of the Parent Teachers Association and the Woman's Club and as chairman for the first March of Dimes in 1934. She taught at Port St. Joe Elementary School and was instrumental in starting the school's first lunchroom. (BE.)

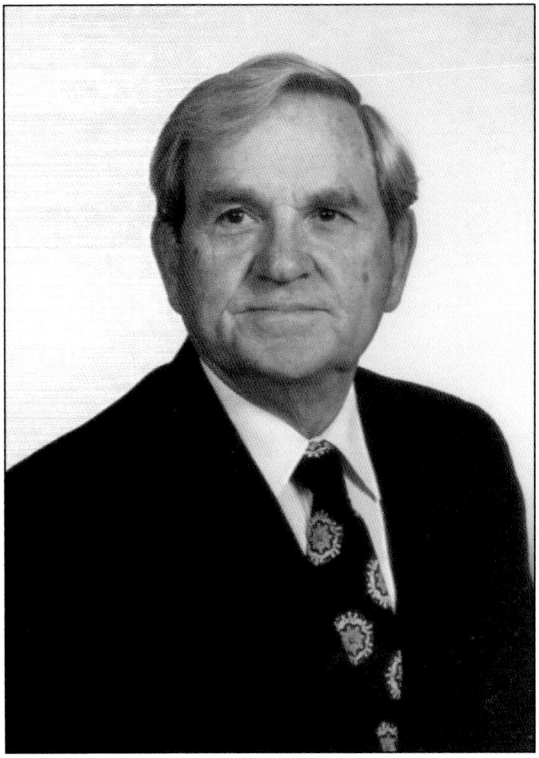

Frank Hannon began a career as a teacher and coach (of all sports) at Port St. Joe High in 1940 after graduating from the University of Florida. In 1941, his six-man football squad won the first high school state championship game. Hannon opened Frank and Dot Insurance Agency, which later became Hannon Insurance. Frank Hannon served as mayor of Port St. Joe from January 1962 to October 1966. (FHS.)

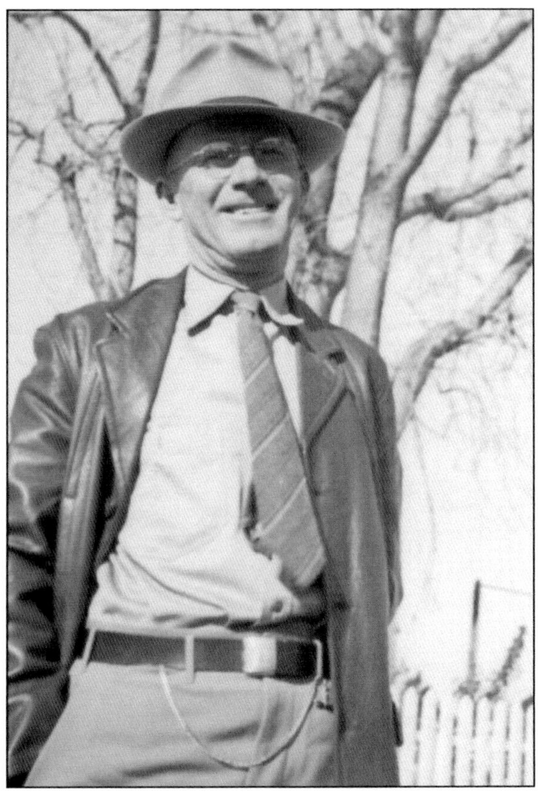

William "Willie" Henry Howell Sr. was born in Gadsden County, Florida. After moving to Port St. Joe in 1913, he began a career at age 15 as a "butcher boy" selling newspaper, magazines, and candy. He worked as an engineer for 43 years with the Apalachicola Northern Railroad before retiring. He was a veteran of World War II and a member of the Brotherhood of Locomotive Engineers and Firemen. (BH.)

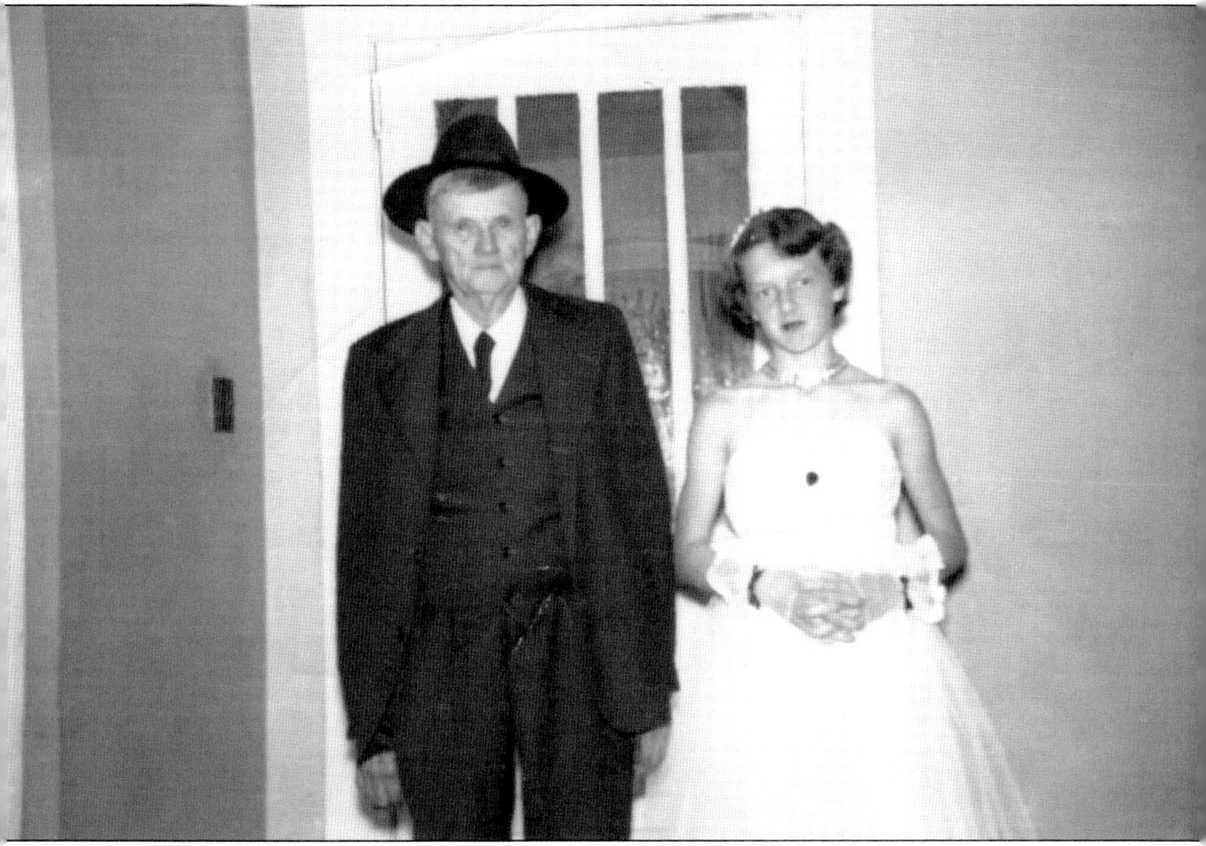

Max Kilbourn moved to Apalachicola, Florida, *c.* 1885 with his family. Later that same year, they moved to Port St. Joe. Max had the distinction of having the longest continuous record as a manufacturer of ice in the state of Florida. The site of his first plant was located on land that later became St. Joe Paper Company's huge paper mill. This photograph shows Max and his granddaughter Eda Ruth Kilbourn on the way to a musical recital in 1954. Eda Ruth K. Taylor graduated from Port St. Joe High School and later became a tax collector. (ERT.)

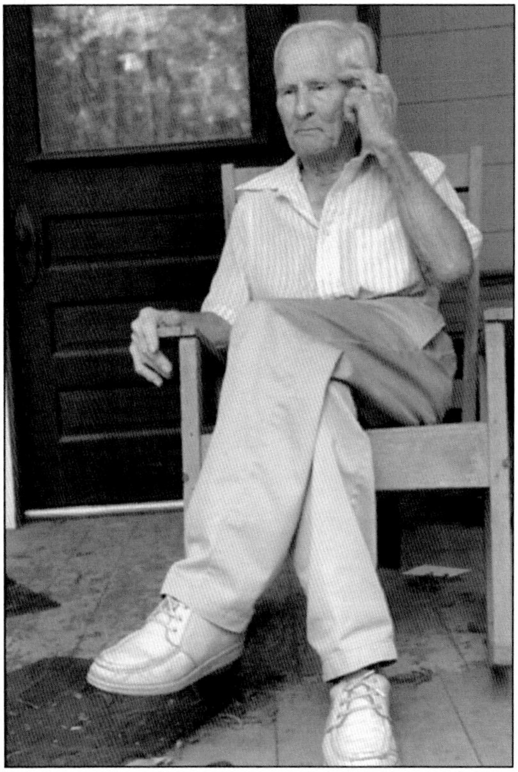

Sid Alderman was the owner of the first hive of bees in the area. Lavernor Laveon Lanier Sr. established the second colony in 1898. He borrowed $500, using his word as collateral, and brought the bees from Bainbridge, Georgia. L. L. Lanier Jr. retired from beekeeping in 1991 and turned the business over to his son Ben, making three generations of Laniers in the honey business in Gulf County. (BP.)

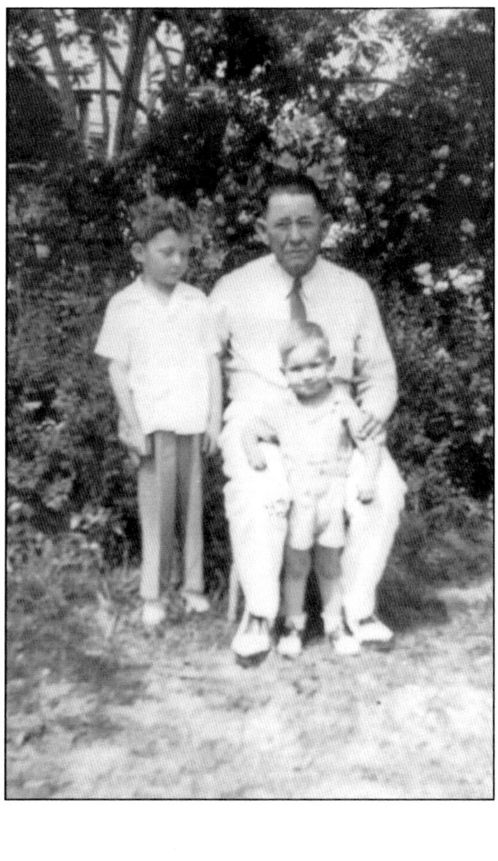

Ivory Carl Nedley opened a general store, Nedley Mercantile Store, and other businesses in 1921 with his brother Bob Nedley. Ivory served 25 years on the Port St. Joe City Commission and for six of those years served as mayor. He also served as city judge for several years. He and his wife, Mary Amanda "Mae," owned and operated Nedley's Café for six years. He retired from St. Joe Paper Company. (RN.)

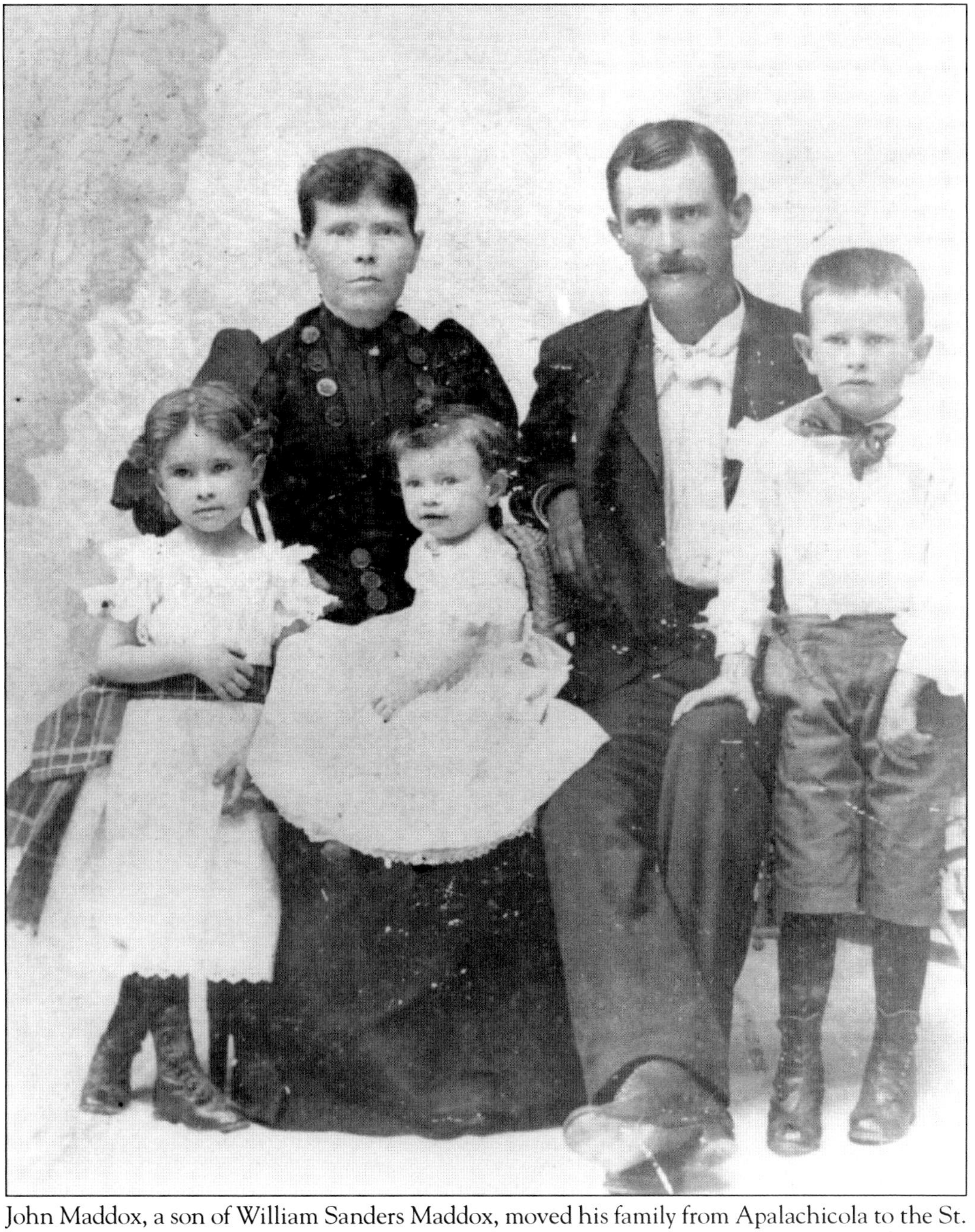

John Maddox, a son of William Sanders Maddox, moved his family from Apalachicola to the St. Joseph Bay area of Gautier Hammock in 1893. This particular area produced an abundance of saltwater Bermuda grass, known as coastal Bermuda today, and provided better grazing for his cattle. John and his wife, Charlotte Wall of Cheltenham, England, had four children: Fred, Eva, Alice, and Roy. Later they relocated to Black's Island. John served in the U.S. Navy during the Spanish-American War. In 1905, he and his sons, Fred and Roy, were hired to sound the bay for a dock site. The Swedish sailing ship *Henrietta*, piloted by John Maddox, loaded the first cargo over this dock in 1910. Captain John also piloted the USS *Constitution*, known as "Old Ironsides," when she came to Port St. Joe in March 1932. (DM.)

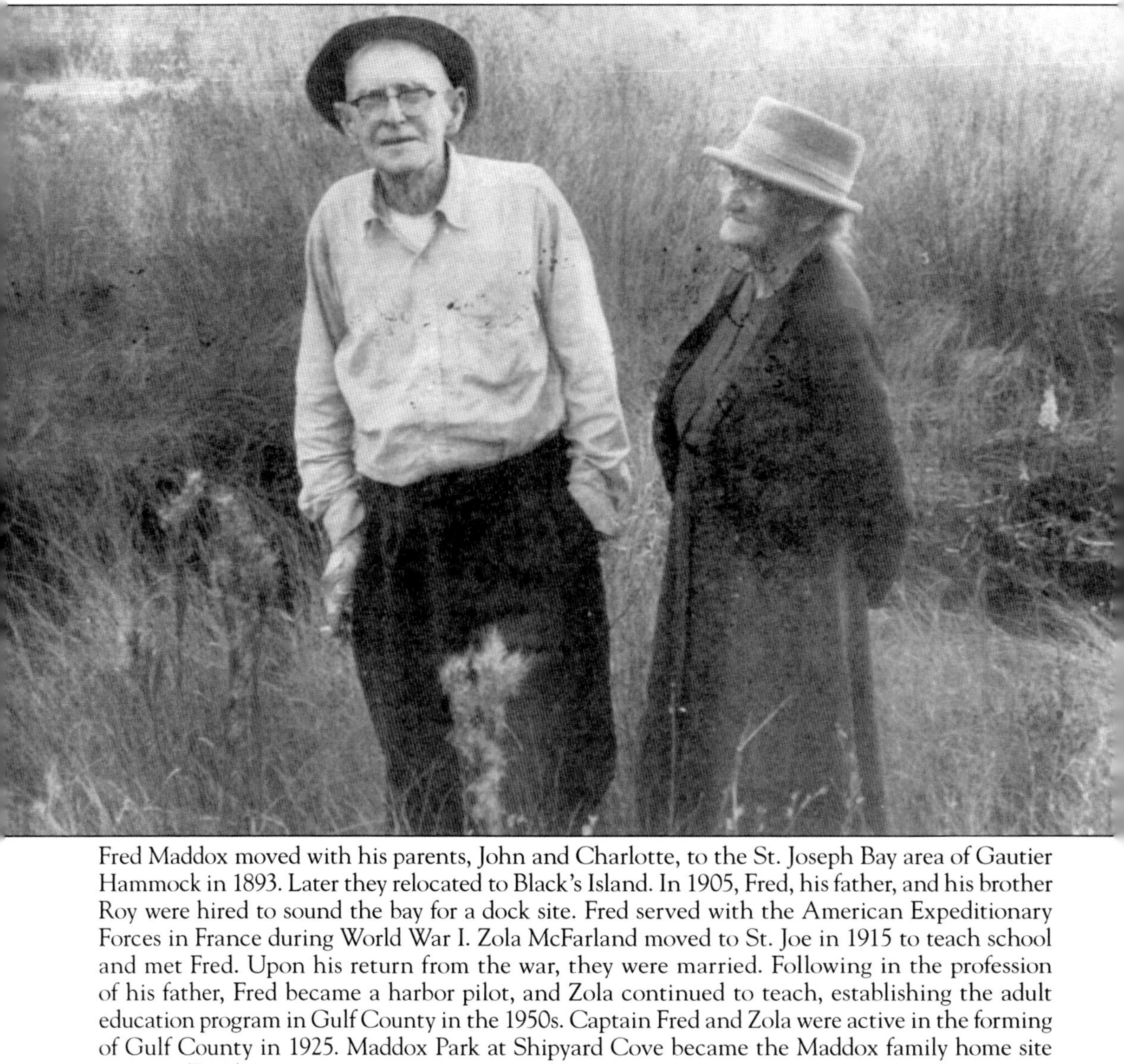

Fred Maddox moved with his parents, John and Charlotte, to the St. Joseph Bay area of Gautier Hammock in 1893. Later they relocated to Black's Island. In 1905, Fred, his father, and his brother Roy were hired to sound the bay for a dock site. Fred served with the American Expeditionary Forces in France during World War I. Zola McFarland moved to St. Joe in 1915 to teach school and met Fred. Upon his return from the war, they were married. Following in the profession of his father, Fred became a harbor pilot, and Zola continued to teach, establishing the adult education program in Gulf County in the 1950s. Captain Fred and Zola were active in the forming of Gulf County in 1925. Maddox Park at Shipyard Cove became the Maddox family home site in 1910. (DM.)

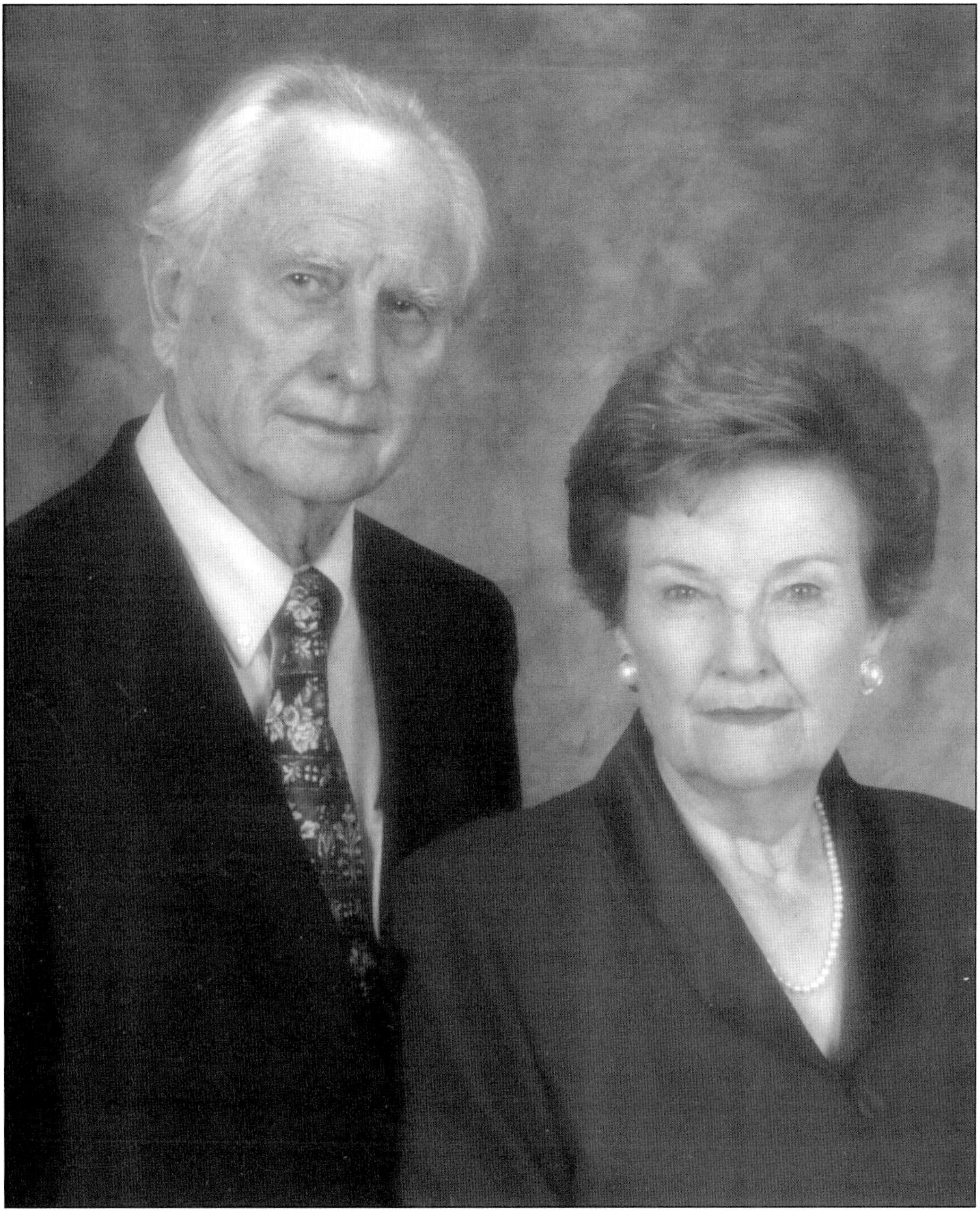

Dave Maddox, the son of pioneer residents Captain Fred and Zola Maddox, graduated from Port St. Joe High School in 1940. While a high school student, he played football and basketball and was a member of the band. After serving in the Merchant Marine and navy during World War II, he returned home to follow the family tradition and become a harbor pilot. In 1948, Dave married Sara Duke of Decatur County, Georgia. Dave served as president of the Shark Boosters when Shark Field was built in 1953–1954. Sara, a registered nurse, worked in different areas of her chosen profession and loved them all. She has taught Sunday school for many years. Her hobbies include reading, sewing, working in the yard, and evening bike rides. Dave and Sara are the parents of four children and have three grandchildren. (DM.)

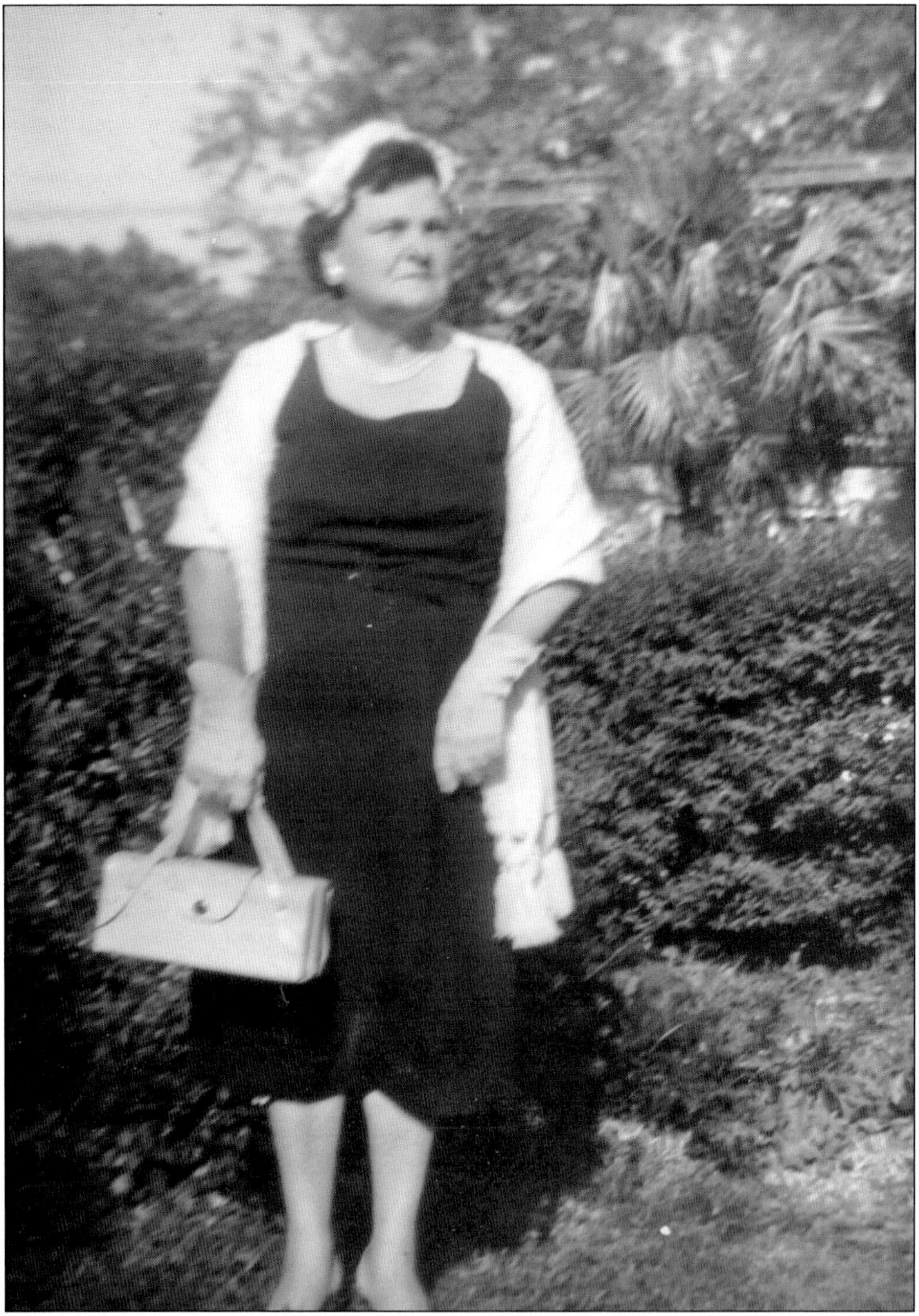

Dessie Lee Benton moved to Port St. Joe in 1924 with her family when she was 12 years old. Her father was employed by Parkwood Lumber Company. Her parents were Oliver L. and Mamie Benton. She later met and married Tom Parker Sr., who had moved to Port St. Joe in 1919 and was employed with the Apalachicola Northern Railroad. Their first four children were born on Blossom Row. In 1934, they moved their family to the corner of Long Avenue and Seventh Street, where their last four children were born. "Miss Dessie" later ran for and became supervisor of elections for Gulf County. She served in that capacity from 1969 until her retirement in 1981. (PPL.)

Tom Parker Jr., lovingly known as "Dooder," is a native of Port St. Joe. He was born on Blossom Row in the home of his grandparents, John and Millie Parker. He worked at the St. Joe Paper Company for 44 years. He is referred to as one of Gulf County's astute and beloved local historians and is known for his beautiful handwriting. He is always willing to share a story with those interested. (PPL.)

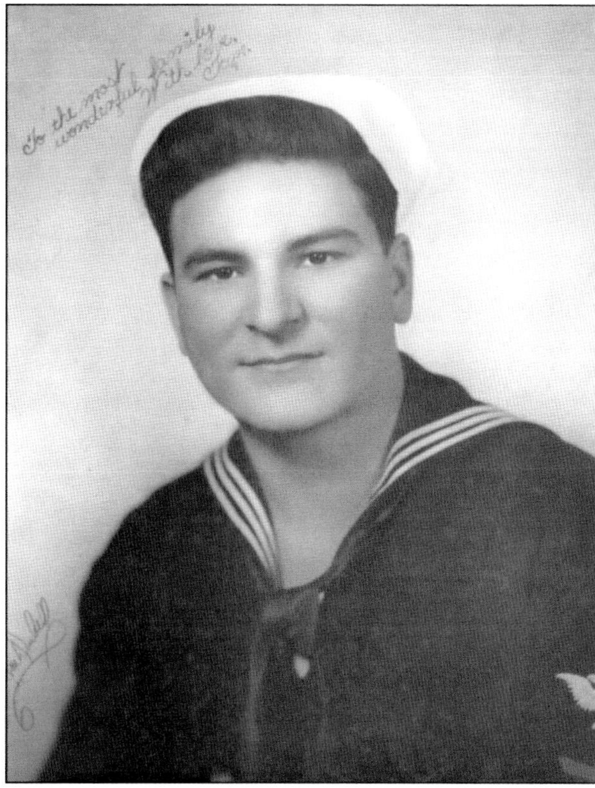

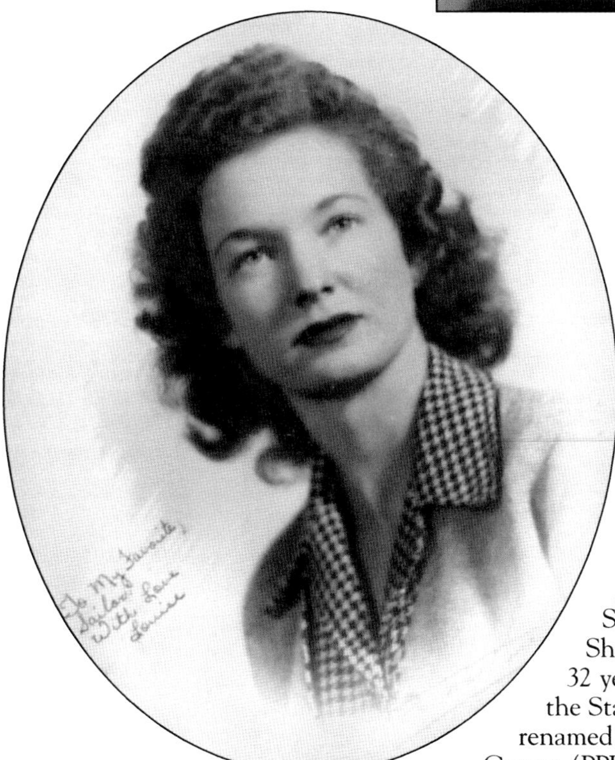

Erma Louise Wilder, known to most of the community as "Miss Erma," graduated from Port St. Joe High School in 1945 in a class of 17 students. She worked with the community youth for 32 years at the local teen center, known as the Stac House. In 2004, the Stac House was renamed in her honor as the Erma Parker Teen Center. (PPL.)

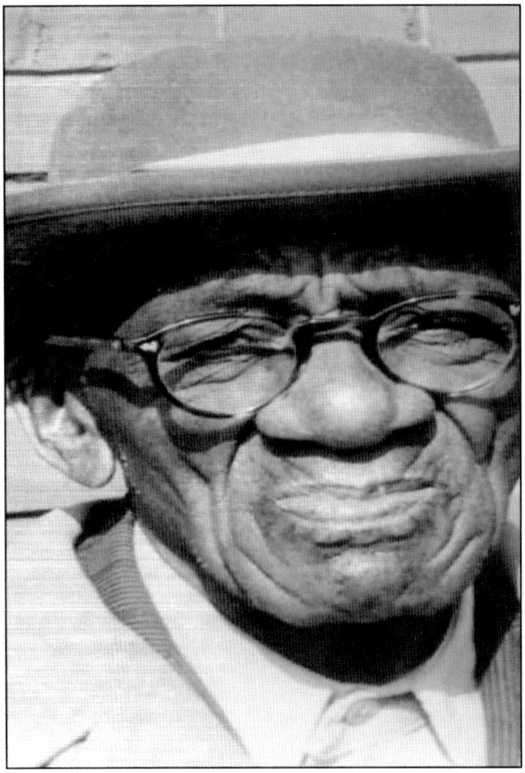

Lewis B. Peters, lovingly called "Uncle Pete," managed the Kilbourn company for many years. It was decided to expand the business to Port St. Joe in 1919. Pete and his son Damon came; Pete ran the fish and seafood house, and Damon worked in the ice plant. Lewis's wife, Sarah, and the children came in early 1920. The Peters boys were in real estate, general merchandise, and laundry service. (JDP.)

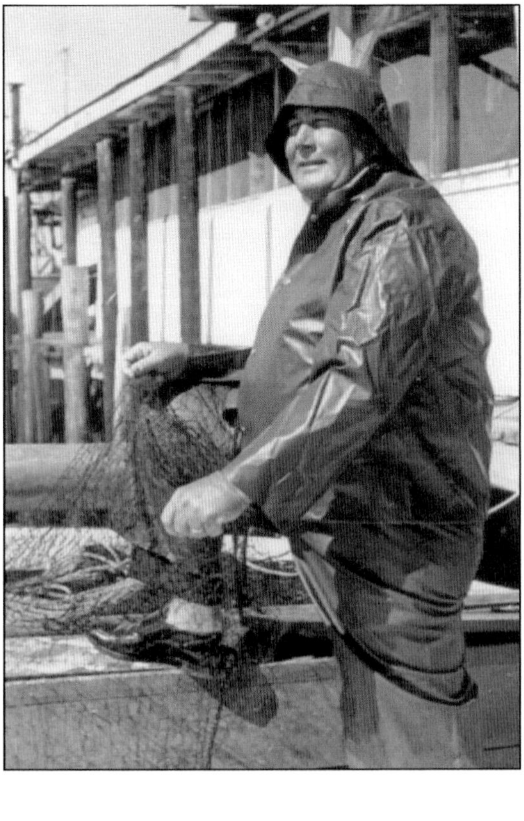

Carl Raffield was dedicated to creating a family business shaped by honesty, hard work, and a love of the sea. Captain Carl is a pioneer in the fishing industry. He is credited with many innovative fishing developments both in gear and boat design. He was known by watermen all along the coast for his ability to catch fish and to make friendships. Raffield family members still work the family-dominated business. (HR.)

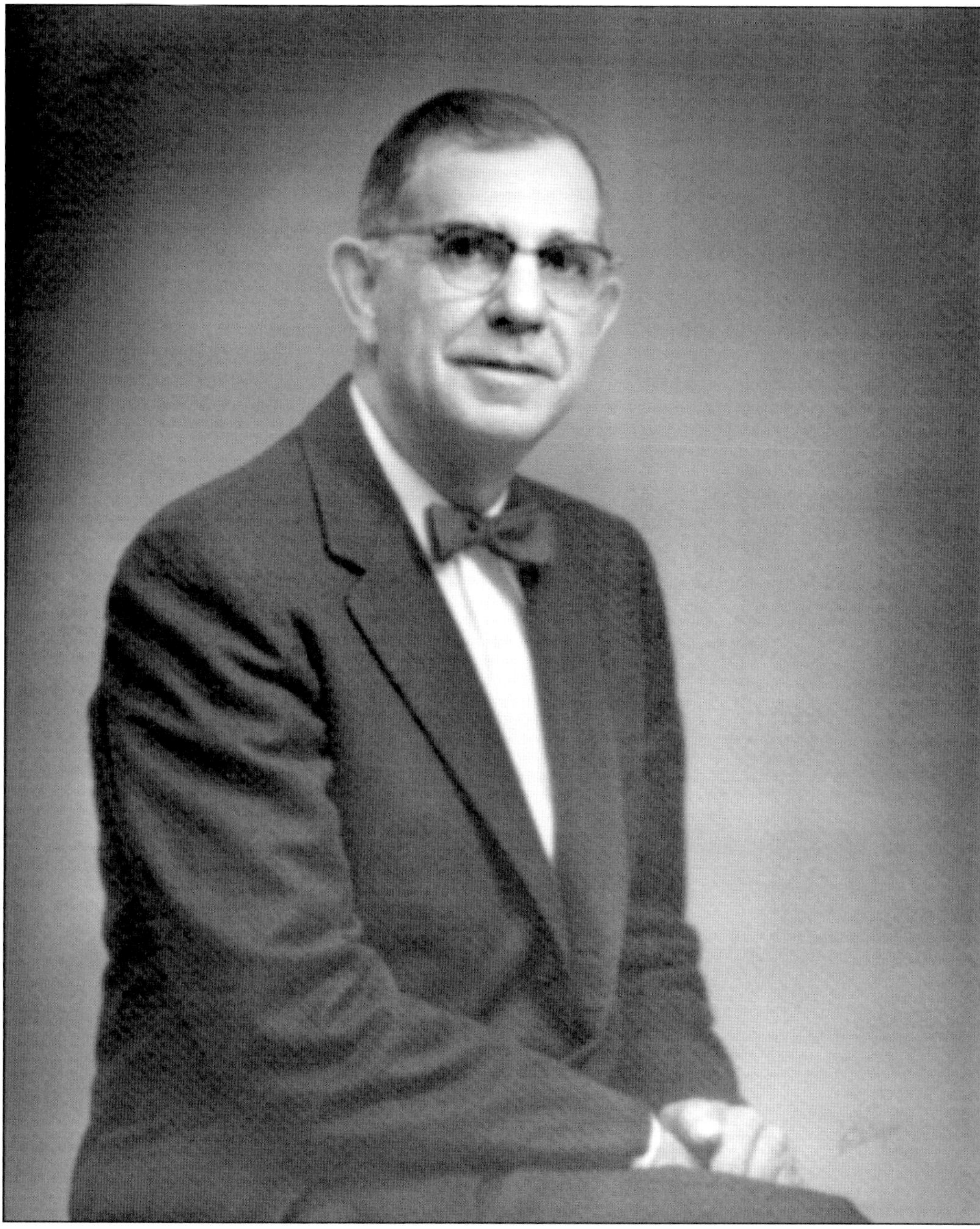

Josiah "Joe" Leonard Sharit has become widely and favorably known as Port St. Joe's mayor. He particularly distinguished himself as superintendent of the Apalachicola Northern Railway and as a state senator. Born January 4, 1895, in Cottondale, Florida, he was the son of James H. and Leah Mildred (Woodward) Sharit. His paternal grandparents came to Florida in 1845. Joe Sharit moved to Port St. Joe in 1917 as a telegrapher for the Apalachicola Northern Railroad Company. He worked his way up and was appointed general manager in 1937. He served the 25th District as state senator from 1936 to 1940. He was vice president and director of the Florida National Bank. At the time of his death, Sharit was completing his 18th year as mayor of Port St. Joe. (JSIII.)

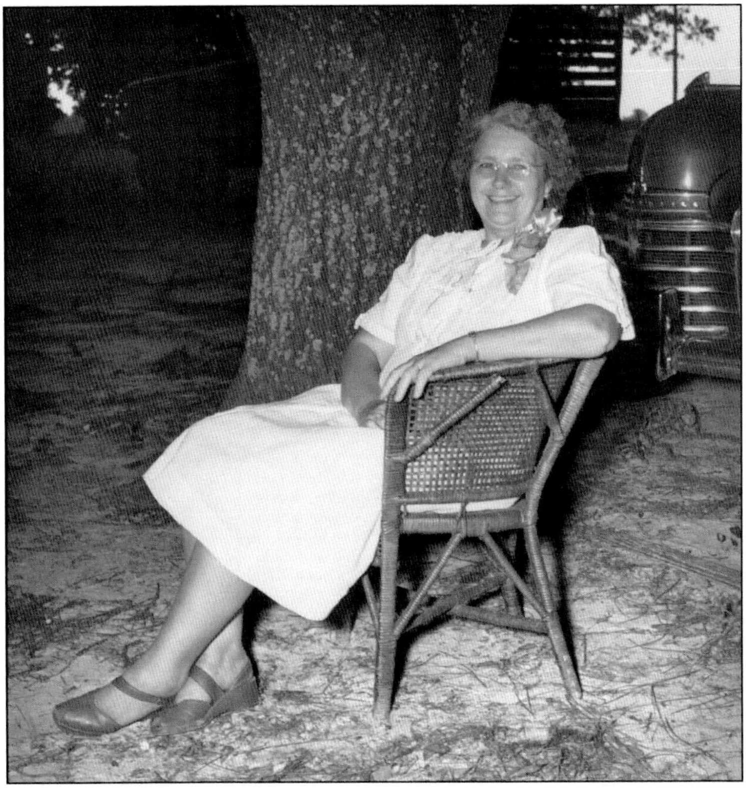

Mrs. Pearl Whitfield was a native of Washington County, Georgia. She attended the University of Georgia. Pearl was Gulf County's first home demonstration agent for the Florida Extension Service. She was a charter member of the Wewahitchka Woman's Club and a member of the First United Methodist Church of Wewahitchka. She was the wife of Joseph A. Whitfield. (AAW.)

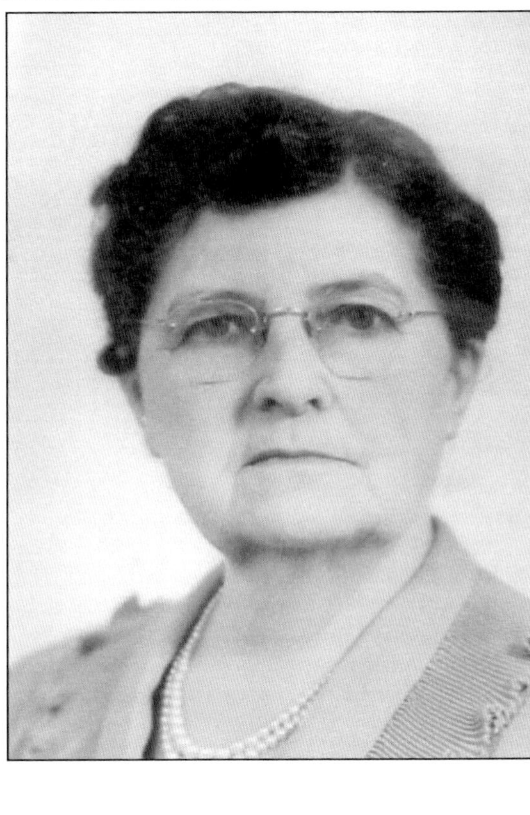

Annie Virginia Wynn Stone of Dubin, Georgia, was the daughter of Jasper C. and Annie (Bracewell) Wynn. Her father was a minister. She married Terrell Higdon Stone, who is known as the founder of Port St. Joe, in 1904. They moved to the wilderness that preceded the development of the town. With her husband, she watched and guided the birth and growth of Port St. Joe and Gulf County. (VSH.)

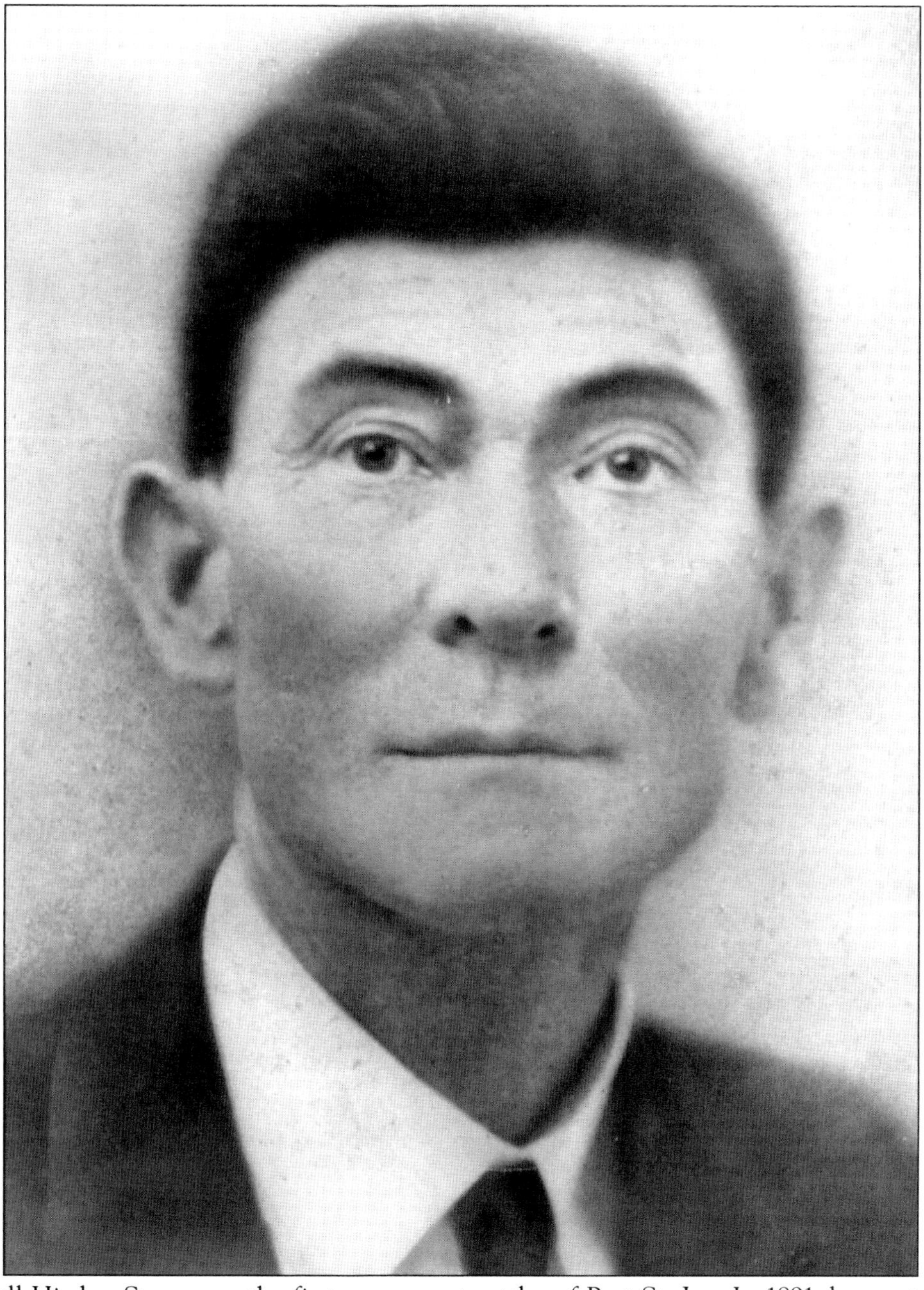

Terrell Higdon Stone was the first permanent settler of Port St. Joe. In 1891, he went into business for himself, opening a general store at Magnolia Landing on the Chipola River, south of Wewahitchka. He was also employed by the federal government as a mail carrier. The mail was left at his store, and he carried it on horseback to the Wewahitchka Post Office. He married Annie Wynn and moved to Port St. Joe in 1904 to establish and operate a naval stores business. He became the first postmaster in 1907 and was instrumental in bringing the Apalachicola Northern Railroad to the shores of St. Joseph Bay in 1910. Stone was instrumental in having the city of Port St. Joe incorporated in 1913 and was successful in having it divided from Calhoun County, forming Gulf County in 1925. (VSH.)

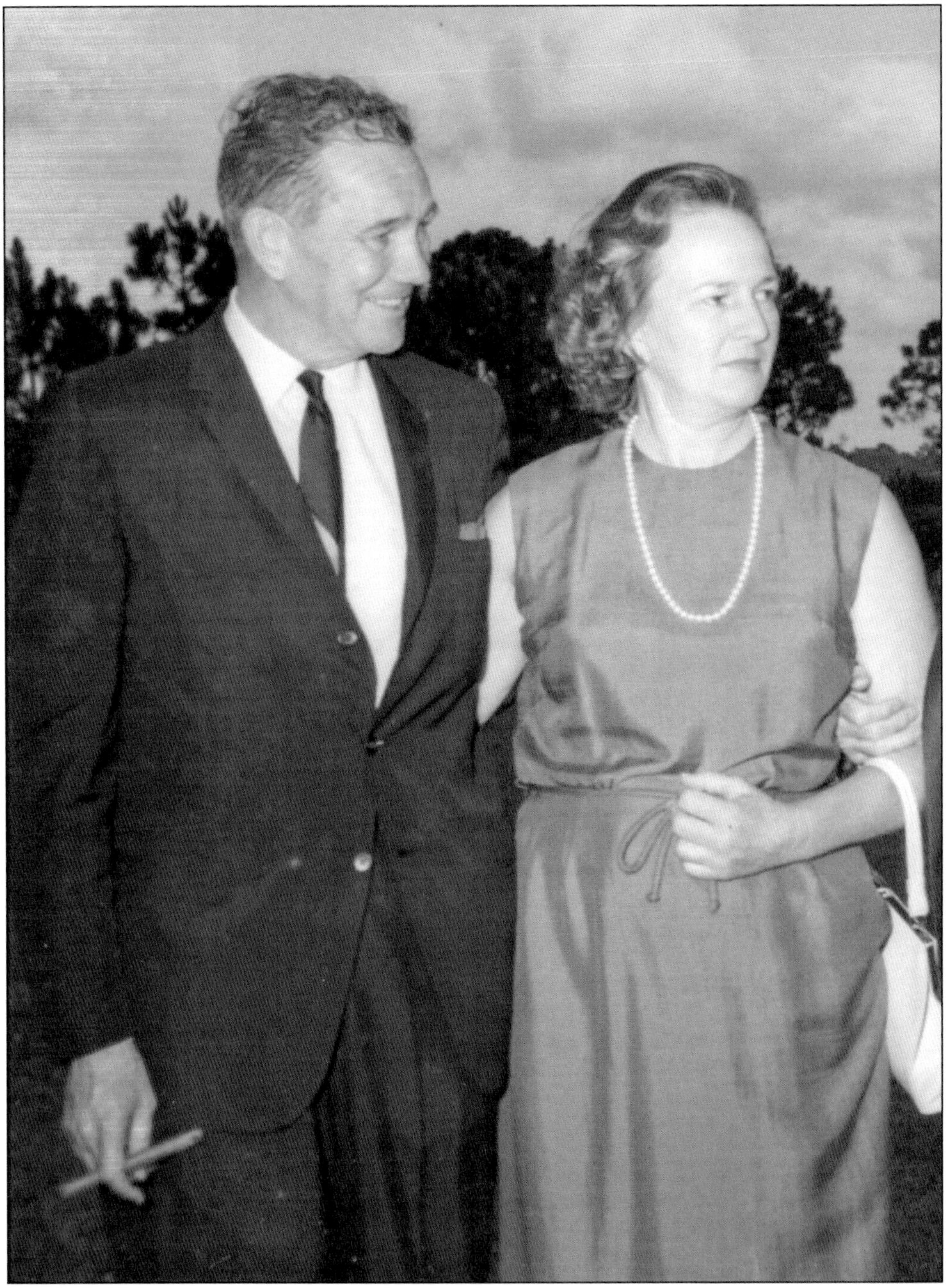

George Tapper learned from his father the life of the sea and private enterprise. He was the first Florida highway patrolman. When the FHP was abolished in 1937, Tapper became director for the paper mill that was under construction. A year later, he became the port director for the Port St. Joe Terminal Company. In 1940, he entered politics and became the youngest Floridian to be elected into office. He married Amelia "Amy" Gibson, who was known as a warm and gentle lady. She was a member of the DAR and served on the Gulf Coast Community College Board, filling her husband's position after his death in 1986. She was most noted for her integrity, excellent communications and management skills, and her insight in guiding college policies. The Amelia G. Tapper Center for the Arts was dedicated on November 10, 1994. (TTW.)

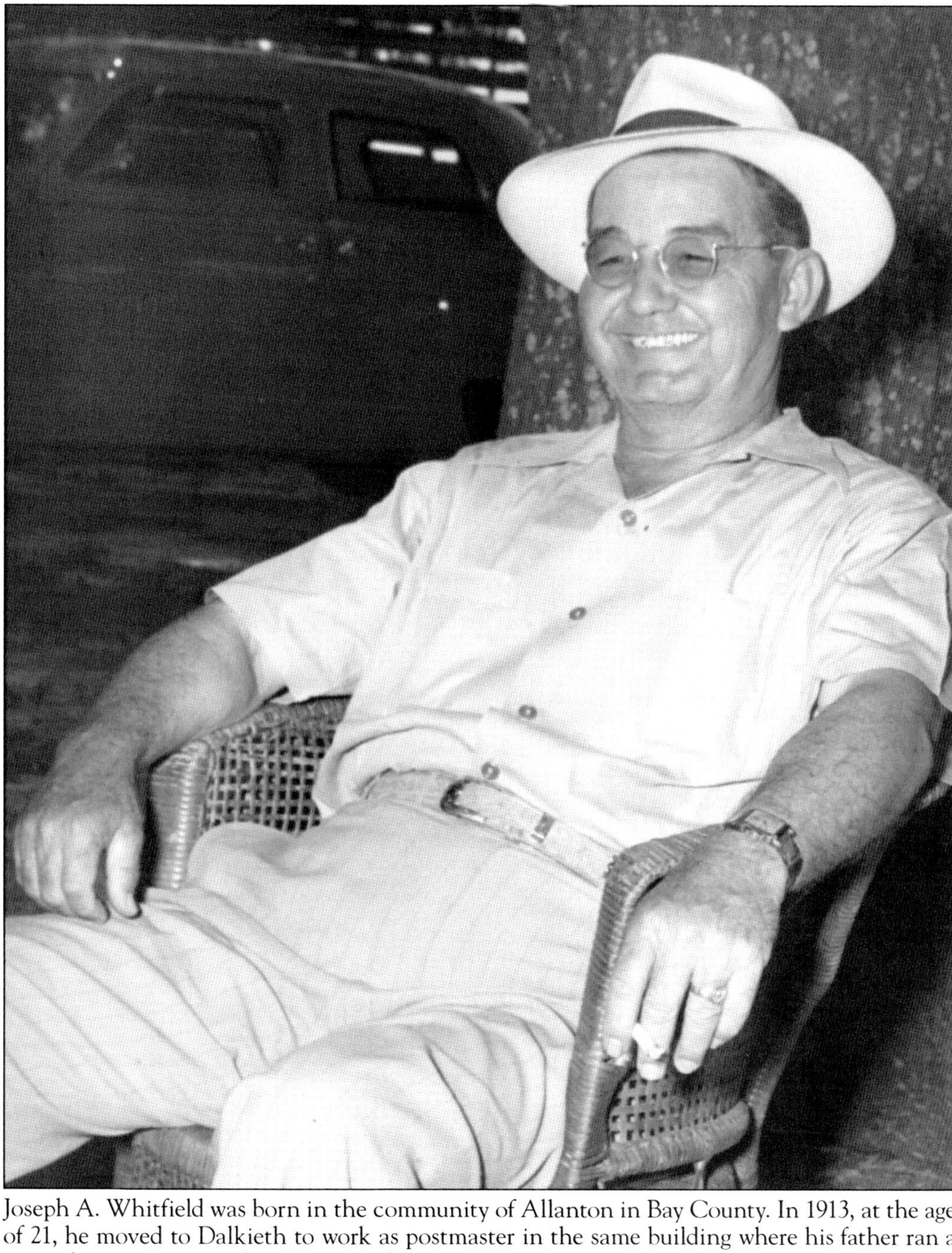

Joseph A. Whitfield was born in the community of Allanton in Bay County. In 1913, at the age of 21, he moved to Dalkieth to work as postmaster in the same building where his father ran a general store. Joe moved to Wewahitchka in 1925 and opened the Pride Mercantile Company. He sold his interest in the business in 1935 and decided to make a living producing tupelo honey. Whitfield Apiaries became the largest producer of tupelo honey in the area. Joe served in the following positions: city clerk, president of the State Beekeepers' Association, sales manager of Gulf County Tupelo Honey Cooperative, member of the Wewahitchka State Bank Board of Directors, member of the District Welfare Board, and the first county supervisor of registration. (AAW.)

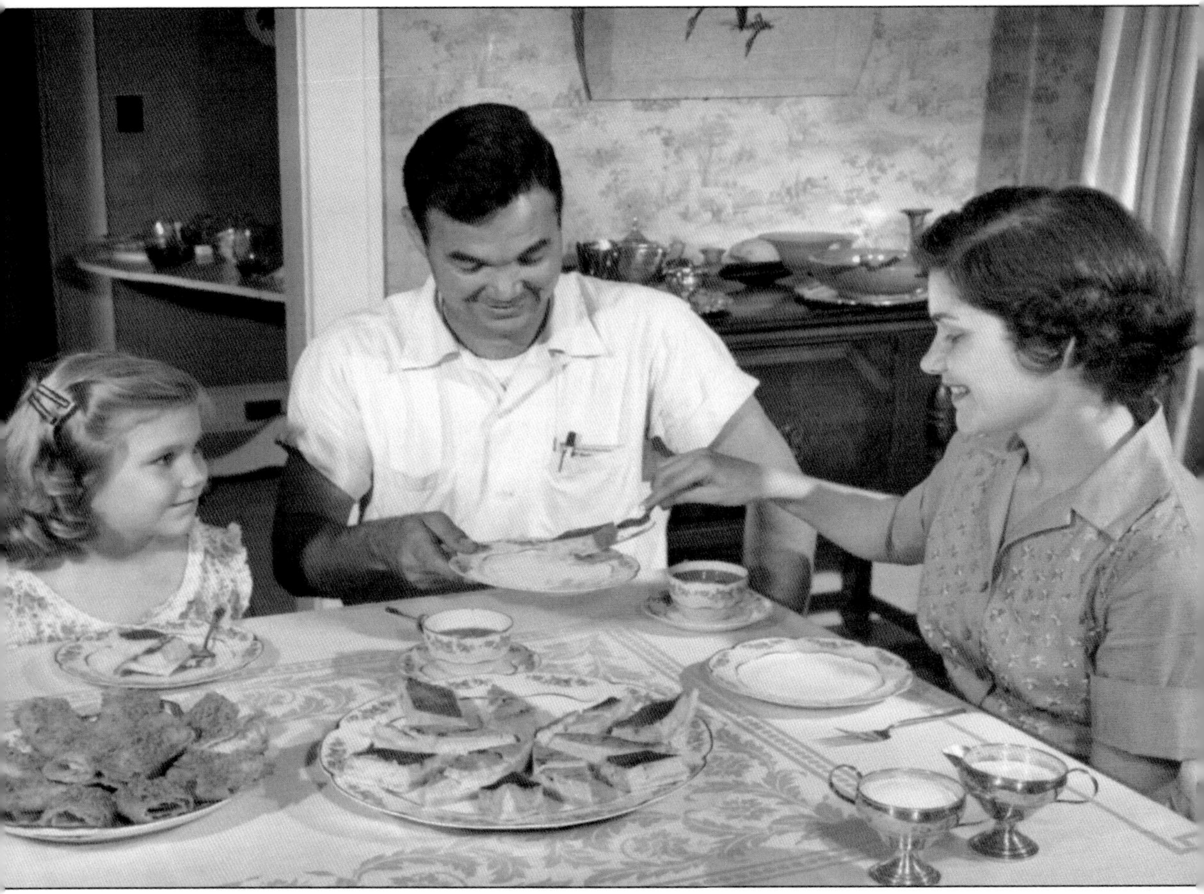

Alfred Whitfield, son of Joseph and Mae (Brown) Whitfield, followed in his fathers' footsteps as he worked in the honey business, while his wife, Angie, taught at Wewahitchka High School. Here is a June 1960 photograph with Alfred, Angie, and daughter Connie sitting down to some wonderful little Greek honey curls and honey cheesecakes that Angie and her mother, Dena Batis, baked. The Whitfield Reunion is one of the largest annual reunions held in Wewahitchka today. (AAW.)

Two

WORKING FOR A LIVING

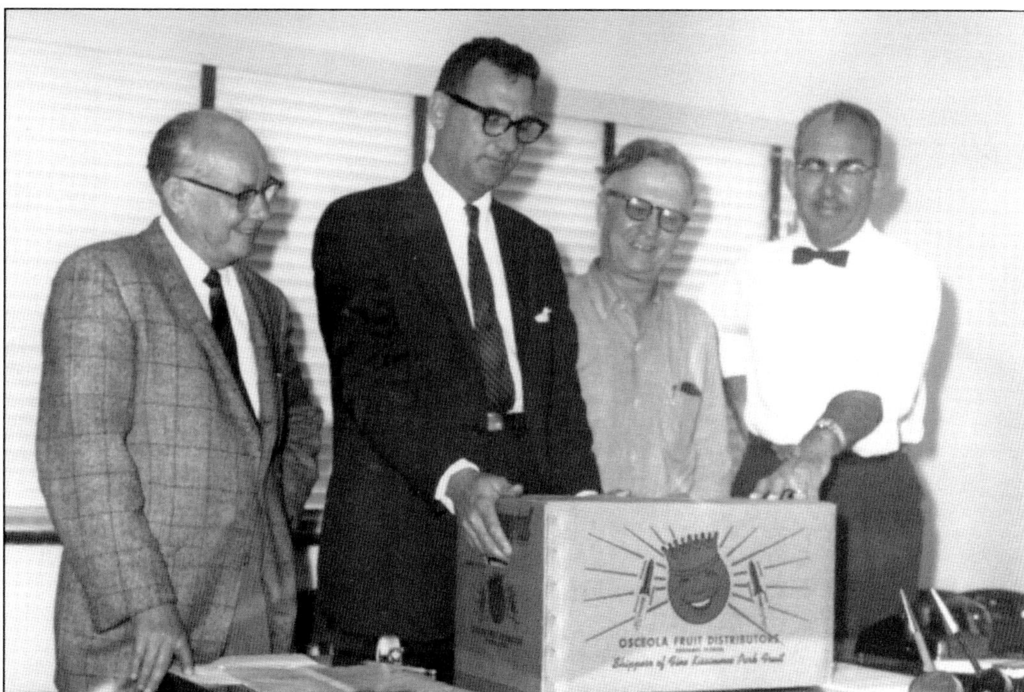

The St. Joe Box Plant is checking out a new package that they produced. From left to right are Wayne Ashley, Jake Belin, Ralph Rich, and Terry Hinote. (St. Joe Co.)

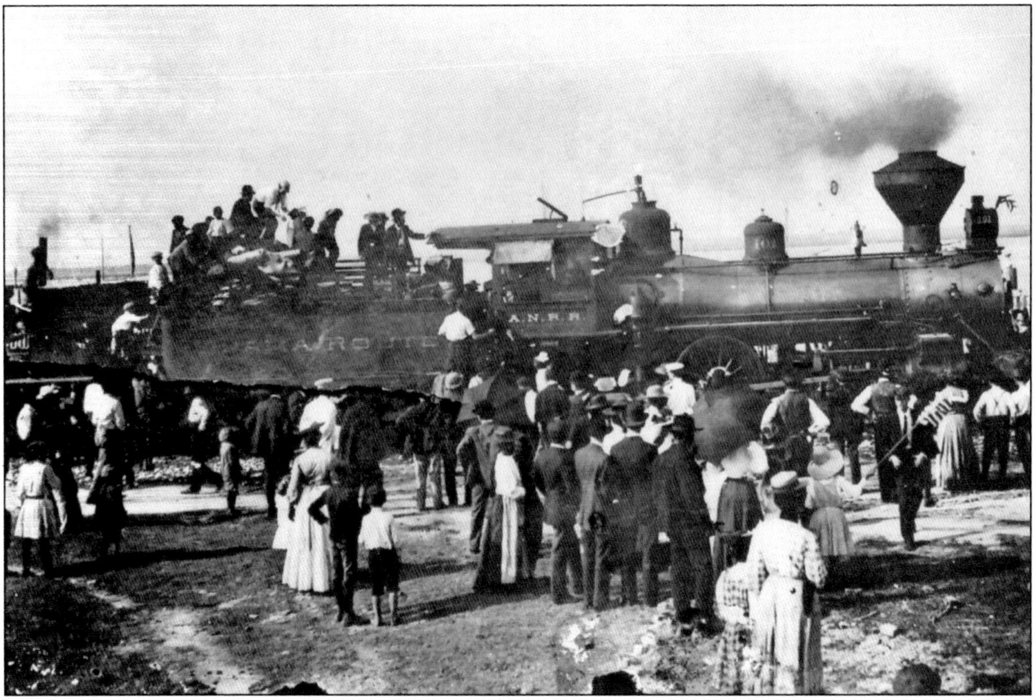

A work train was the first train to reach Apalachicola on April 30, 1907. It was pulled by No. 101, a Baldwin 4-4-0. Engineer George Johnson was at the throttle, there was a fireman named Rambo, and Sy Williams was the conductor. (BH.)

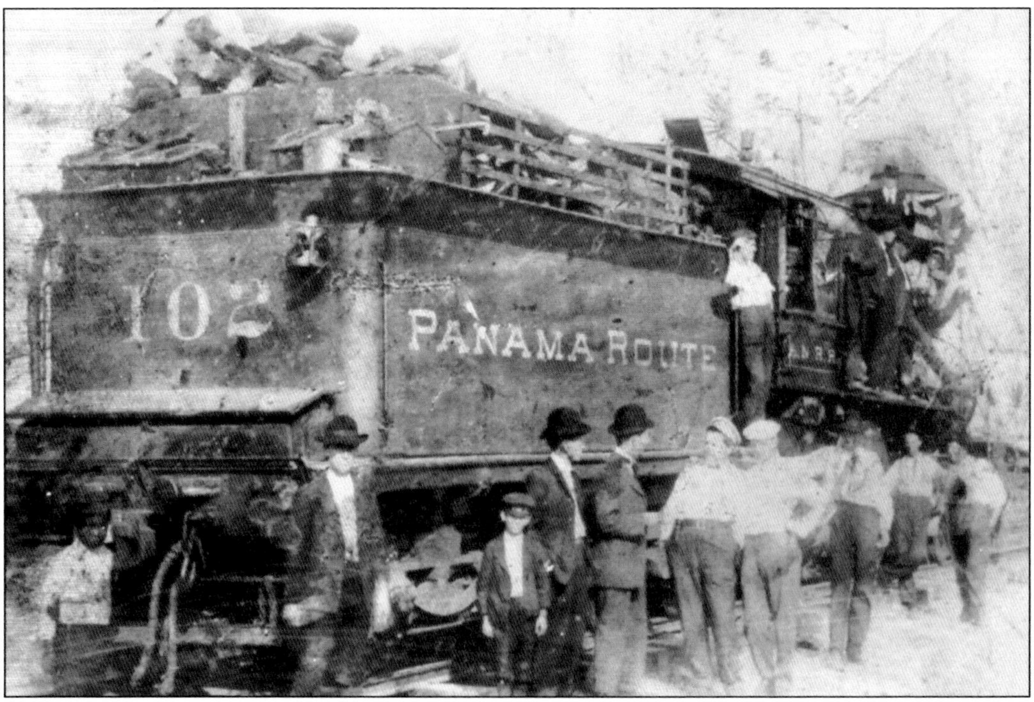

The first train came into Port St. Joe in 1909. It was owned by Apalachicola Northern Railroad and proved to be something big for all the citizens of the town. (BH.)

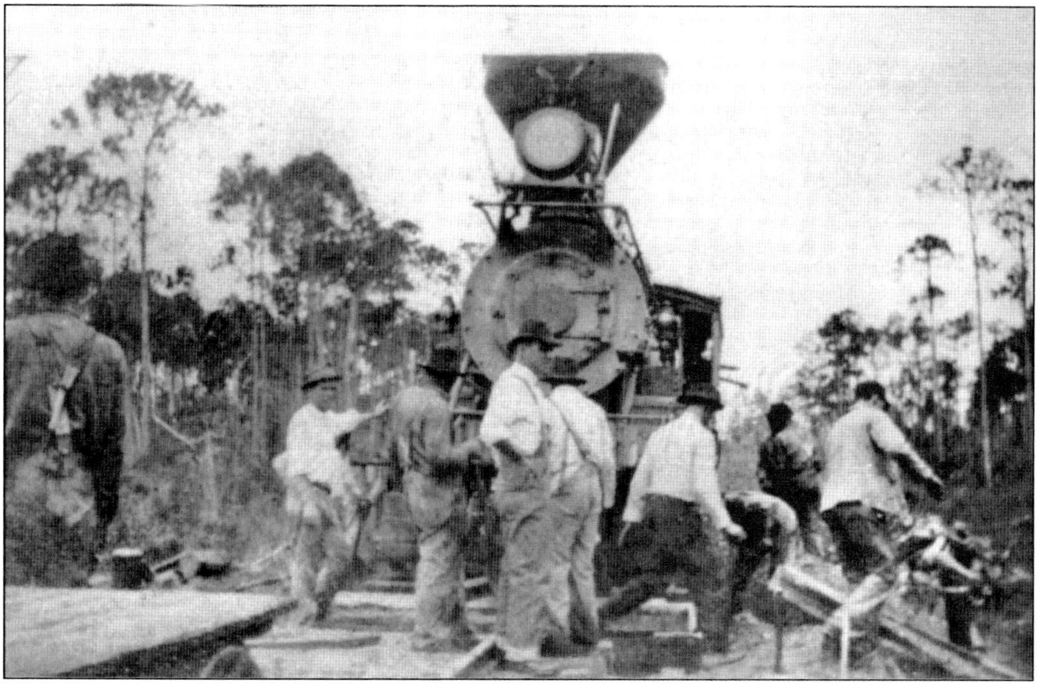

Engine No. 101, a passenger train, was involved in a wreck at Fort Gadsden Creek on a burn trestle around 1914. It was later repaired and put back into service. (BH.)

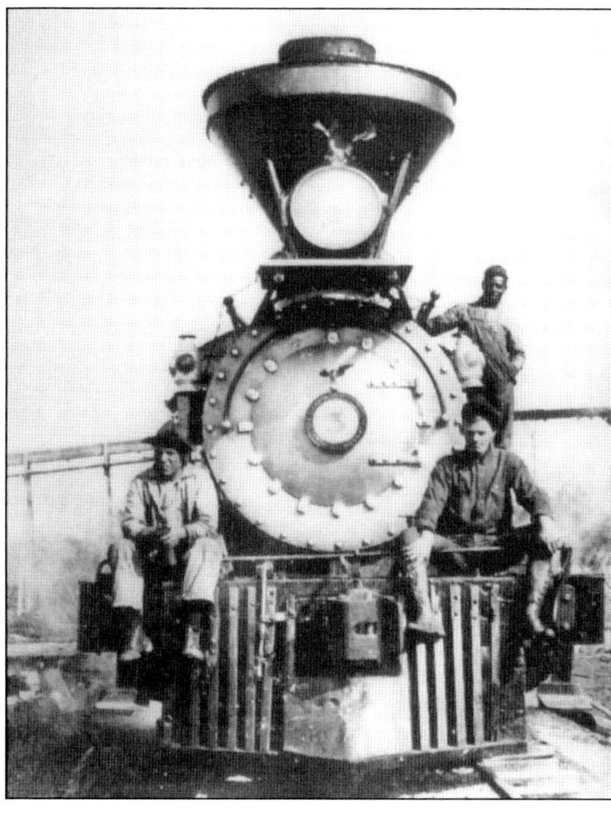

This photograph of Apalachicola Northern Railroad Engine No. 3 shows a man known as "Rambo" sitting on the left and Lewis R. Holiday on the right. The man in back is unidentified. This train was hauling lumber to Hosford in the 1920s. (BH.)

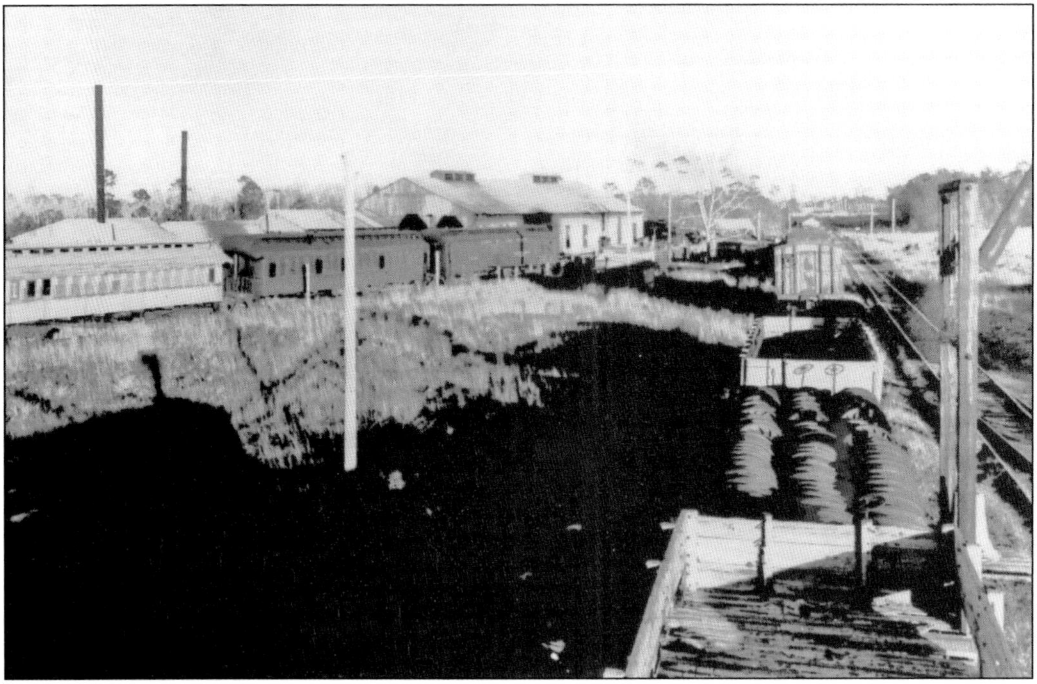

This photograph, taken in 1937, shows the scenery from the second-floor window of the railroad depot overlooking the train yard. This was prior to the opening of St. Joe Paper Co. (BH.)

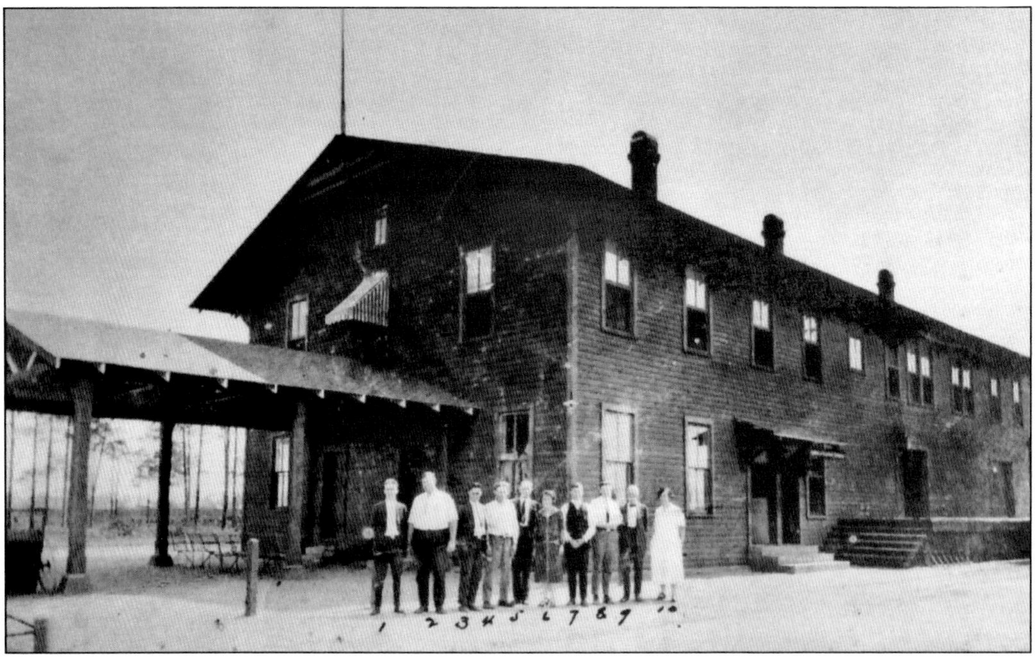

The original building for the Apalachicola Northern Railroad Depot and the St. Joseph Telephone and Telegraph Company was built in 1909. In the 1960s, it was demolished and a brick building replaced the original one. Shown from left to right are M. C. Edwards, C. B. McCranie, O. L. McCranie, F. M. Rownan, A. M. Jones, A. Smith, Henry A. Drake, B. W. Spear, B. S. McCranie, and ? Coleman. (BH.)

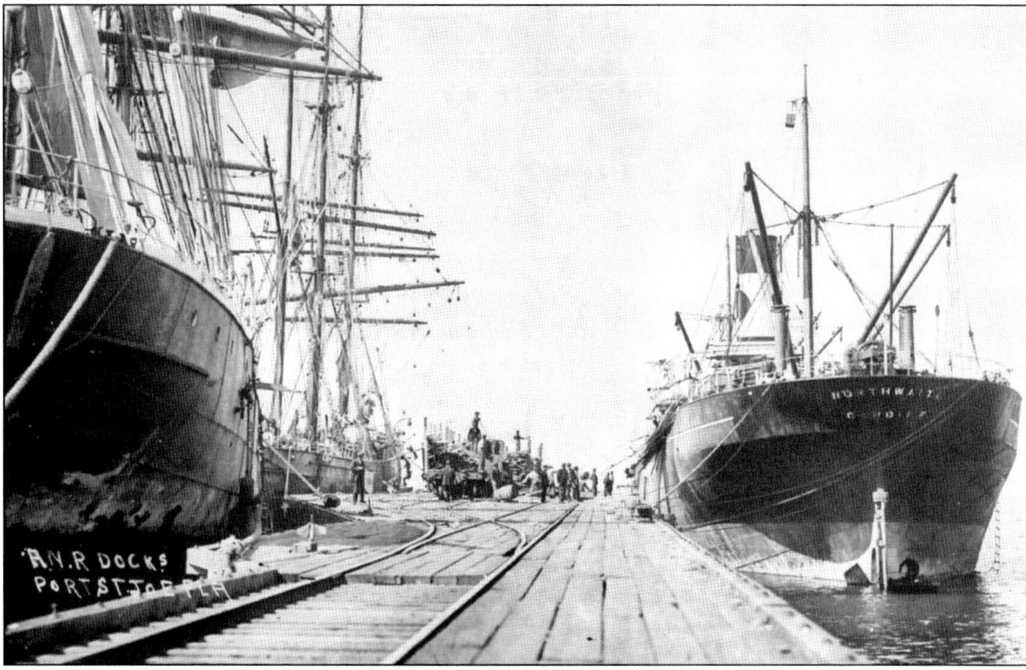

Shipping in Gulf County dates back to the days of Old St. Joseph, and the industry was resumed in 1910, when the Apalachicola Northern Railroad was completed to Port St. Joe. The docks were built before 1914 and were constructed out into the bay to accommodate large freighters. ANRR stopped using the docks in the mid-1930s. Many vessels loaded lumber from St. Joseph Lumber and Export Company. (BH.)

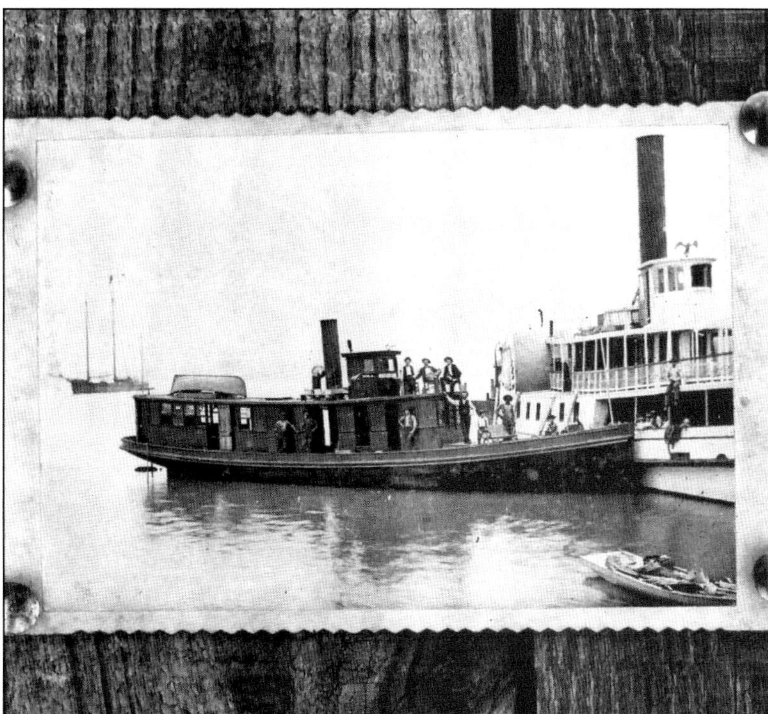

The *Iola* and the steamboat *Eufaula* were primary ships for passengers, express cargo, and mail carriers for many years. They traveled to and from Carrabelle and Apalachicola. The *Iola* was a hand-fired boiler that burned fat lighter wood and was built around 1918. (BH.)

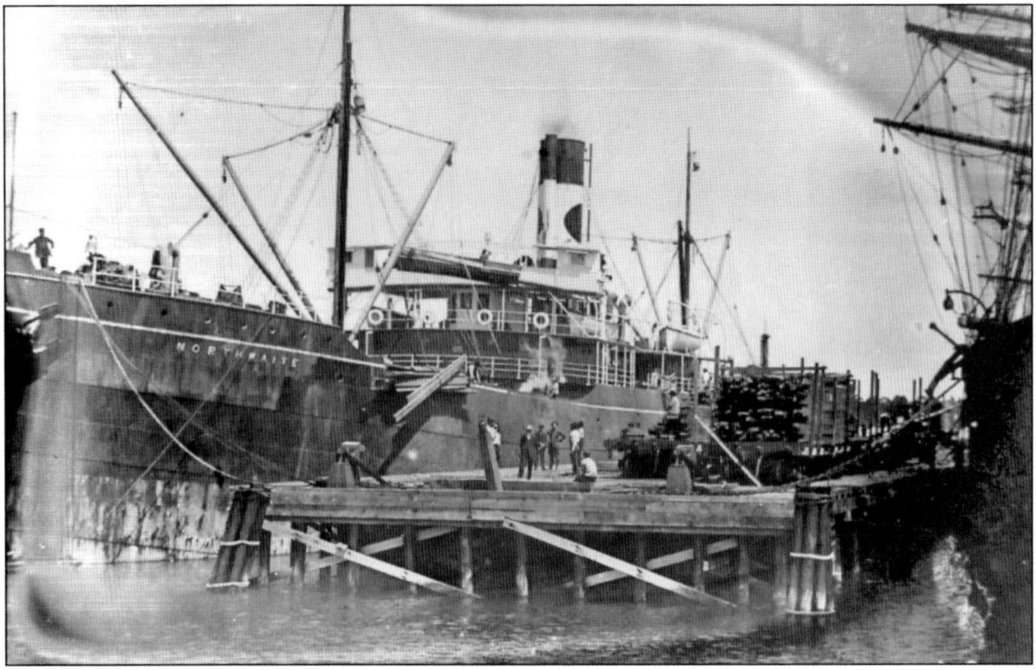

Sailing vessels loaded lumber and barrels of rosin here from approximately 1912 to the 1930s. Ships such as the *Northwaite*, *Henrietta*, *Birchwood*, and the *Belmont* docked at Port St. Joe. The *Northwaite*, shown here, is a steamer taking on lumber for exporting. (BH.)

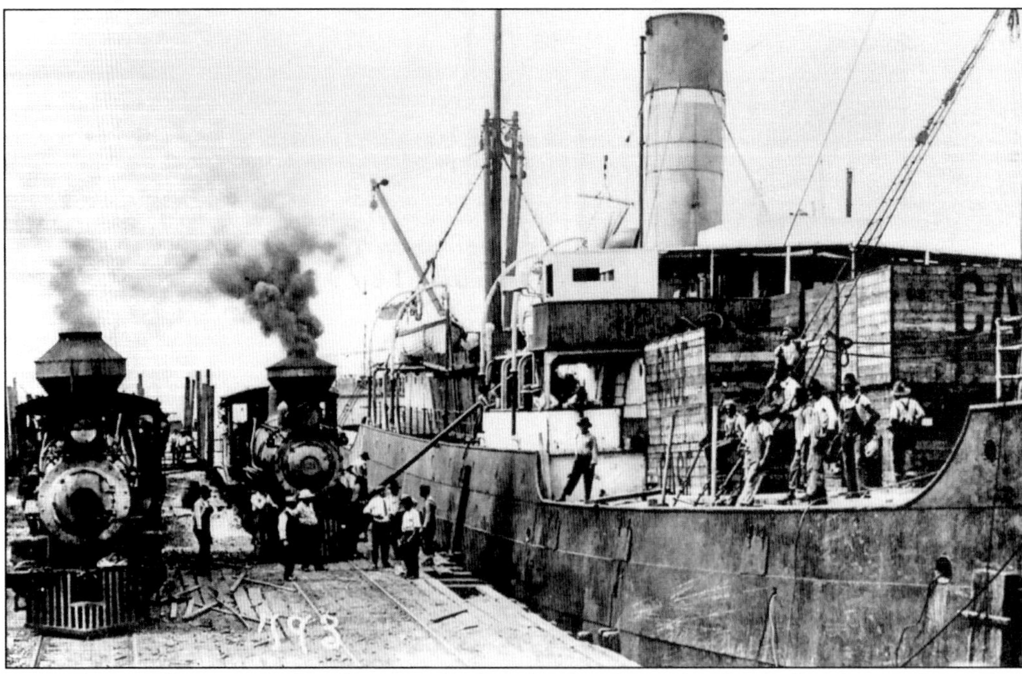

Around 1914, the steamer *Farnham* was loading lumber from the Apalachicola Northern dock at Port St. Joe. The locomotive at left is 4-4-0 No. 101, and 4-6-0 No. 123 is alongside the ship. Located just south of the paper mill, the docks fell into disuse during the Depression years. Most of the docks were removed in 1937 during the construction of the paper mill. (BH.)

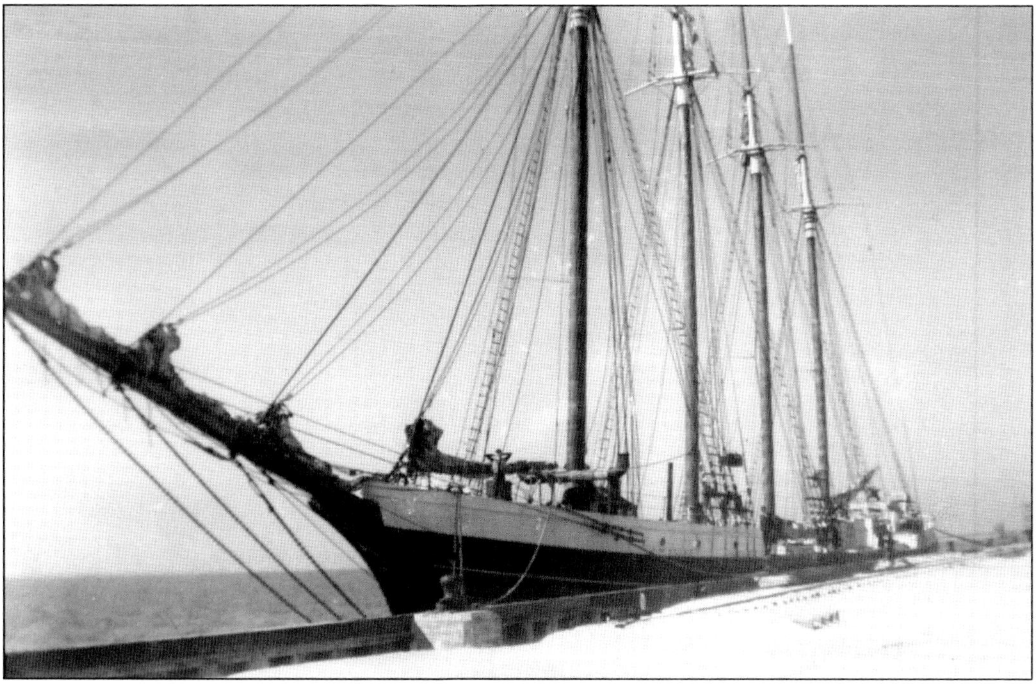

Fred Maddox was pilot of the *J. W. Clis*, the last of the four-masted schooners to load lumber for exporting from the St. Joe docks, around 1937. She was built about 1904 and was owned from the 1920s until 1939 by the Putnam Lumber Company, based in Shamrock, Florida. It was captained by Richard Copsey. The ship became disabled several hundred miles south of Mobile during an August 1940 hurricane. (BH.)

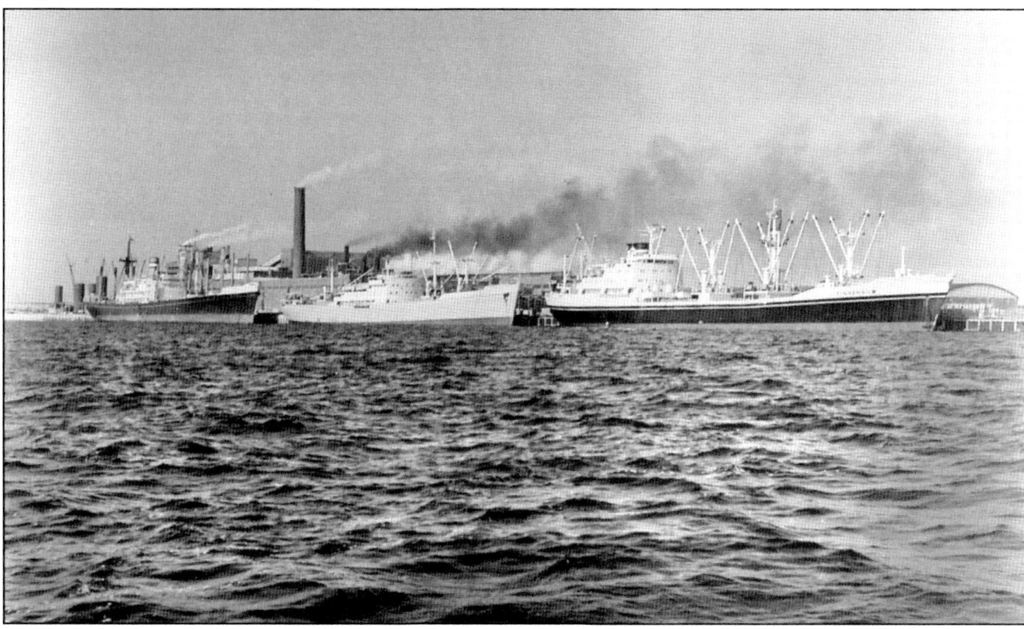

Ships could be seen loading paper for exporting at the St. Joe Docks. At far left is the SS *Alpasserdyk*, a freighter owned by the Holland-American Lines. The middle ship is from Yugoslavia, and to the right is a freighter named the MS *Finnboard*. (BH.)

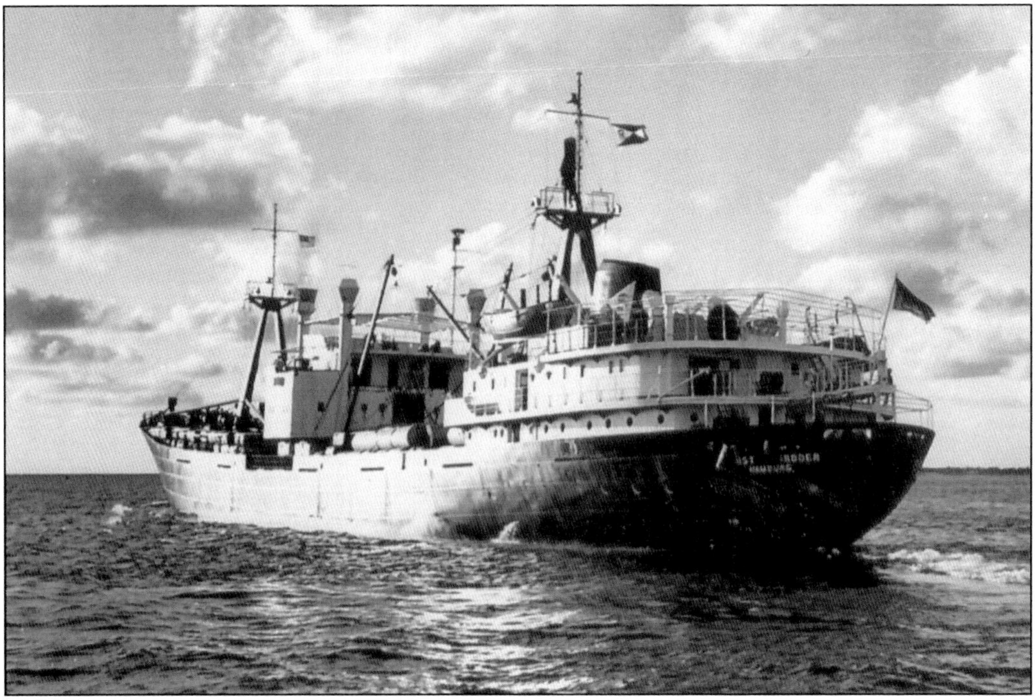

Dave Maddox was the pilot in the 1960s when this German freighter came for a load of paper from the St. Joe Paper Company. (BH.)

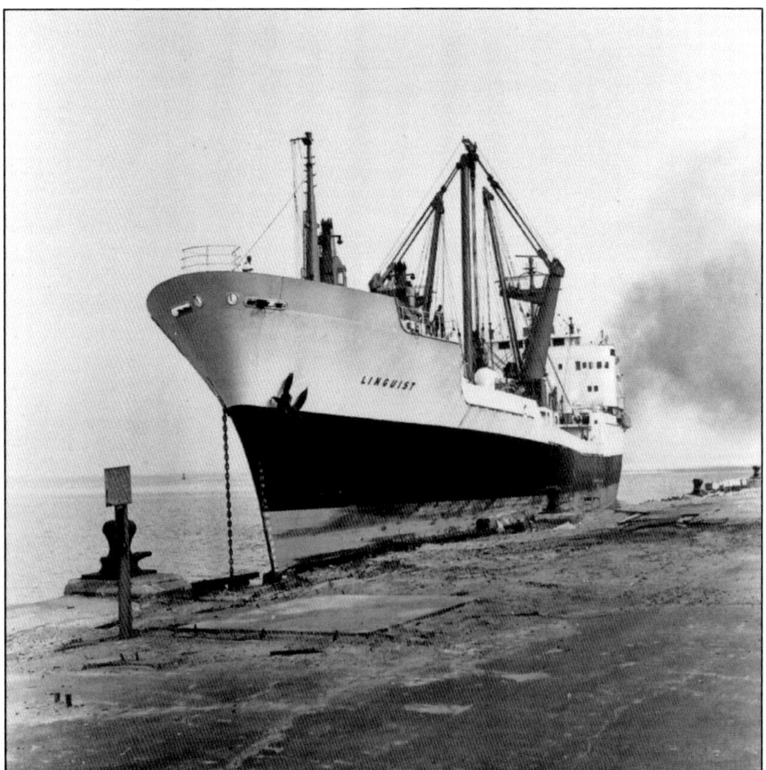

The MS *Linguist*, a British ship, is shown here in the 1970s on the first port of call in America, picking up paper from the St. Joe Company. (BH.)

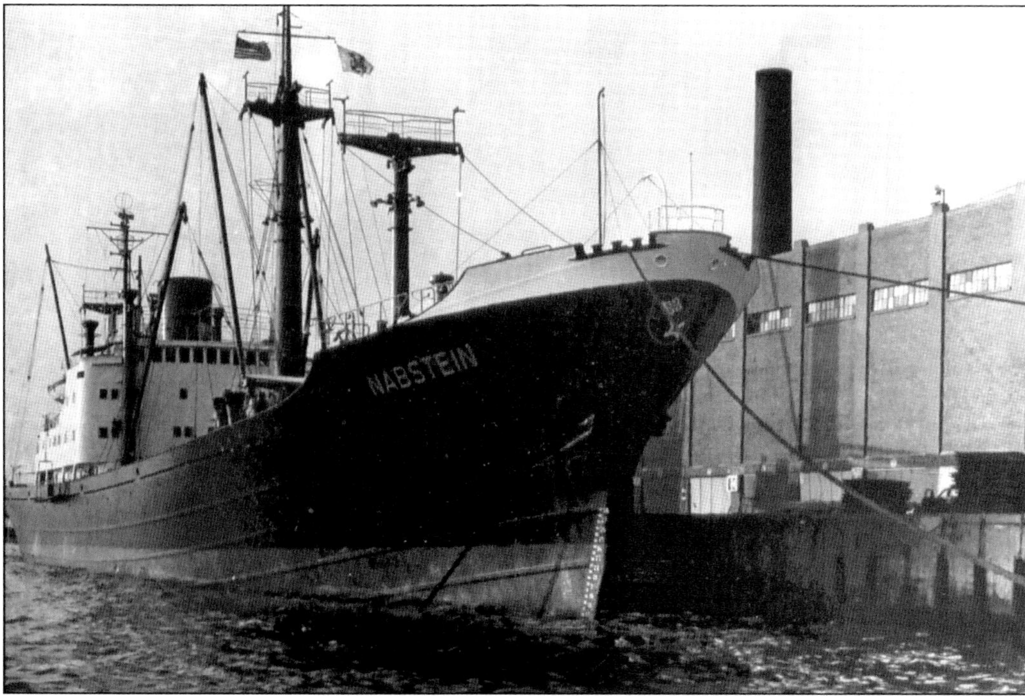

The MS *Nabstein*, another fairly large German ship, is shown loading paper from the Port St. Joe docks. (BH.)

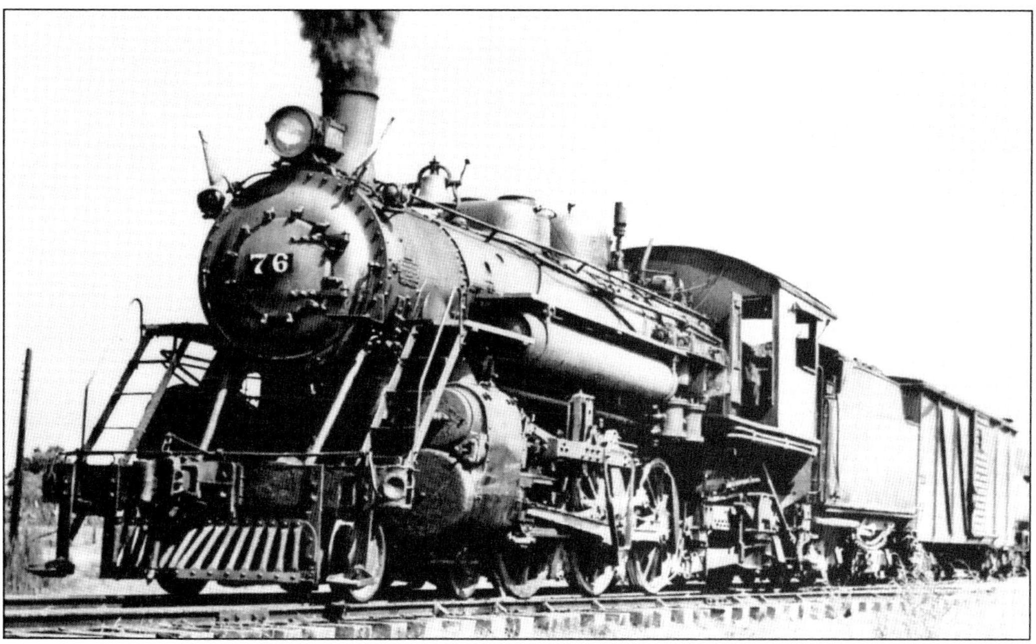

Engine No. 76 was one of five locomotives that ANRR acquired from the Florida East Coastal Railway. This company operated an overseas railroad from Miami to Key West until it was destroyed by a hurricane in 1935. These locomotives were light and very fast, which made them prefect for passenger service. (BH.)

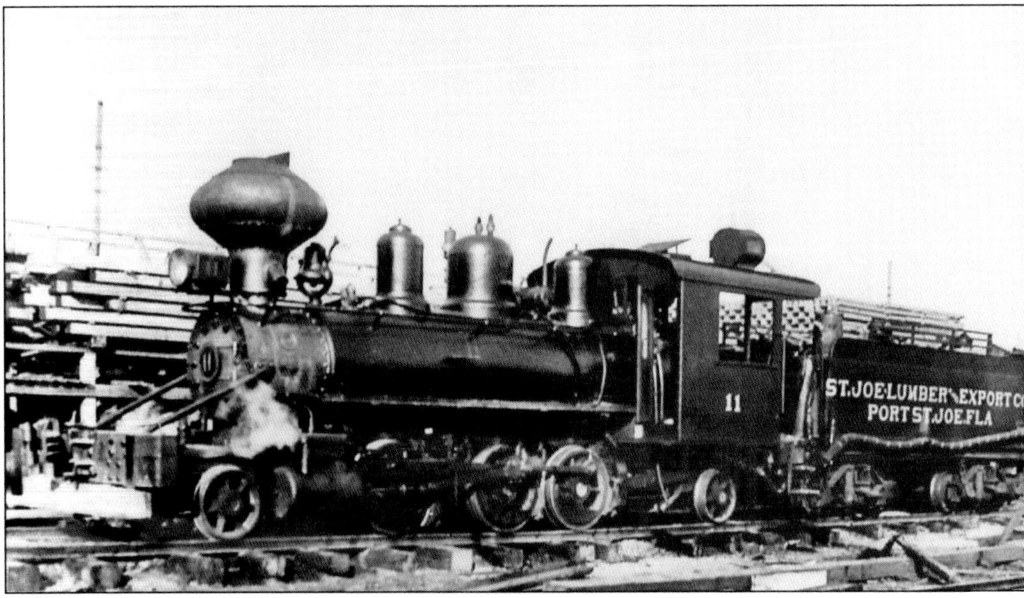

By the 1940s, railroad logging in the Panhandle of Florida was in imminent danger of becoming just a footnote in the history books. The new St. Joe Lumber and Export Company was incorporated in Gulf County on June 16, 1940. Her sister engine, No. 11, is on display at the Centennial Building in Port St. Joe. (BH.)

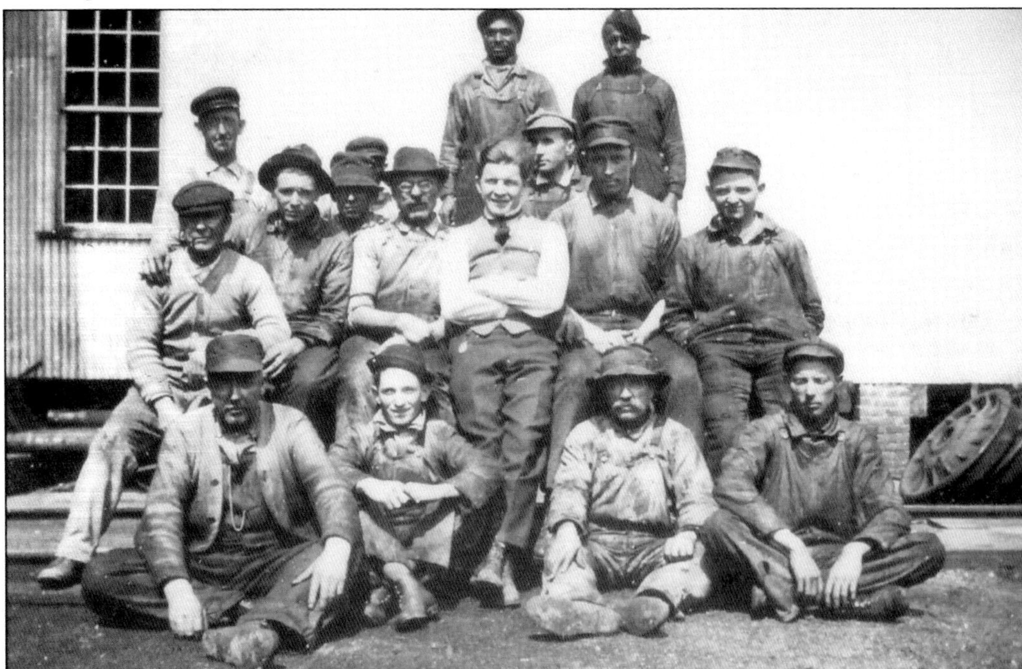

Apalachicola Northern Railroad crew members from the railroad shop in Port St. Joe are shown here. They worked on many jobs, including cleaning the inside of coaches. Some worked as car repairers or "car knockers," as they were called, and some painted railroad cars and did other menial tasks. This photograph was taken about 1918. The gentleman on the far left of the first row is Max Dunaway, great-uncle to the actress Faye Dunaway. (BH.)

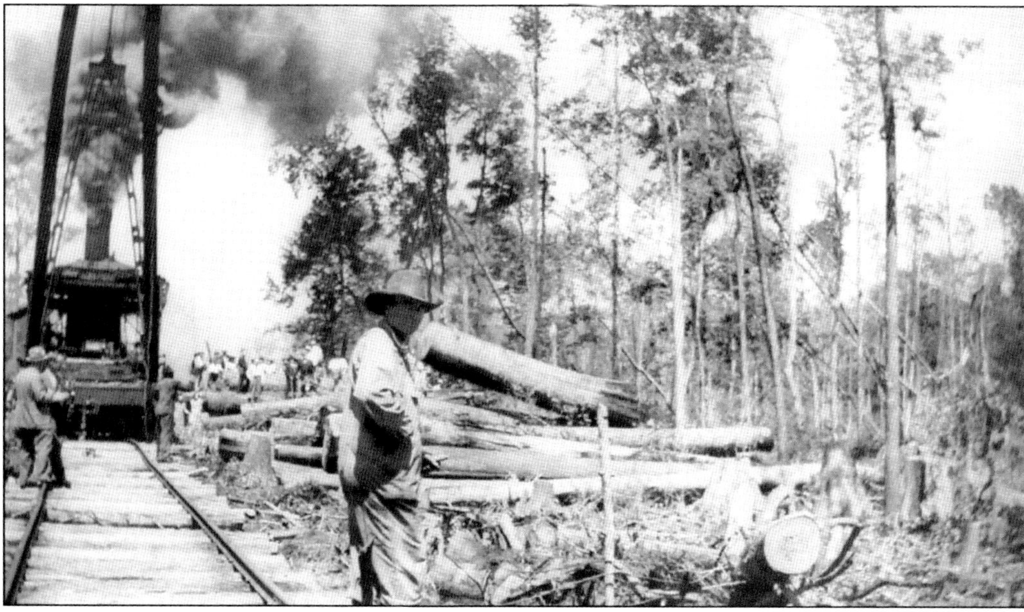

Work was hard as men were building railroad tracks into Port St. Joe. The swamps and wetlands made it hard on the skidders, loggers, and those laying tracks. This photograph was taken between Port St. Joe and Apalachicola. (BH.)

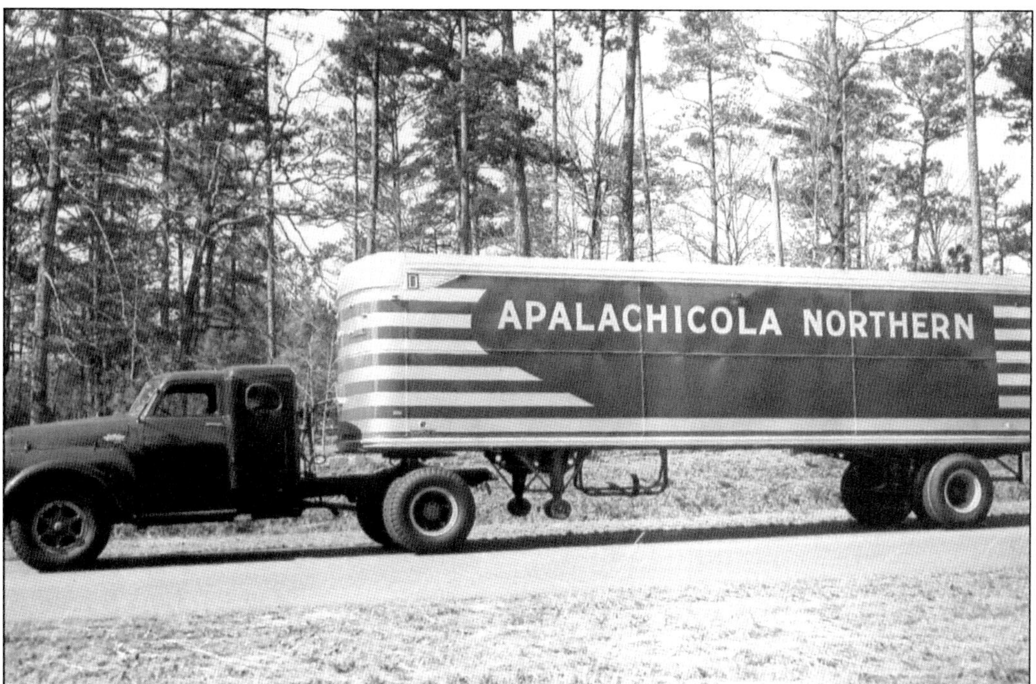

Train service ended in 1952. The ANRR contract for hauling express and U.S. mail needed to be completed, so the railroad company bought a truck to deliver the mail, which came from Climax, Georgia, to Apalachicola and to Port St. Joe. The truck was always on time and would arrive by 7:00 or 7:30 each morning. (BH.)

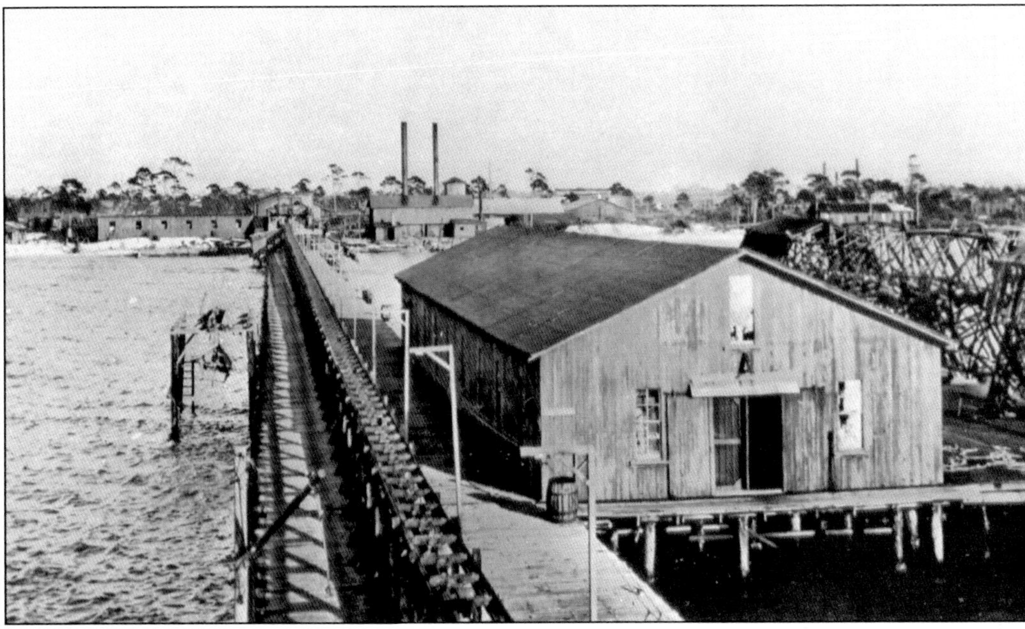

The Southern Menhaden Corporation was headquartered in Jacksonville, Florida, and controlled by the duPont Power Company of Wilmington, Delaware. It operated a fleet of seine-equipped fishing boats in the waters of the eastern gulf. Fish were caught for the oils that could be used in paints, perfumes, and soap. The scrap parts were shipped to fertilizer plants throughout the South. Some parts were mixed into feed for poultry, hogs, and cattle. (BB.)

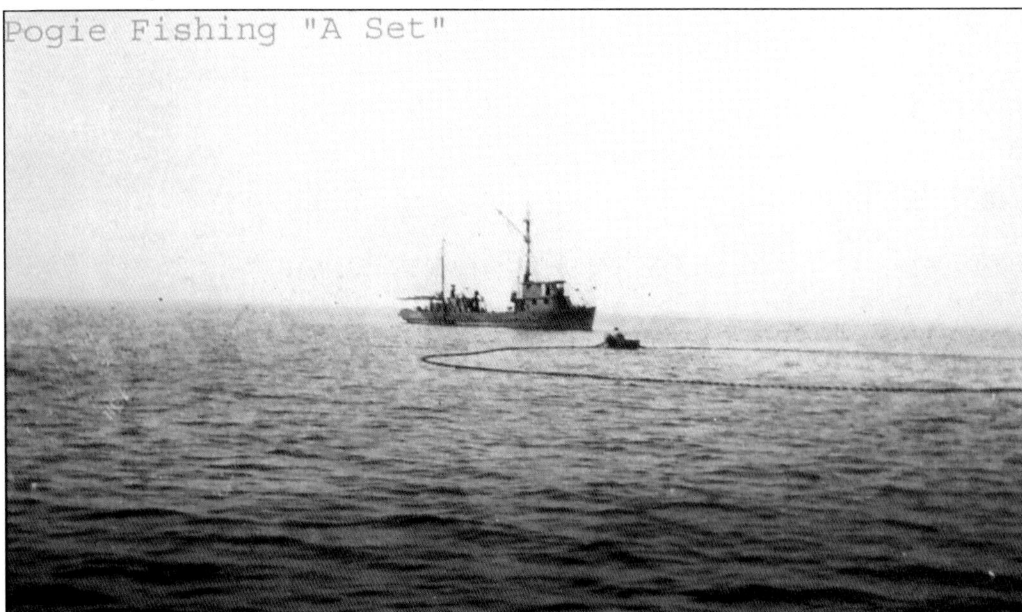

Pogie fishing began in Port St. Joe about 1920. The *Carnival* and the *Novia* were two pogie boats. The *Novia*, commanded by Capt. B. Harrison with a crew of 30 aboard, was lost at sea in August 1939, according to reports from the *Star*, the Port St. Joe newspaper. A daily catch of pogie fish averaged more than 500 barrels. When the area was "fished out," the operation was moved to the Mississippi and Louisiana coast. (BB.)

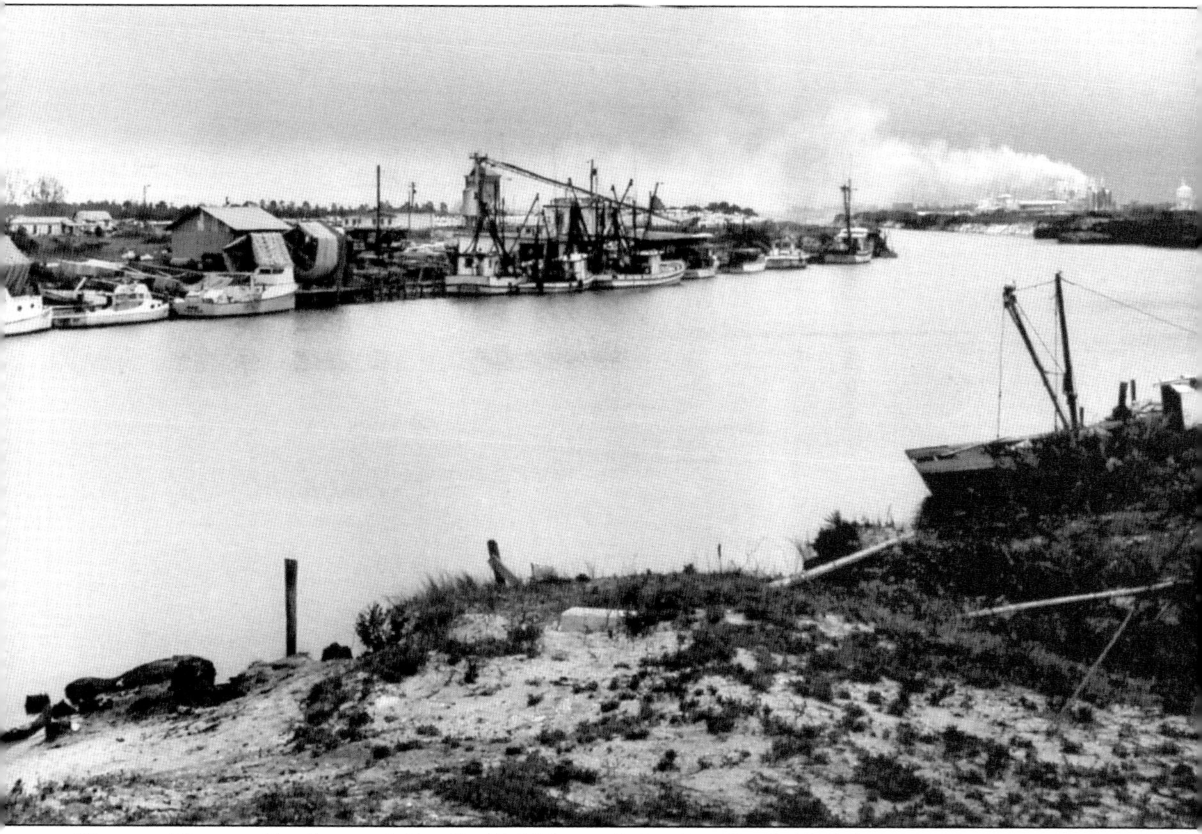

Clayton, Henry, Charlie, and Coy Raffield formed the first Raffield Fisheries in Panama City, Florida. During World War II, many areas around Panama City were closed to fishing, so the families moved to Port St. Joe. Leasing a small tract from St. Joe Paper Company along the newly dug St. Joe Canal, Coy Raffield built a small fish house. This facility was named Gulf Fisheries. A year later, Carl Raffield move to St. Joe and began fishing. Carl soon bought out Gulf Fisheries, and the present-day Raffield Fisheries, seen here some time in the late 1950s, was created. "The Lord has always provided," says Captain Carl. And provide he did—in great abundance. (BH.)

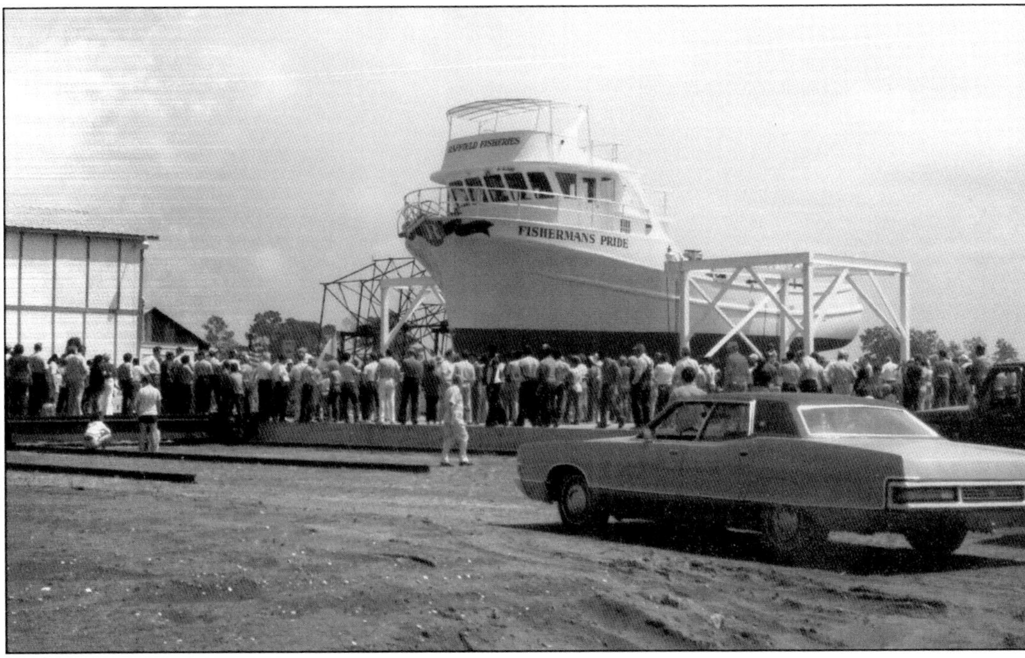

The launching of the *Fisherman's Pride* around 1981 was a memorable time for Highland View. The Raffield and Woods families were great shipbuilders. Today there are many shrimp and fishing boats in the area and in the surrounding counties built by Gabe, M. C., and L. C. Wood. They can be seen still in service working in the bays. (PPL.)

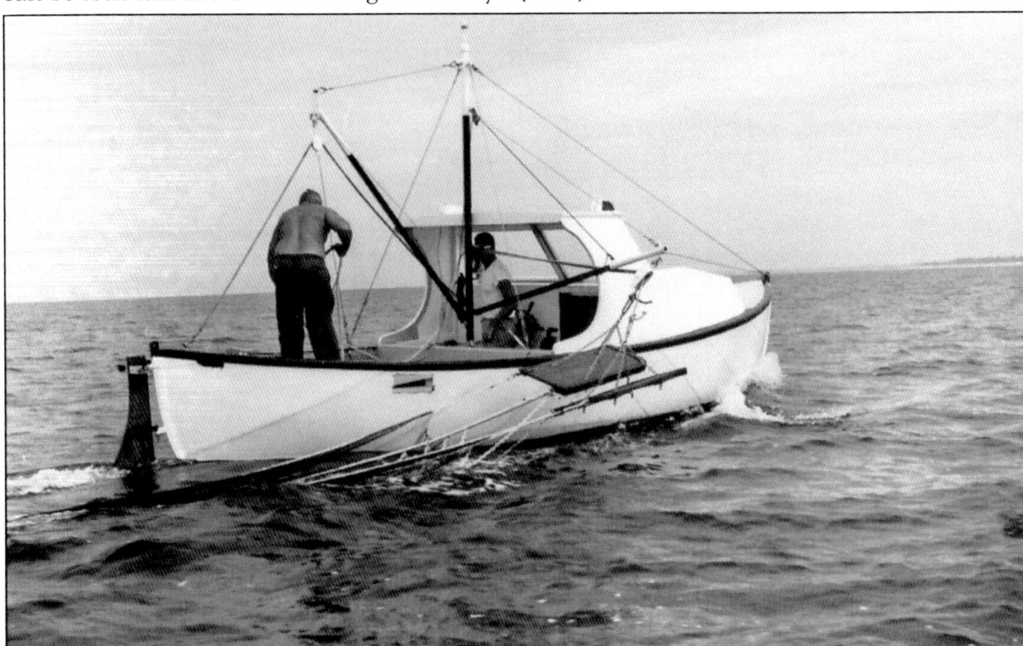

Many locals built their own boats and shrimped in the area bays. *The Sweet Gum* was a small boat built by Clinton Peterson and Billy Howell. This little boat was rebuilt from a lifeboat taken from the Liberty ship *Big Foot Wallace*. She was a hand-crank, four-cylinder, imperial gasoline engine. (BH.)

Gabe Wood and brothers L. C. and M. C. were some of the best boat builders in the area. The Wood brothers were known for their talent by many fishermen and shrimpermen. Everyone along the coast knew them well. Shown here is the *Morning Star* still on the dock just before launching. (BH.)

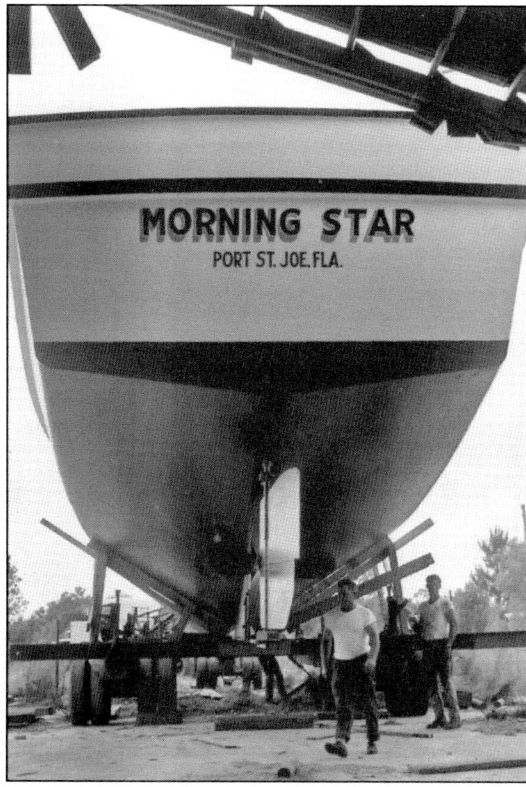

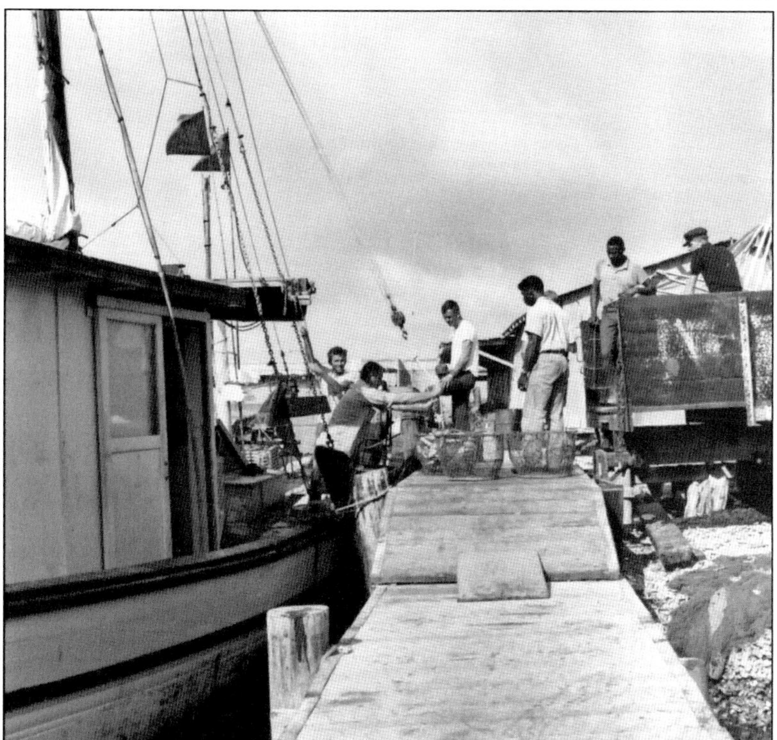

Gene Abrams and Blake Tomlinson owned and operated the Dixie Seafood Company in the early 1960s. Here men are unloading a load of red snapper onto a truck for transporting. (BH.)

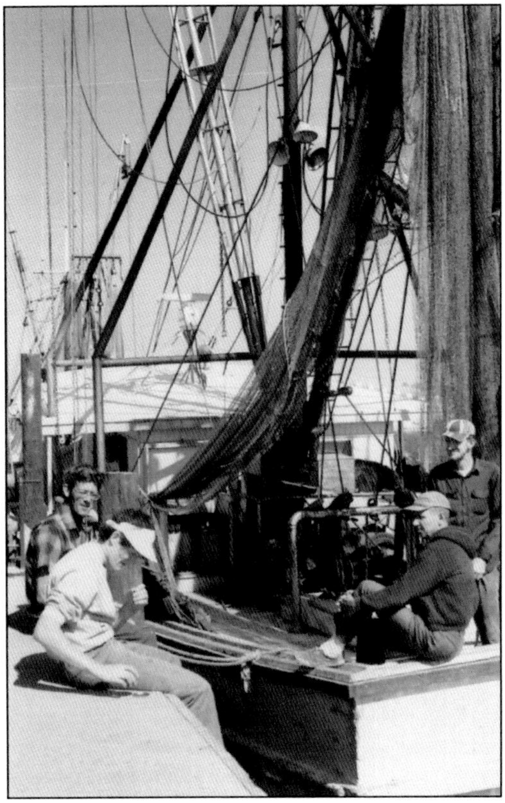

Commercial shrimping and fishing were very important sources of income for many citizens around Gulf County. On the back of the *Morning Star* are, from left to right, Royce Chancey, Marion Huff, Fred Buskins, and unidentified. In the 1960s, L. C. Wood was the captain. (BH.)

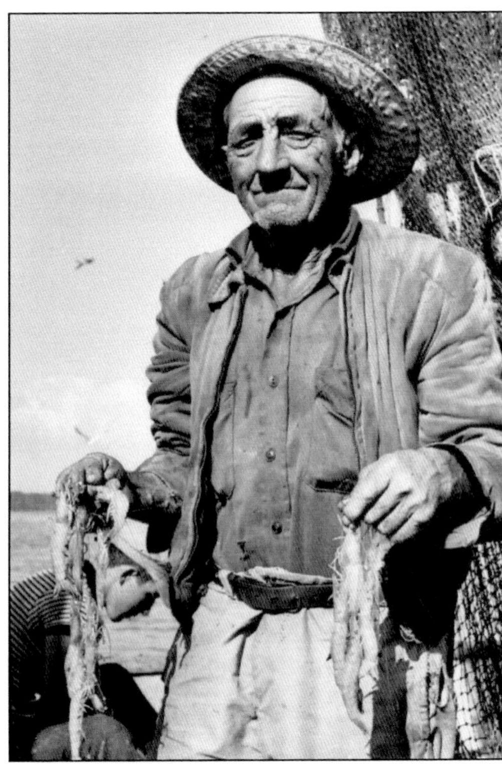

Ben Williams, a longtime shrimper from Indian Pass, shrimped for the McNeil family for many years. (BH.)

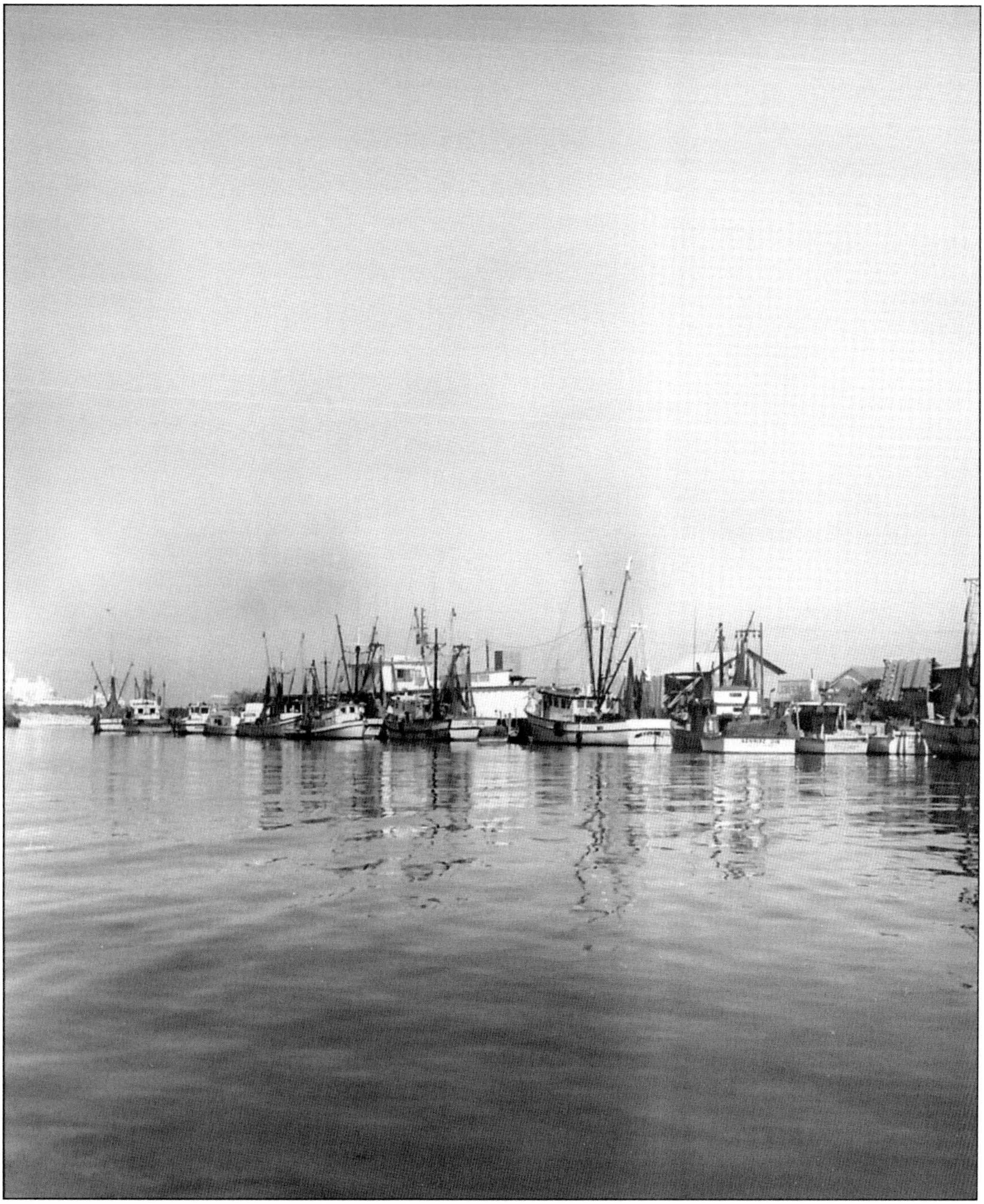

Raffield Fisheries and Wood's Fishery are located on the Intracoastal Canal just between Port St. Joe and Highland View, Florida. With careful planning, both companies have been able to cope innovatively and effectively with the new laws, regulations, and restrictions. Because of the perseverance, dedication, and sheer grit of these families, a unique legacy has been carried on and a treasured way of life preserved. This photograph was taken about 1970. (BH.)

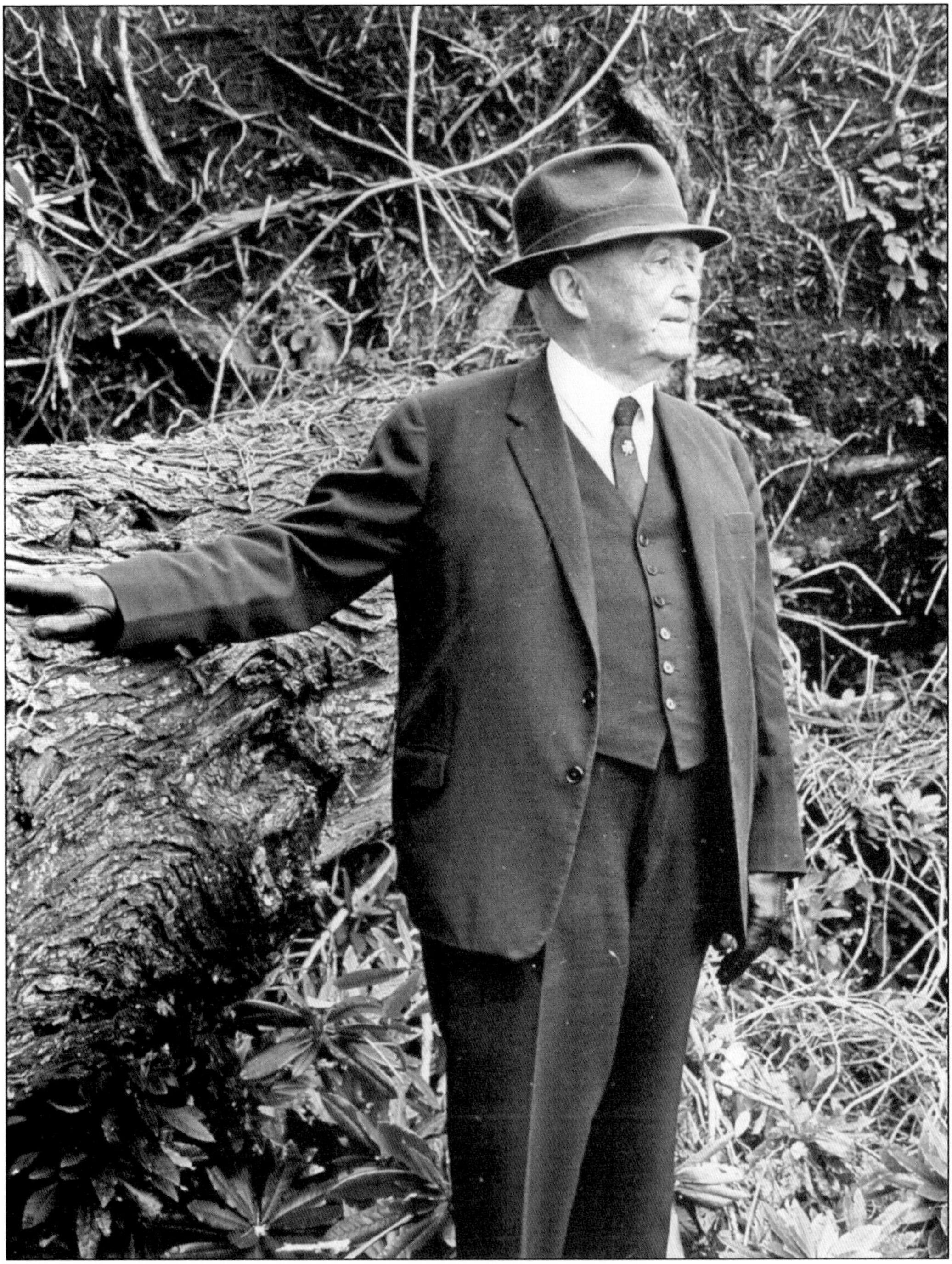

Edward Ball arrived about 1933 in Florida when asked by Alfred I. duPont, and in the span of Florida business and political history, no man ever made a deeper mark on the state than Ball. He came to Florida half a century ago, built an empire from the foundation started by his brother-in-law Alfred I. duPont, and nurtured that empire through political criticism, tangles with American labor, and countless legal attacks. There is still probably no more powerful man breathing Florida air than Ed Ball. (St. Joe Co.)

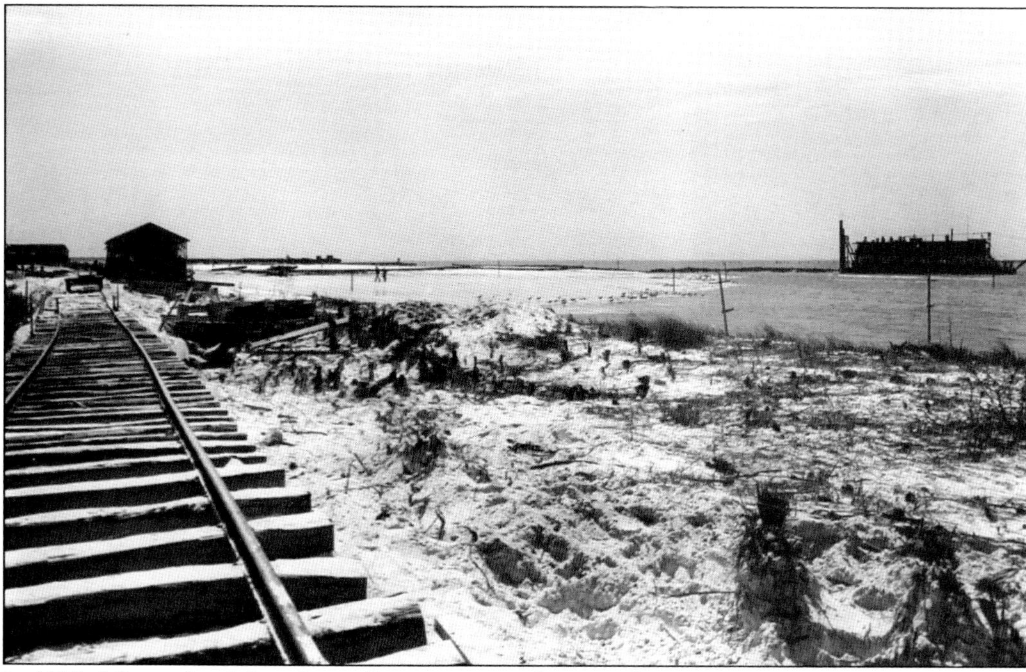

In 1936, folks realized that the mill was coming when Hardaway Construction Company moved two barges into the bay with steam pile drivers and began driving sheet steel pilings for the paper mill docks. Haffman Dredging Company brought in two dredges, which began pumping sand up from the bay bottom behind the sheet pilings where the paper mill is located. (GA.)

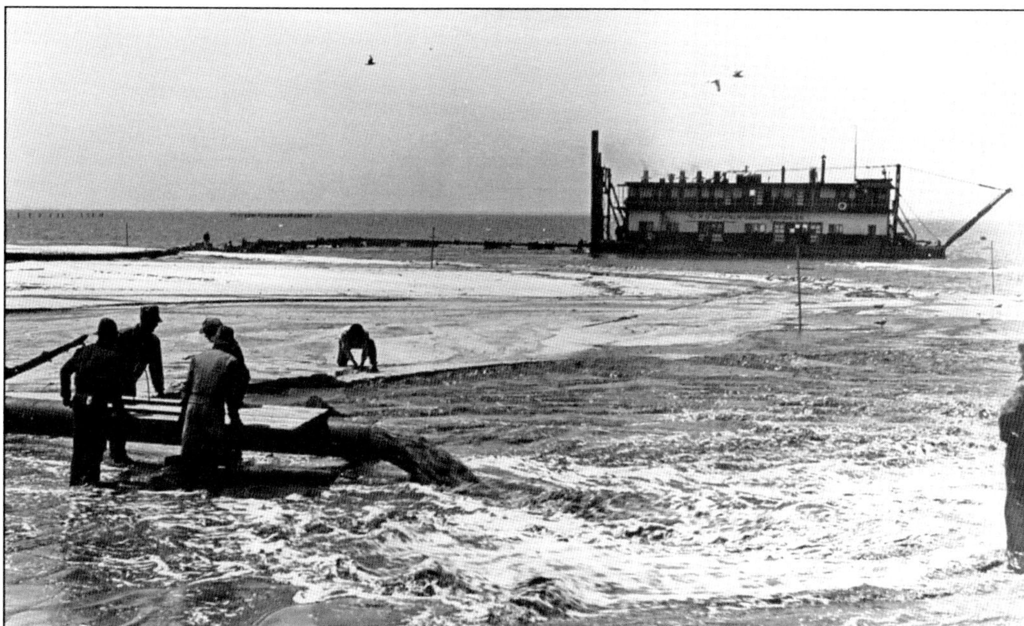

When enough sand had been pumped in, it was leveled and pilings were driven for the mill's foundations. Carpenters began building forms over the pilings for the steel structure. People were coming from all around the area hoping to get jobs building the mill. These two photographs were taken in April 1837. (GA.)

L to R

.L.Sharit	Jesse Dawson	R.C.Brent,Jr.
dd McMillan	W.H.HOwell	Mrs. Brent
ohn Harris	G.F.Suber	Fred Hummel,Sr.
. Lowery	J.C.Belin	Mrs. Fayard
.R.Parish	H.H.Saunders	W.T.Edwards

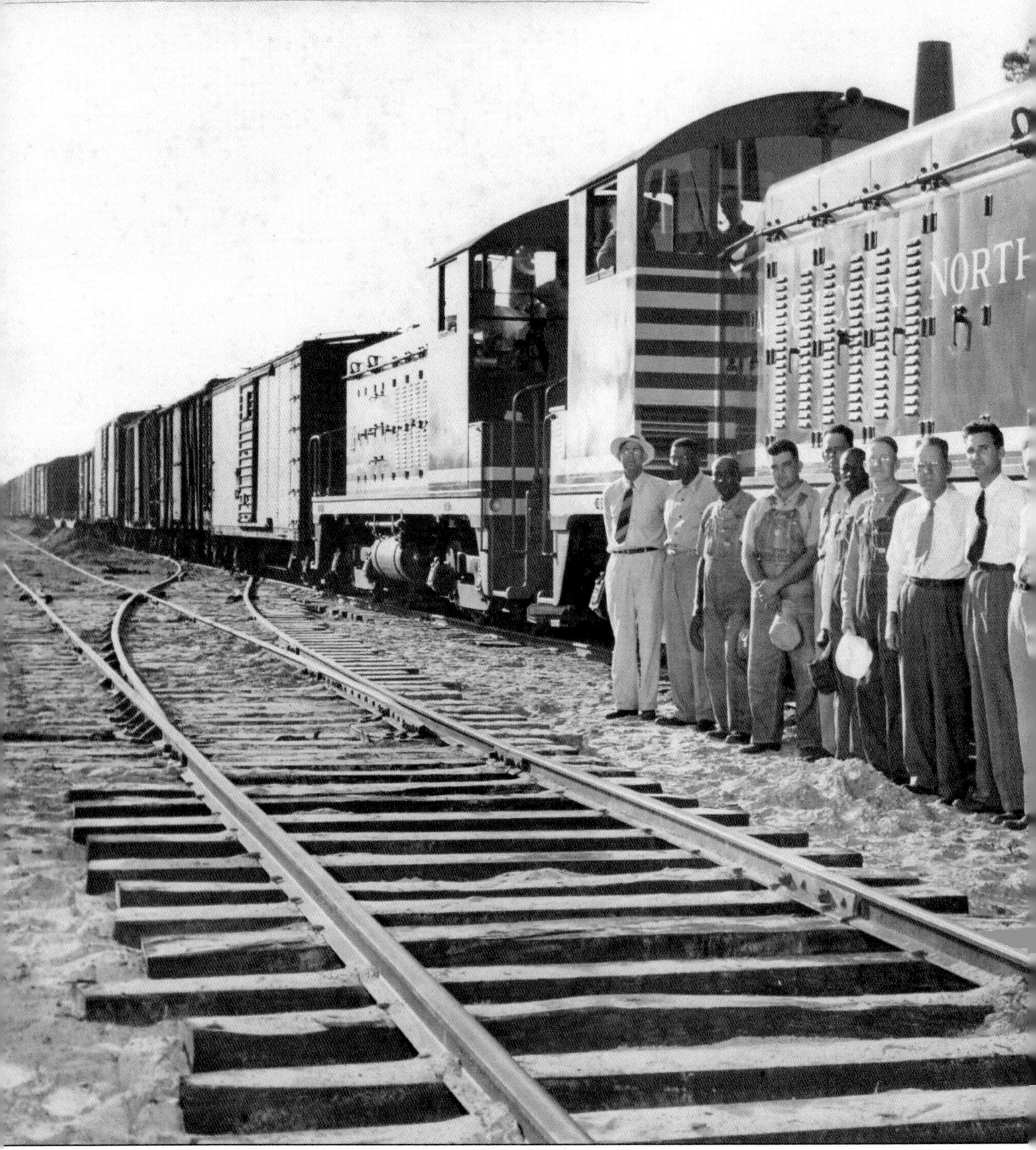

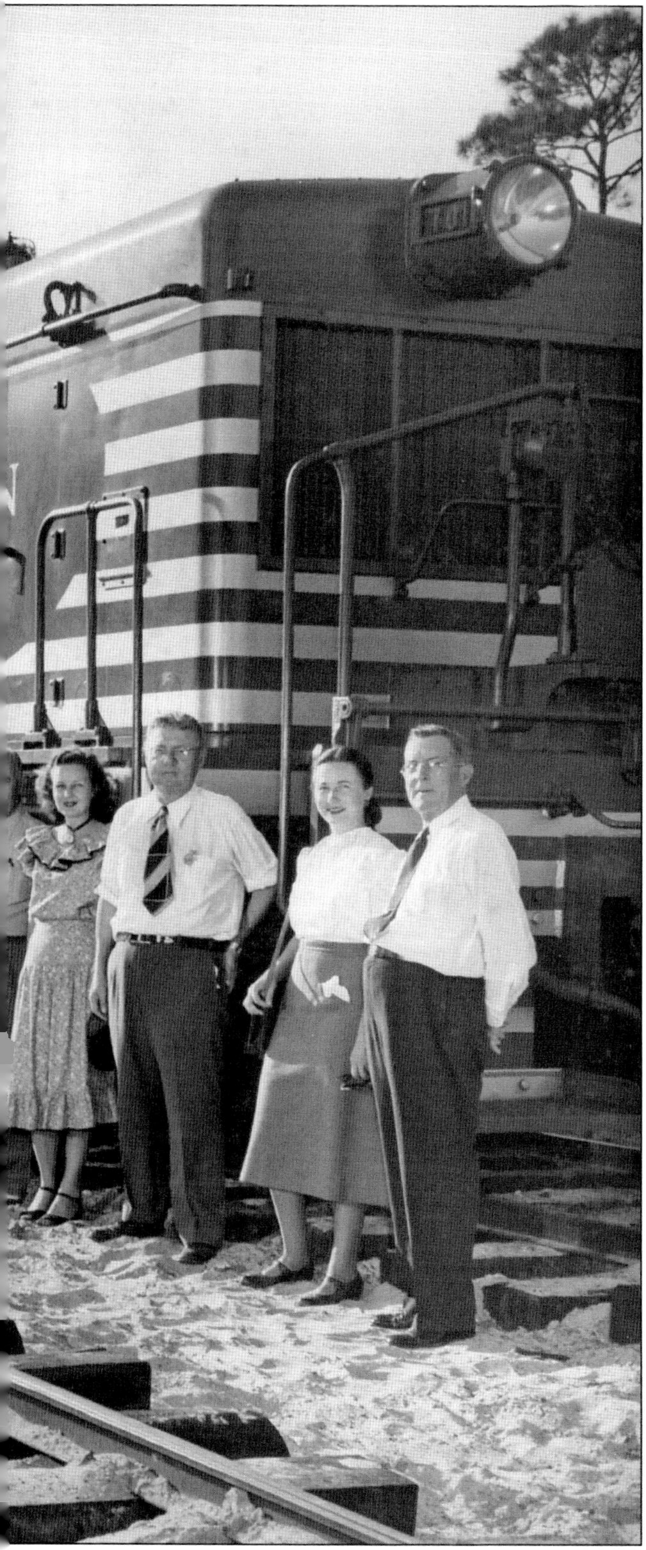

The first diesel-operated locomotive to come into Port St. Joe, Florida, was in 1947, with Willie Howell as the engineer. The Apalachicola Northern Railroad employees shown are, from left to right, J. L. Sharit, Edd McMillan, John Harris, E. Lowery, J. R. Parish, Jesse Dawson, Willie H. Howell, G. F. Suber, J. C. Belin, H. H. Saunders, Ray C. Brent Jr., Dolly Brent, Fred Hummel Sr., ? Fayard, and W. T. Edwards. (St. Joe Co.)

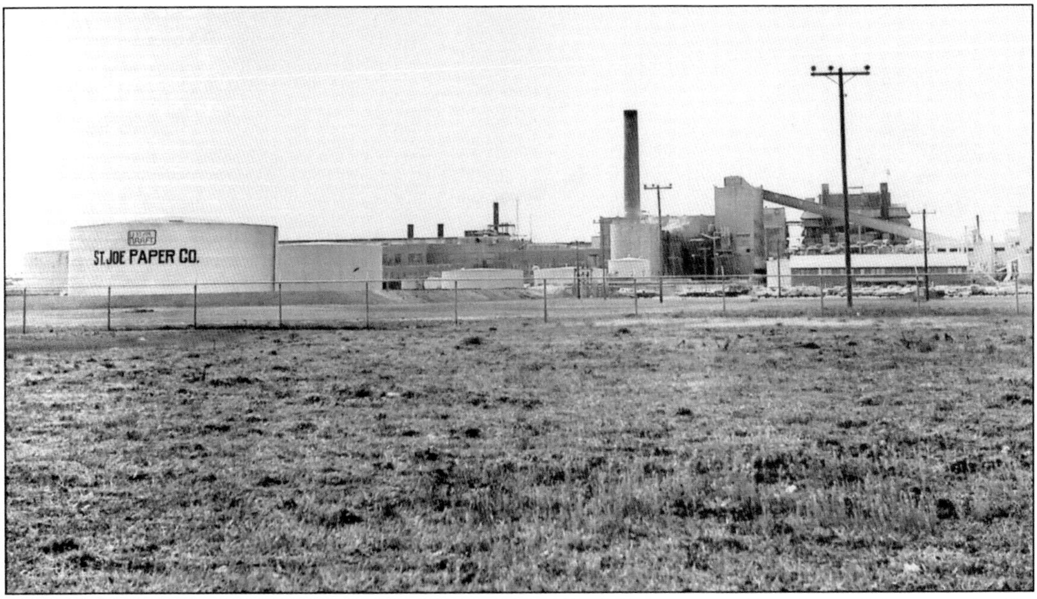

The St. Joe Paper Company went into operation in 1938. The paper mill and its affiliates—the St. Joseph Container Division, the St. Joseph Land and Development Company, and the Apalachicola Northern Railroad—not only make up the largest industry in the city but one of the largest in the state of Florida. Sadly the mill was closed in 1998 and demolished in 2002. (BH.)

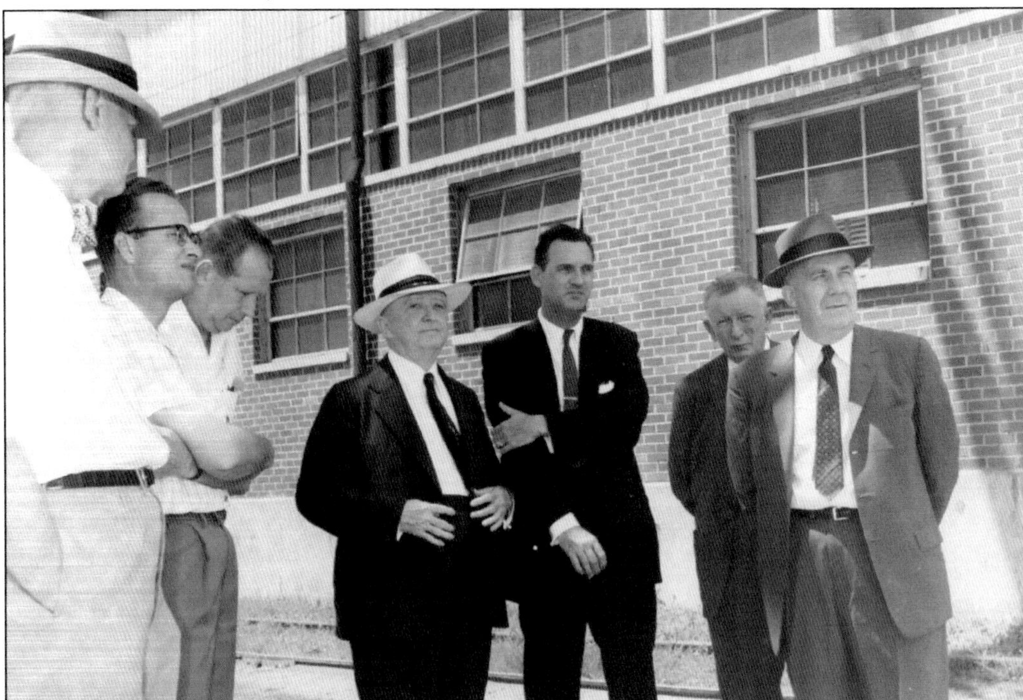

The present industrial expansion began with the newly formed St. Joe Paper Company. As the company grew, so did the mill and the community. In 1953, the paper company installed a second paper machine and more men were employed in its operation. From left to right are Ralph Rich, Joe Paffee, Tom Coldeway, Ed Ball, Jake Belin, Harry Saunders, and S. L. Barke. (St. Joe Co.)

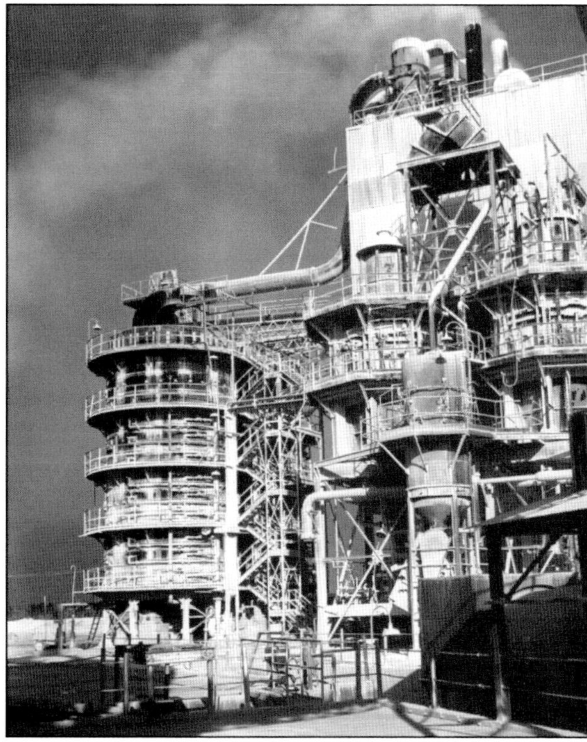

Michigan Chemical Company and the Cunningham, Limp Construction Company came to Port St. Joe in September 1958. They manufactured magnesium oxide from seawater. This product is used in the manufacture of textiles, firebrick, rubber, paper, and many other raw materials. The plant was located northeast of the old St. Joe Lumber and Export Company site. (Gulf County Chamber of Commerce.)

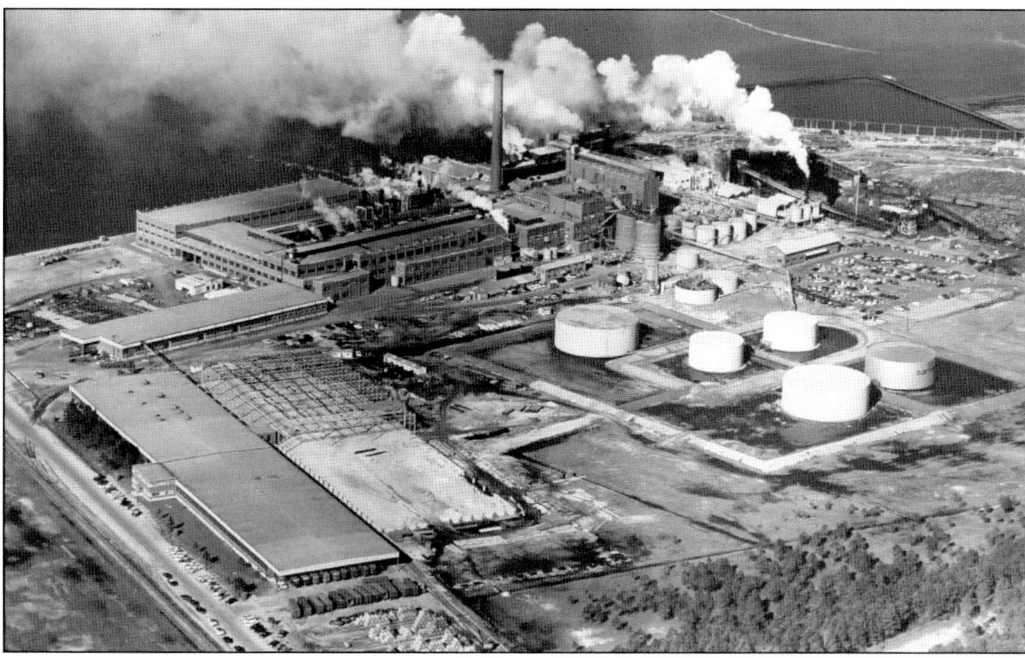

In 1958, the St. Joe Paper Company ventured into the foreign field, acquiring a paper mill and box plant in Ireland. These were later supplemented by a second mill and two more box plants, also in Ireland. The Irish operations were supplied with paperboard from the big mill at Port St. Joe, thus expanding its outlets. St. Joe is continuing to expand its position in the international economy. (St. Joe Co.)

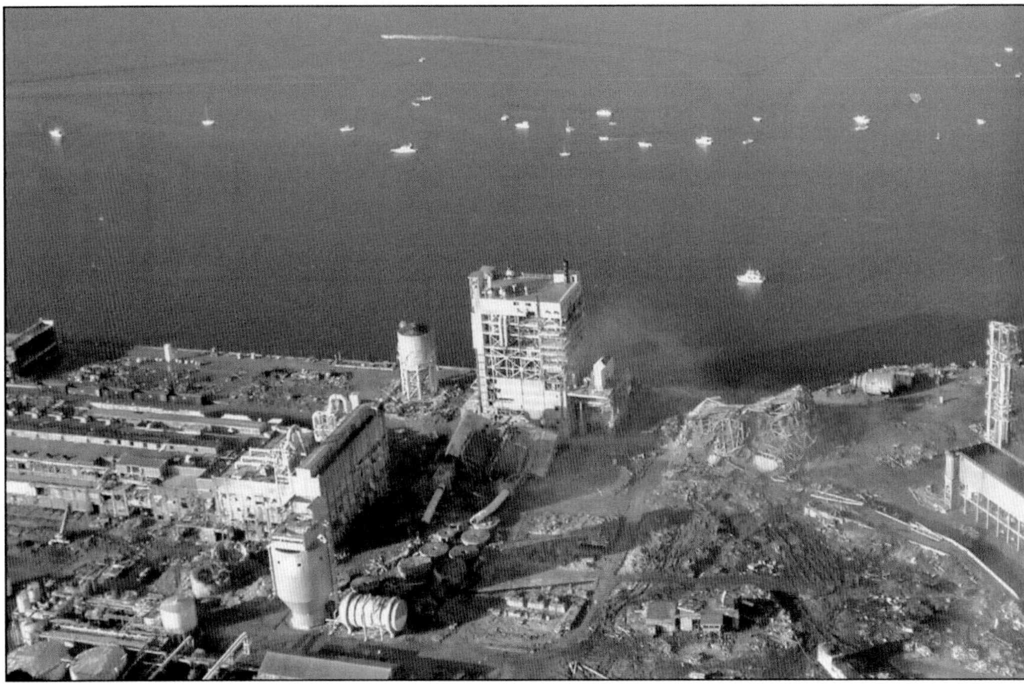

"In a staccato burst of flash and fury, what took years to construct came tumbling to the ground in seconds at the paper mill site. Hundreds watch as three structures imploded," wrote Tim Croft in the *Star* about one stage of the mill's demolition in November 2002 in Port St. Joe. (DH.)

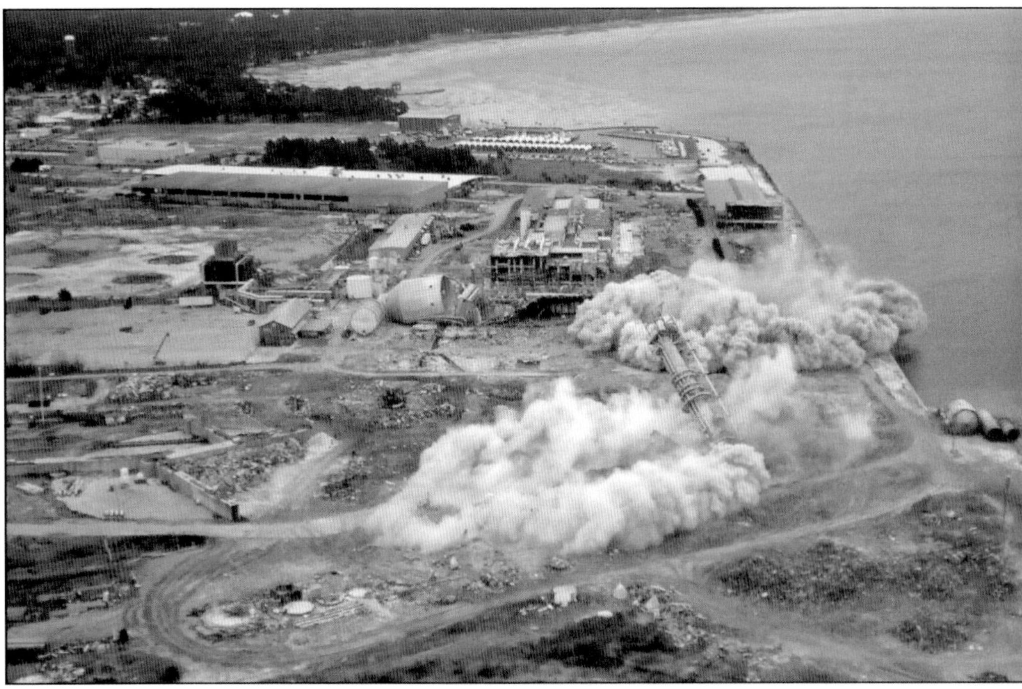

"The demolition charges begin detonating, the buildings start their collapse, buildings are falling, buildings hit the ground, dust obscures the site, the dust clears, and a way of life has slipped away for the residents of Gulf County," Croft wrote in the *Star* on January 12, 2003. (DH.)

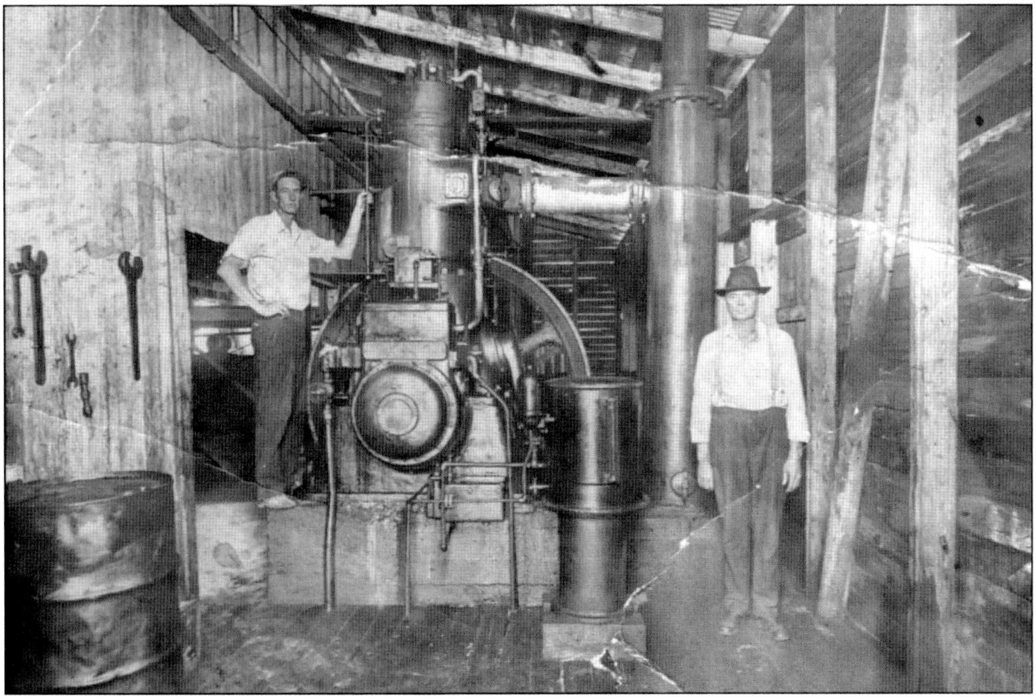

This was the engine room of the old ice plant owned by Max Kilbourn in the 1930s. It was located partly over the water where the paper mill was built in 1937. Max is the man on the right; his son Jimmy is to the left. A fish house occupied the westernmost part of the plant. Uncle Pete Peters worked in the fish house cleaning fish and keeping the place orderly. (ERT.)

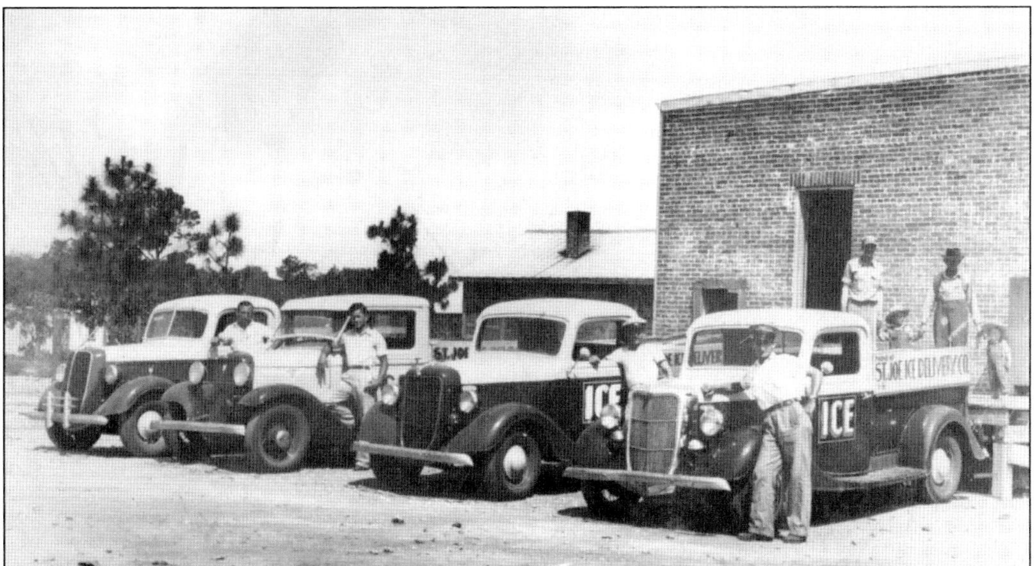

St. Joe Ice Company on Garrison Avenue was owned and operated by Max Kilbourn during the 1940s. From left to right are (standing beside the trucks) Bo Brown, Billy Hammock, Ralph Player, and Henry Raiford; (on the platform of the ice plant) Jimmy Kilbourn (Max's son), James Max (grandson), Max Kilbourn, and Charles Vincent Kilbourn (grandson). Max Kilbourn was short of stature (five feet, seven inches) and always wore dark suspenders and a black hat. (ERT.)

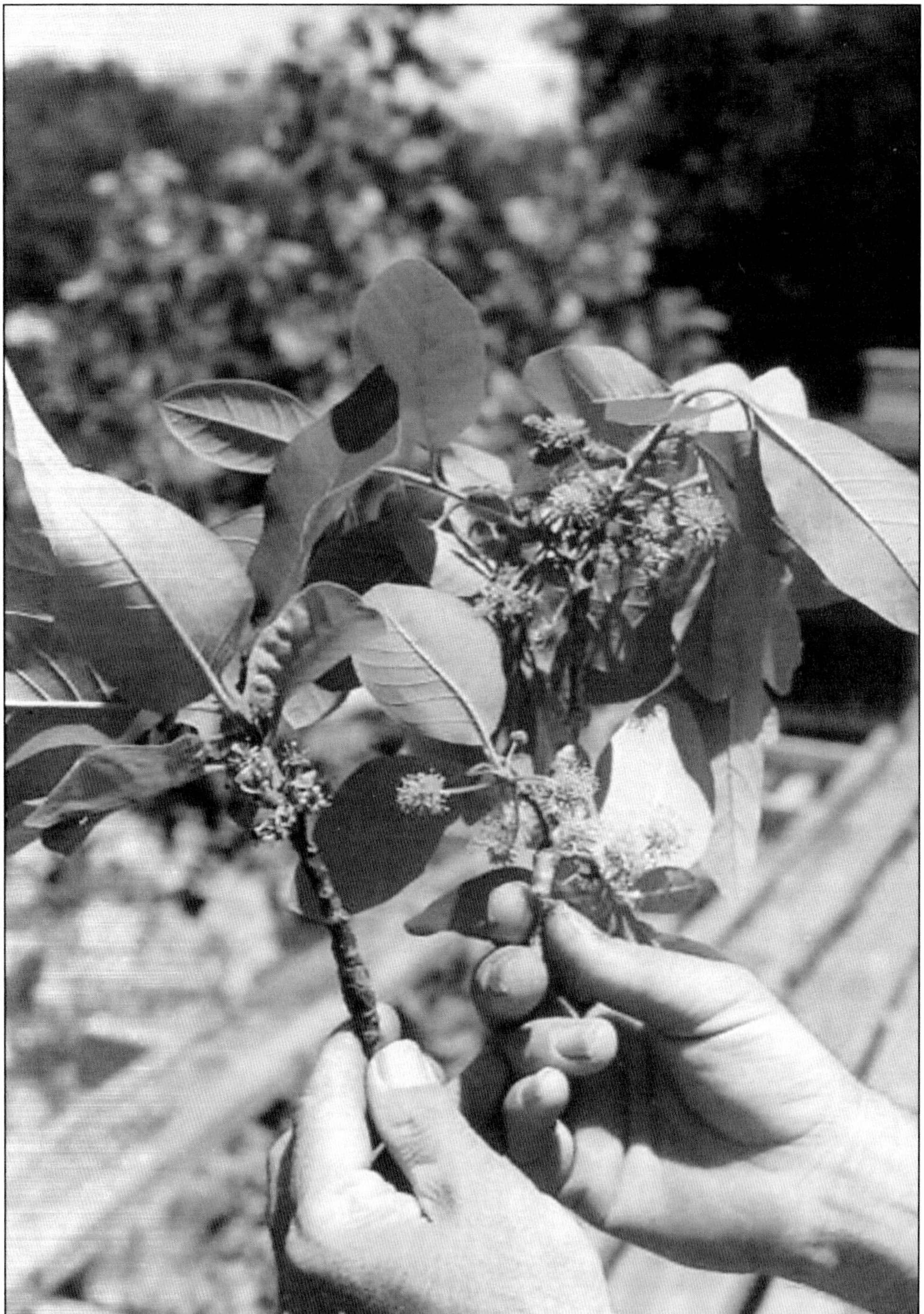

Tupelo honey derives its name from the white and black tupelo gum whose blossoms yield the nectar. For two weeks every spring, down 10 miles of the Apalachicola River, the tupelo trees are in bloom. Nowhere else in the entire world are there so many tupelo trees blooming white in such profusion. During these two weeks, the honeybees retrieve the pollen and return to their apiaries. (AAW.)

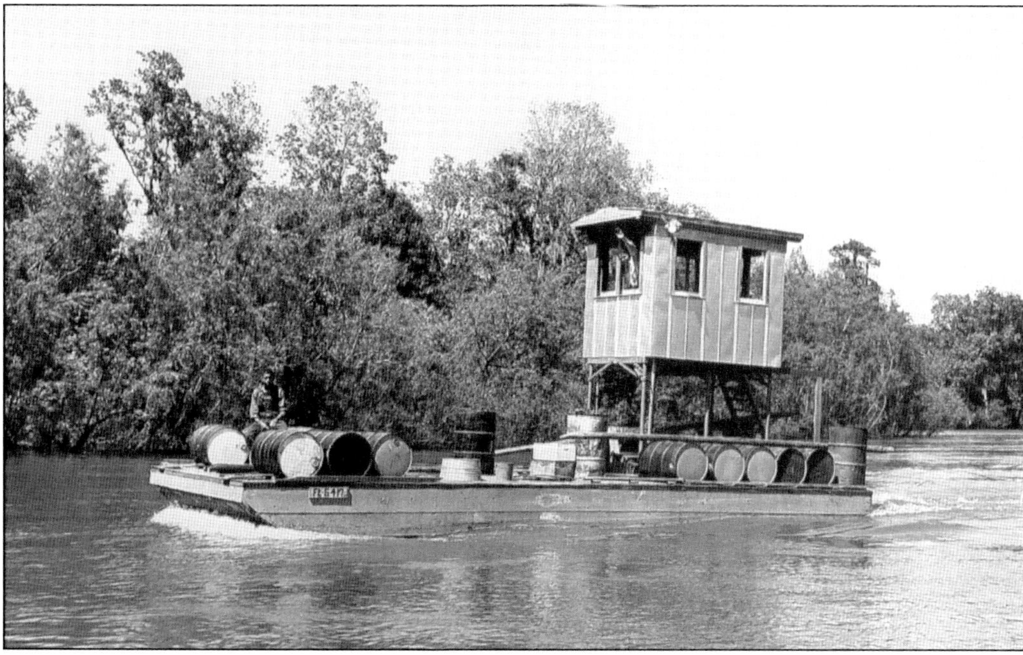

The region along the lower Apalachicola River ships over 20 freight carloads of tupelo honey each year. The shipments are distributed over America and Europe to meet an ever-growing demand. Wewahitchka is the center of the small area where this famous product is made. Some beekeepers here were the Whitfields and Aldermens; today there are the Rishes and the Laniers. (AAW.)

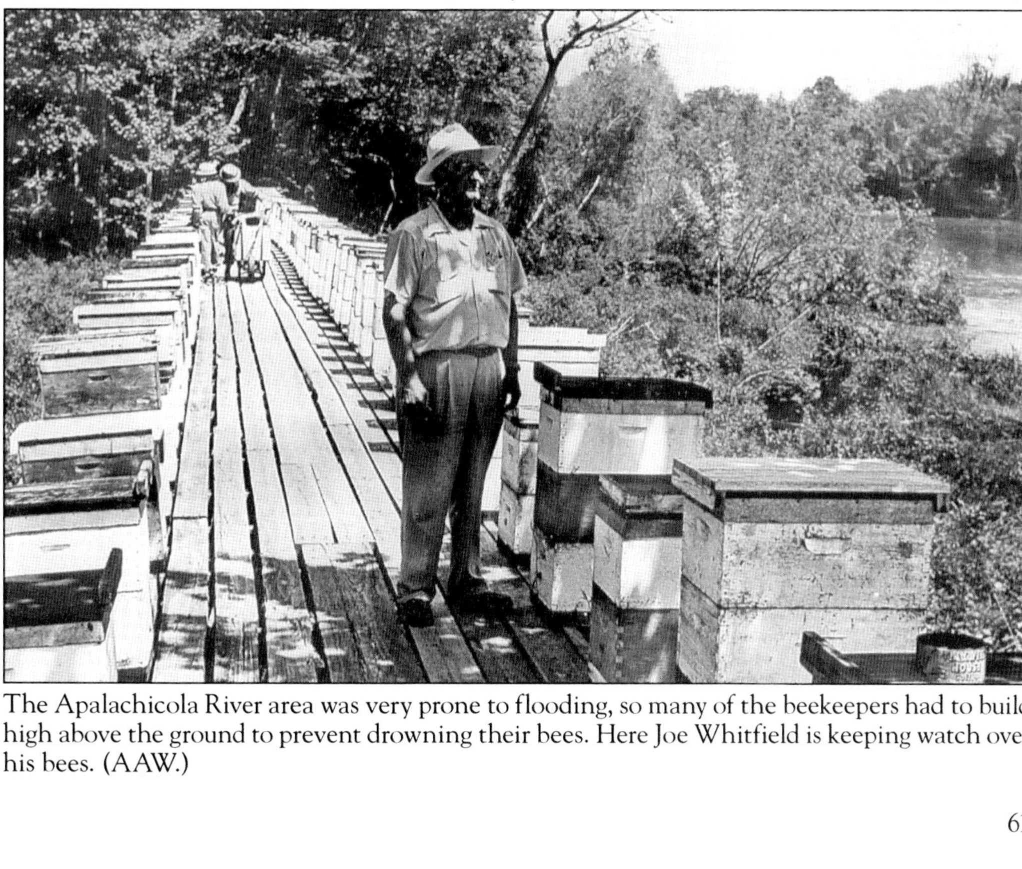

The Apalachicola River area was very prone to flooding, so many of the beekeepers had to build high above the ground to prevent drowning their bees. Here Joe Whitfield is keeping watch over his bees. (AAW.)

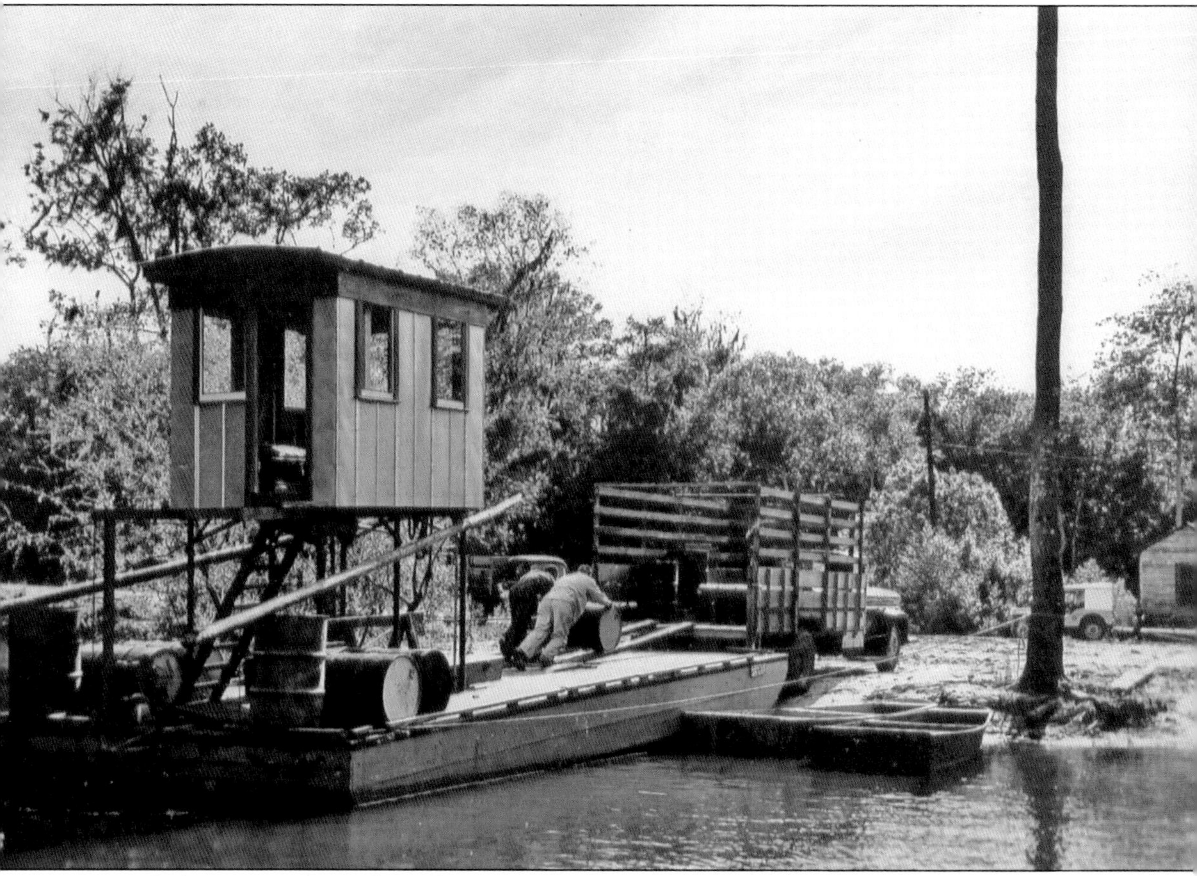

Tupelo honey was shipped to all parts of the world and was loaded off of the barges onto trucks for delivering. (AAW.)

Three

A City with a Past

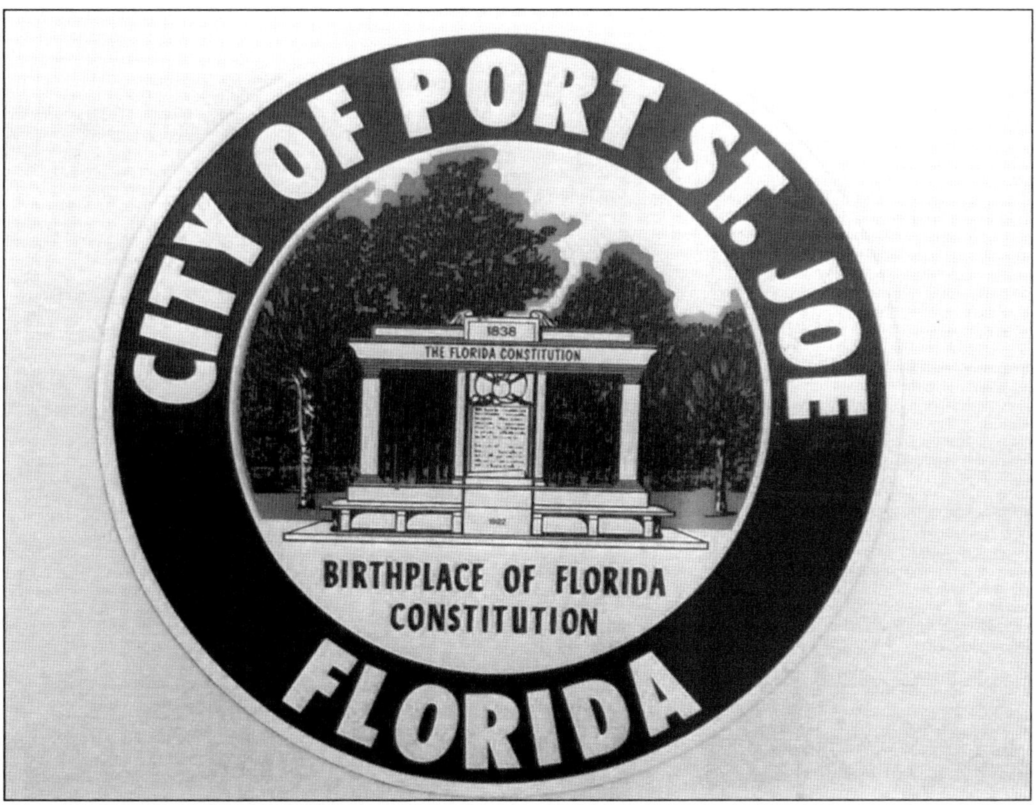

This is the logo for the City of Port St. Joe, Florida, a city with a past. (CPSJ.)

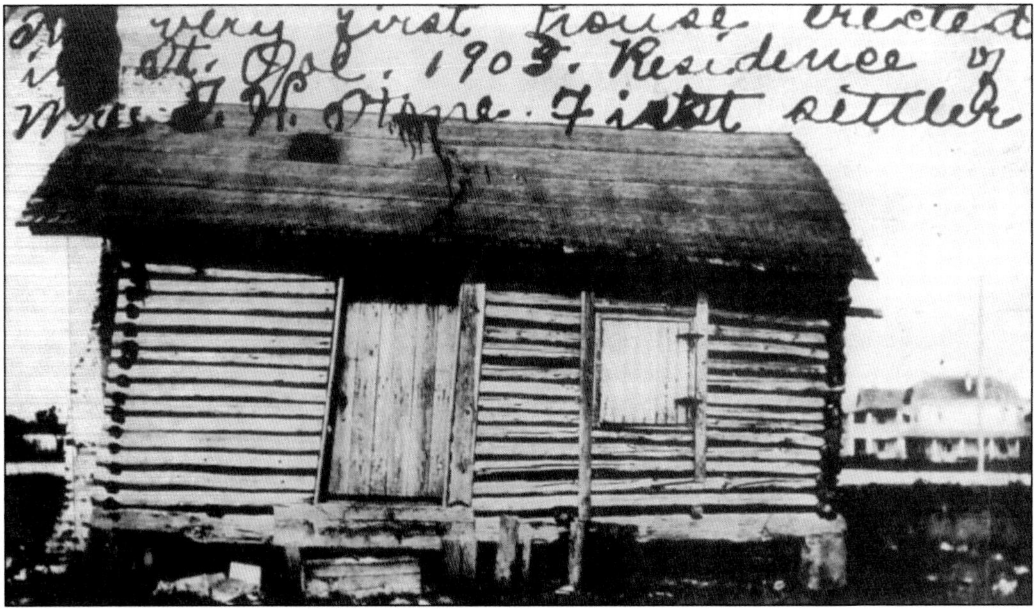

T. H. Stone came here in 1904 and built this house, a small log cabin to which he could later bring his wife and family. The land on which the Stones settled was a large acreage in the southern part of the county on the incomparable St. Joseph Bay. (VSH.)

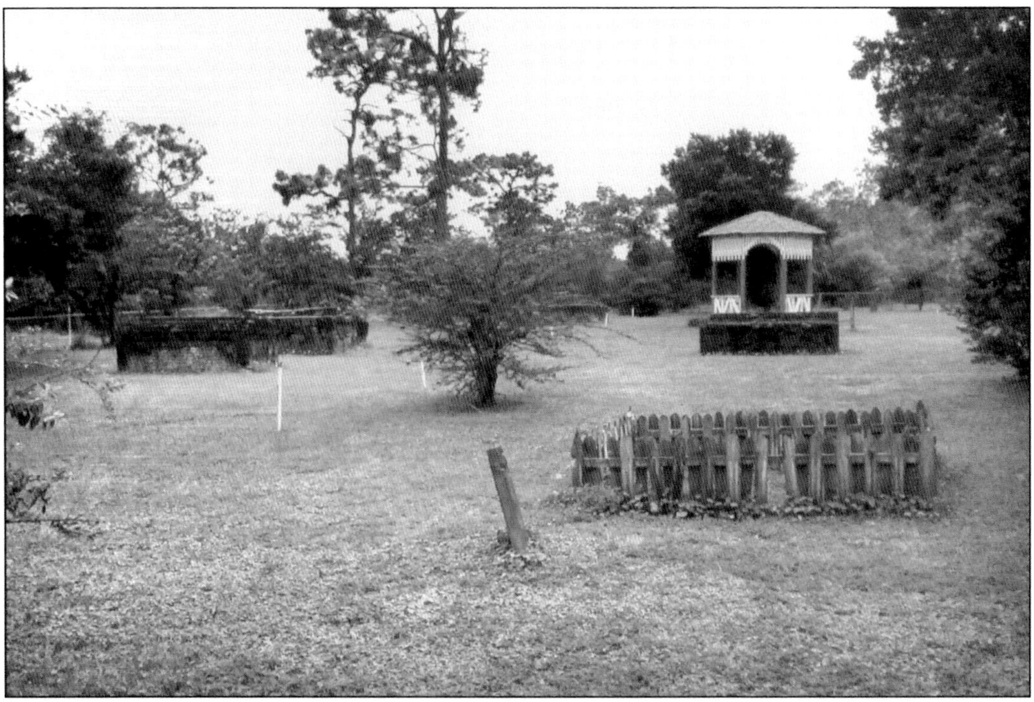

These aboveground tombs and a few headstones are said to have been built of brick brought from Italy as ballast in sailing vessels. The bricks are of clay not found in this section of the country. St. Joseph was once a flourishing city until destroyed more than 100 years ago by fever, fire, and storm. Located in the Old St. Joseph Cemetery, this graveyard is no longer used as a burial place. (BMD.)

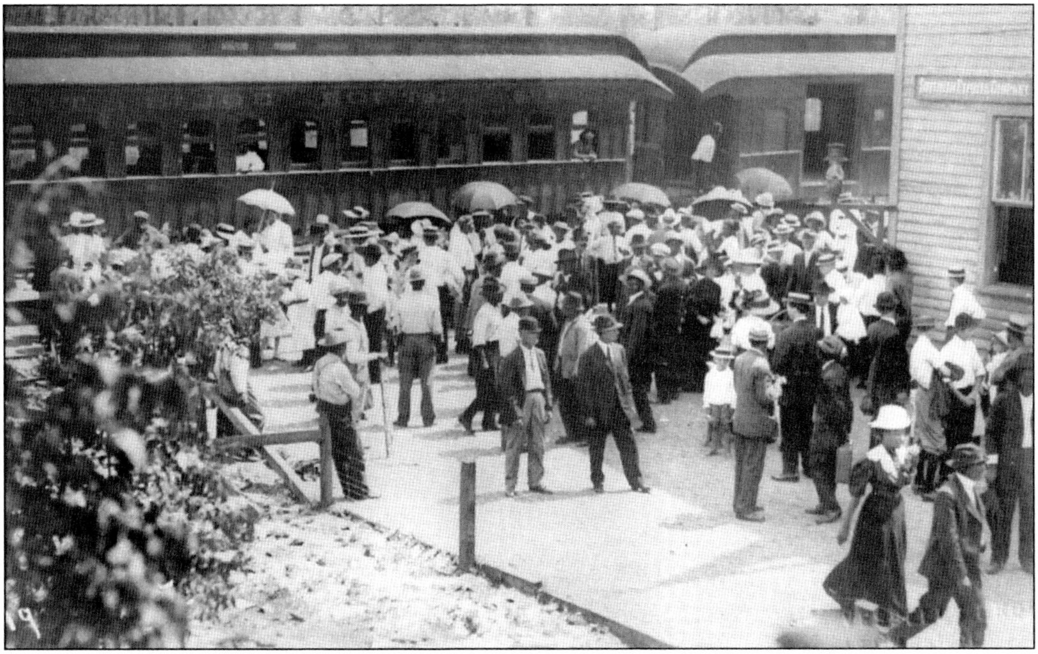

The first train driven into Port St. Joe was in 1909. There were some 400 to 500 passengers on that day as there was no other transportation here at that time. It had four coaches and an express car. Rain or shine, people came to Port St. Joe on "excursion days," like on Sundays and holidays. This photograph was taken about 1915. (BH.)

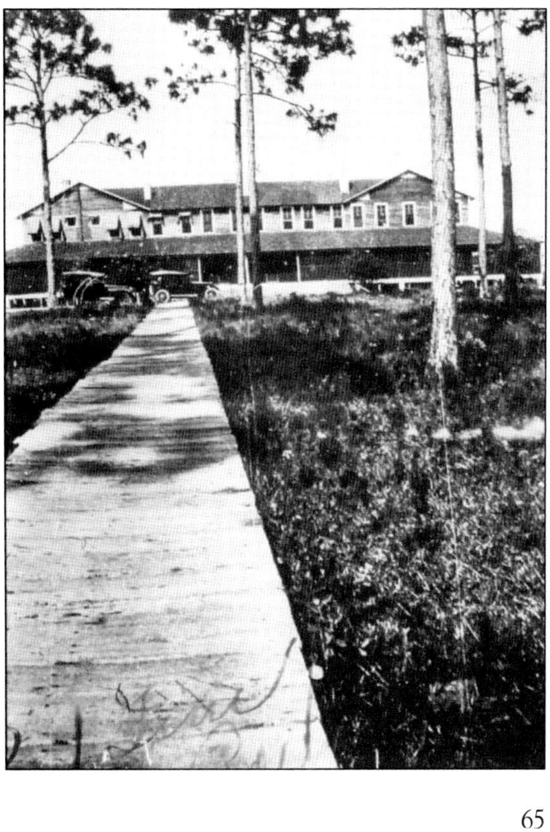

Early Port St. Joe was a fun town. In the park in front of the Port Inn was a bandstand and tables for picnicking; a boardwalk reaching from the hotel to the pier extended far out into the bay. There were spacious bathhouses and a large slide with steps reaching upward for 75–100 feet in the air and descending into the water. (BH.)

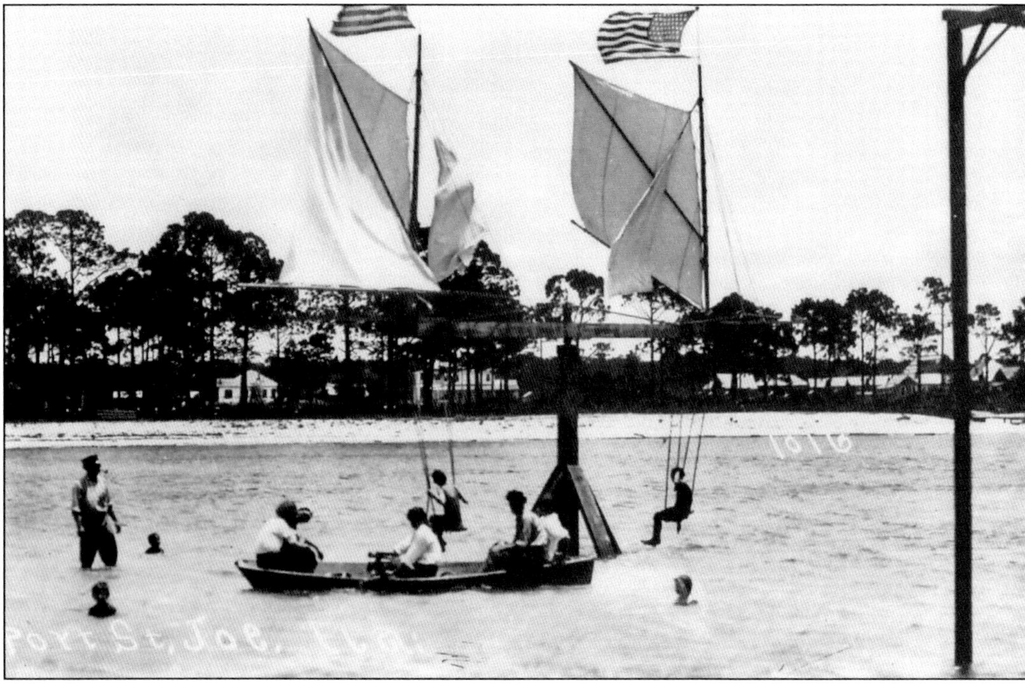

The early days in Port St. Joe were fun for the large and small, with a Sunday picnic, swimming off the city pier, or shoot-to-shoot and swinging on the merry-go-round. Port St. Joe is a great little city. Yesterday's bay is still here, and nowhere on earth can there be found a more gorgeous sunrise or sunset. (BH.)

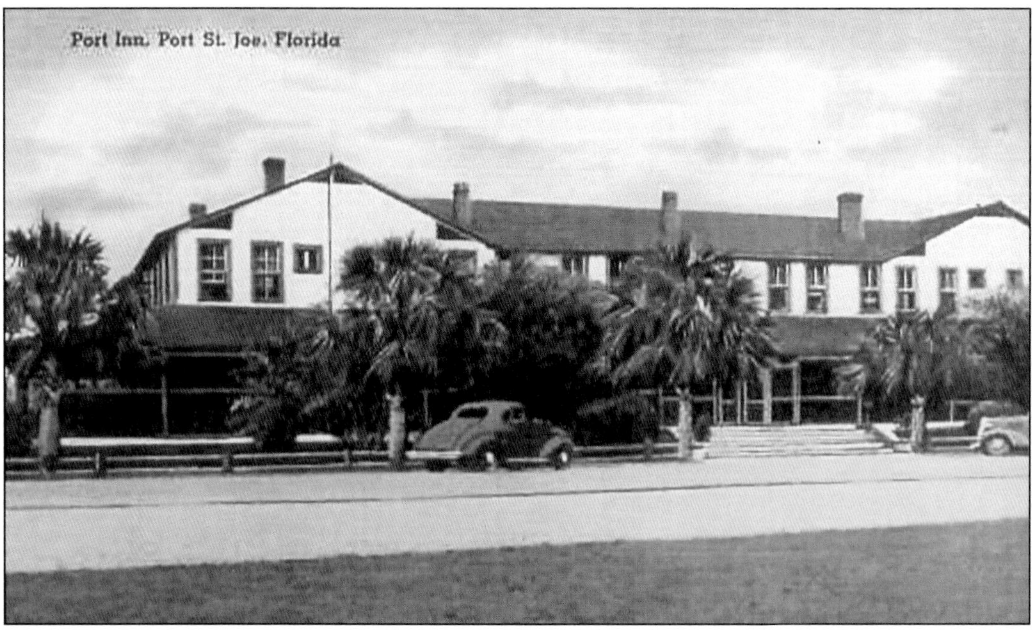

The Port Inn, built in 1909, remains a prominent landmark in Port St. Joe. From its spacious veranda, a boardwalk extended through the park out into the bay. A great fire destroyed the inn in 1944, and it was later rebuilt in 1947. For several years, it was known as the St. Joe Motel. The Port Inn has been renovated and is enjoyed by many locals and visitors to the city. (BH.)

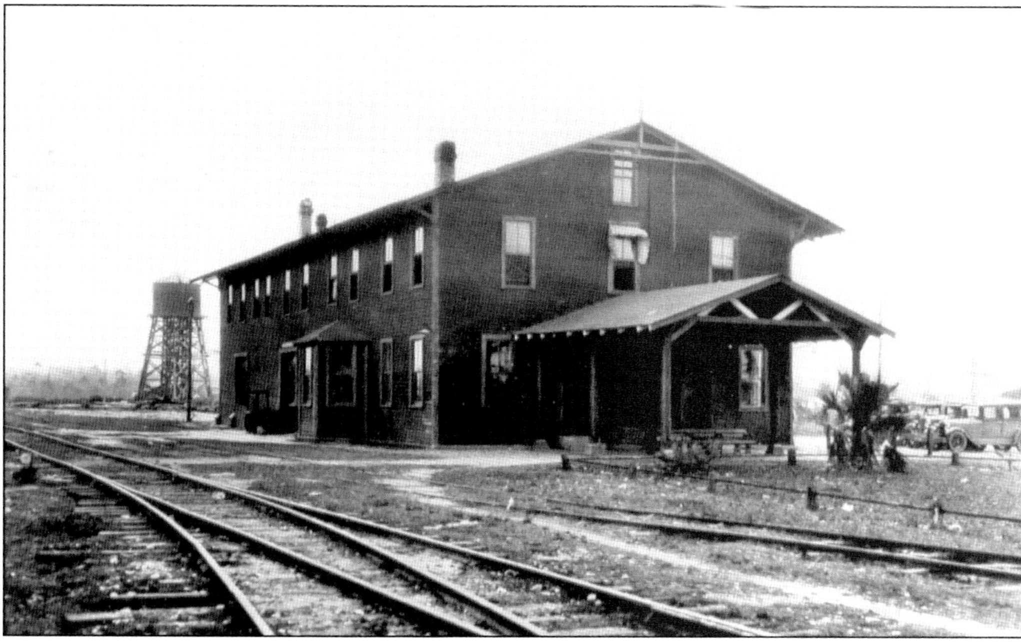

The Apalachicola Northern Railroad began here in 1909, and passenger service to Port St. Joe started on May 10, 1910. The railroad dock located at the end of Marina Drive extended out into St. Joe Bay for approximately 1,000 feet and ushered in Port St. Joe's shipping industry. The ANRR Depot was located at the north end of Reid Avenue. (BH.)

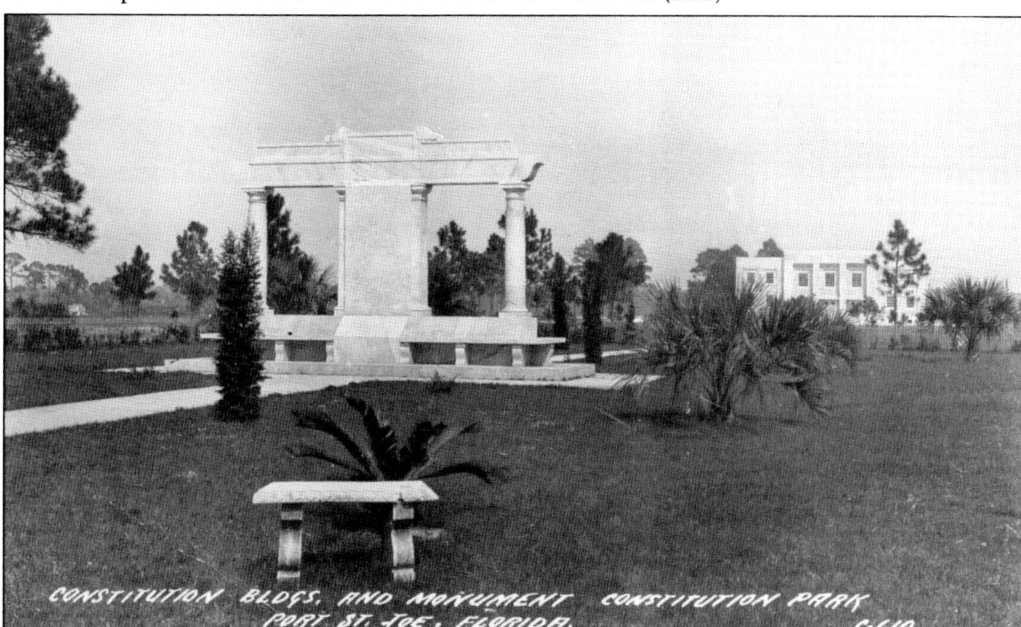

On January 11, 1923, this beautiful monument was unveiled on the site where the Constitution Convention Hall stood, in which delegates from throughout territorial Florida gathered. Cary A. Hardee, then governor of Florida, gave the dedication address. The monument was unveiled by Elizabeth Jones and Mabel Stone. A beautiful park surrounds this marble marker, which was the center of the Centennial Celebration that was held in December 1938. (PPL.)

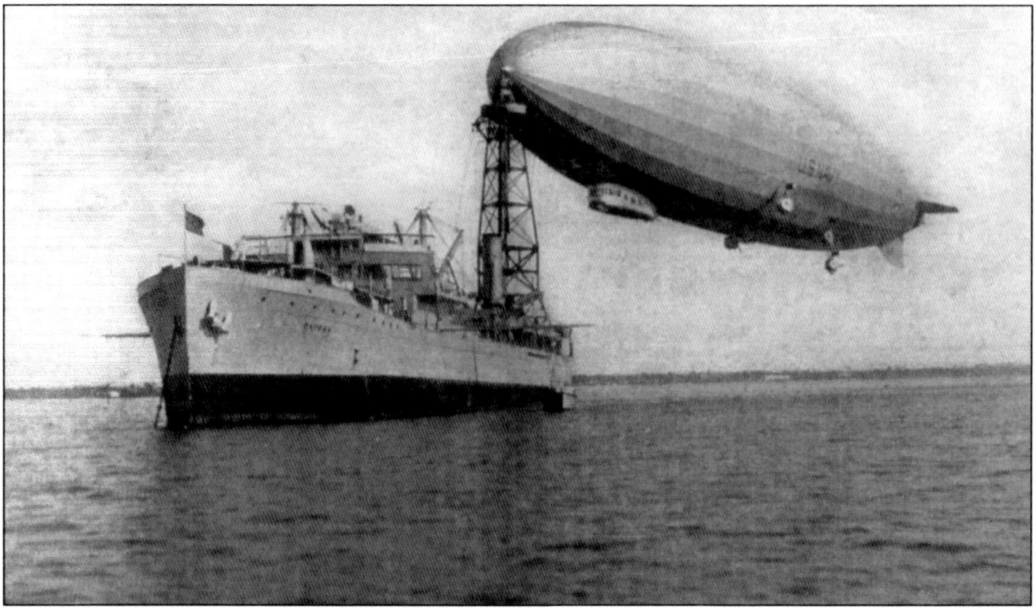

The *Los Angeles*, a giant navy dirigible, left its mooring at the U.S. Patoka, stationed in St. Joseph Bay off Port St. Joe. Hundreds of people visited the giant airship during the stay in January 1929 at Port St. Joe. The *Los Angeles*, which is commanded by Lt. Cmdr. Charles E. Rosendahl, was purchased in 1924 by the United States from the Zeppelin Company of Germany, at a cost of $1.5 million. (BH.)

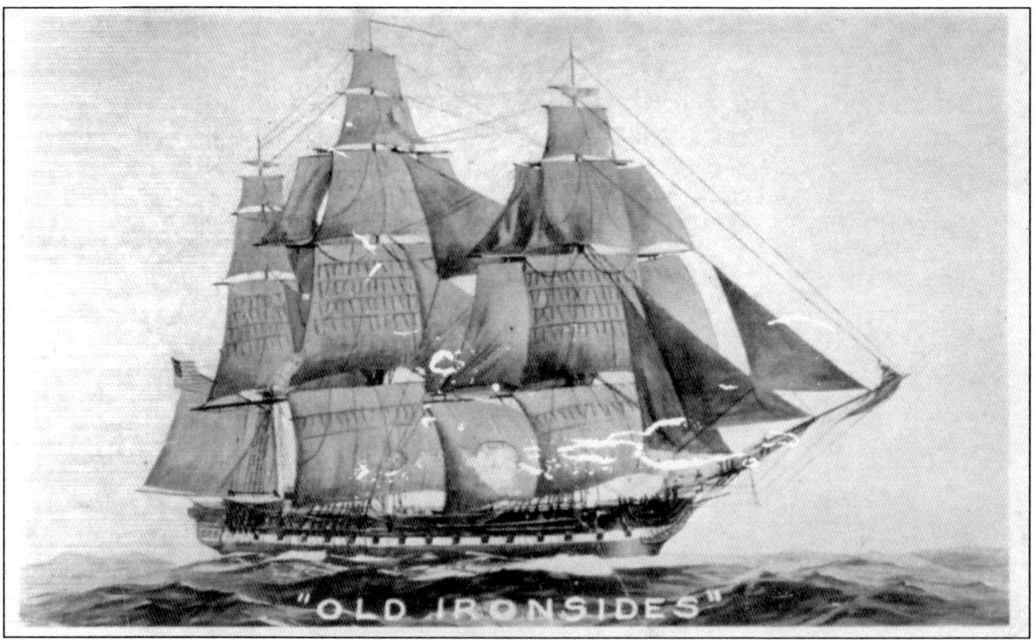

"Old Ironsides" visited for three days in 1932, and schoolchildren got their history lessons dockside as they looked at the riggings of the 170-year-old vessel. The USS *Constitution* was accompanied by its tender, the USS *Grebe*, and its only other stop along the Gulf Coast was St. Petersburg. People came by bus, car, train, and special boat excursions to see the scarred old hero riding at anchor. (BBO.)

Built in 1937 by the Works Project Administration to commemorate the drafting and signing of Florida's first Constitution, the Centennial Building remains the center of Port St. Joe's civic and social life. Designed in the art deco style by architect Hughell Crockett, the building features a distinctive decorative ceiling. (BP.)

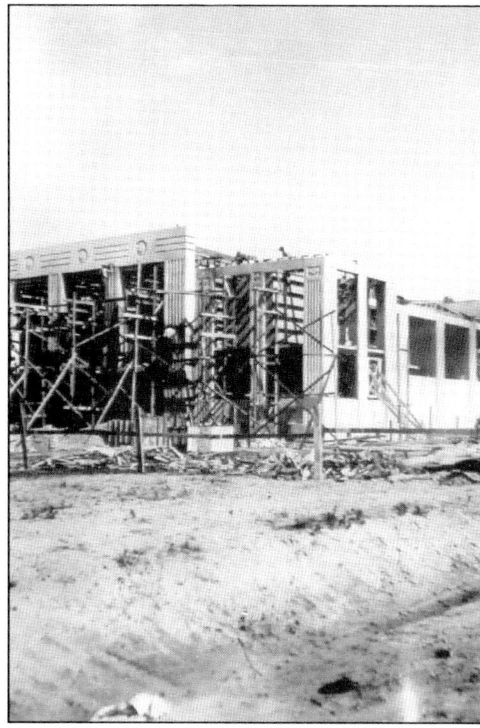

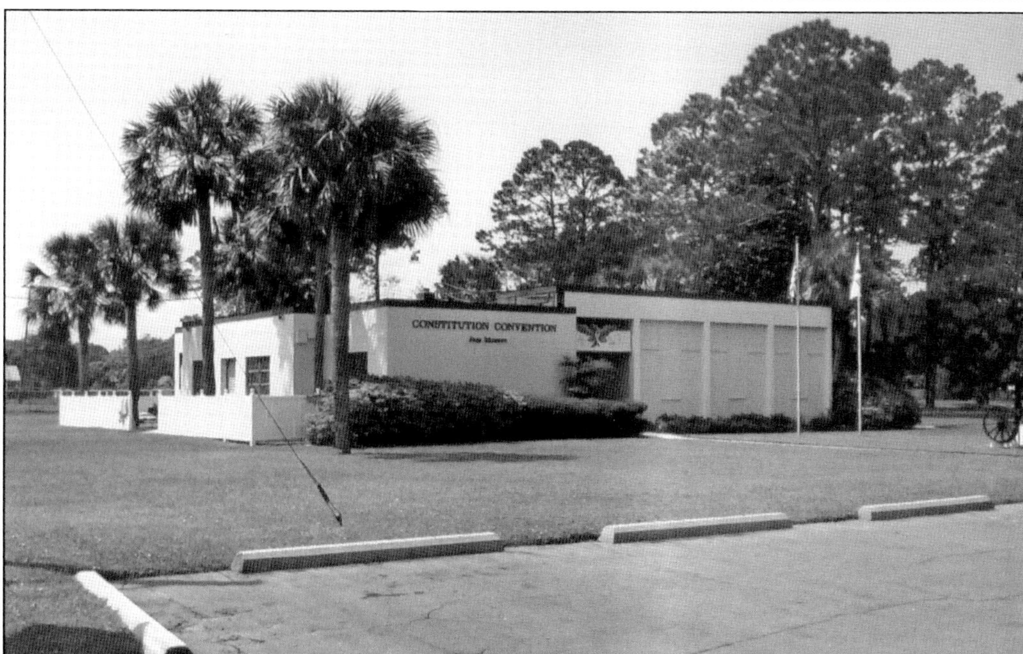

Opened December 16, 1955, the Constitution Convention State Museum was founded for the purpose of depicting the brief but momentous history of St. Joseph, Florida's "Constitution City." There have been many changes—renovations and additions—inspired and promoted by the St. Joseph Historical Society. The museum today, in addition to office space, a reception area, and a large storage room, has a sizeable entrance, an area devoted to early history. (SJHS.)

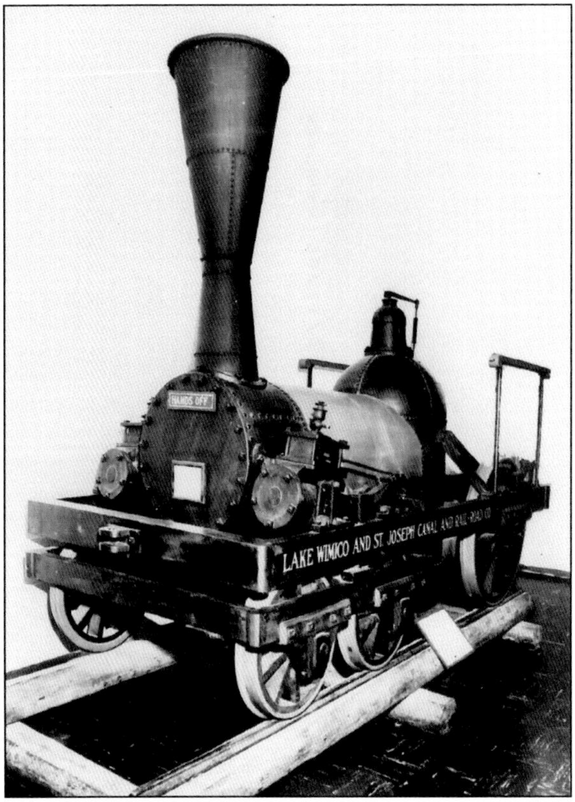

A replica of the first locomotive in the state was built for exhibit on display at the museum. The first railroad in Florida was operated from Port St. Joe to Lake Wimico, a distance of eight miles, for the purpose of transporting freight from boats that came down the Apalachicola River to the wharves that lined the shores of St. Joseph's Bay. (BH.)

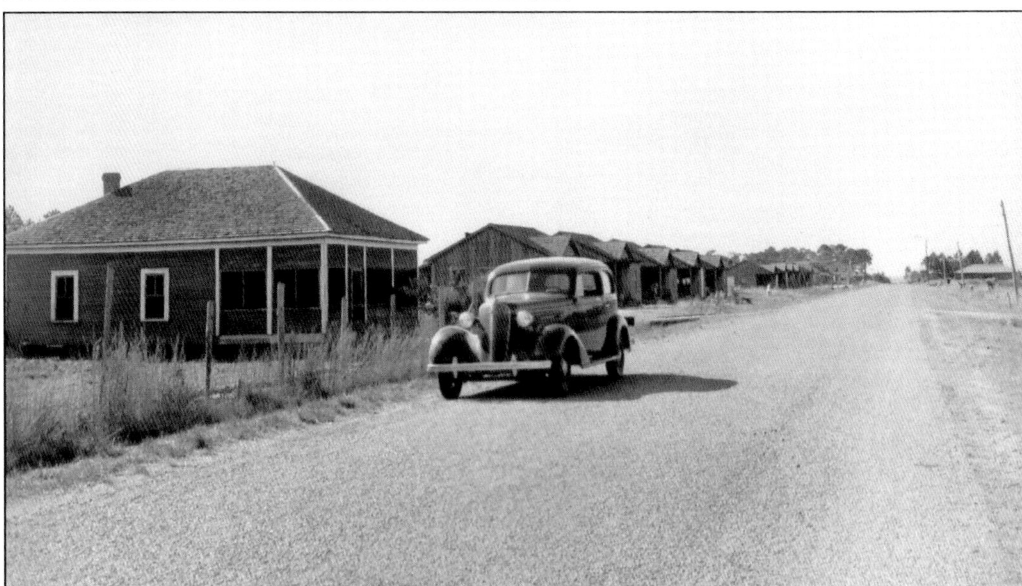

Blossom Row was a single-lane road, seen here looking west as it vanishes toward St. Joseph Bay. The house in the left foreground was the Parker home. The 12 humble houses continue toward Long Avenue. Most of the families who came to St. Joe lived on Blossom Row. No one has been able to learn who built the row houses, but Higdon Stone owned and collected rent on them. (TP and BH.)

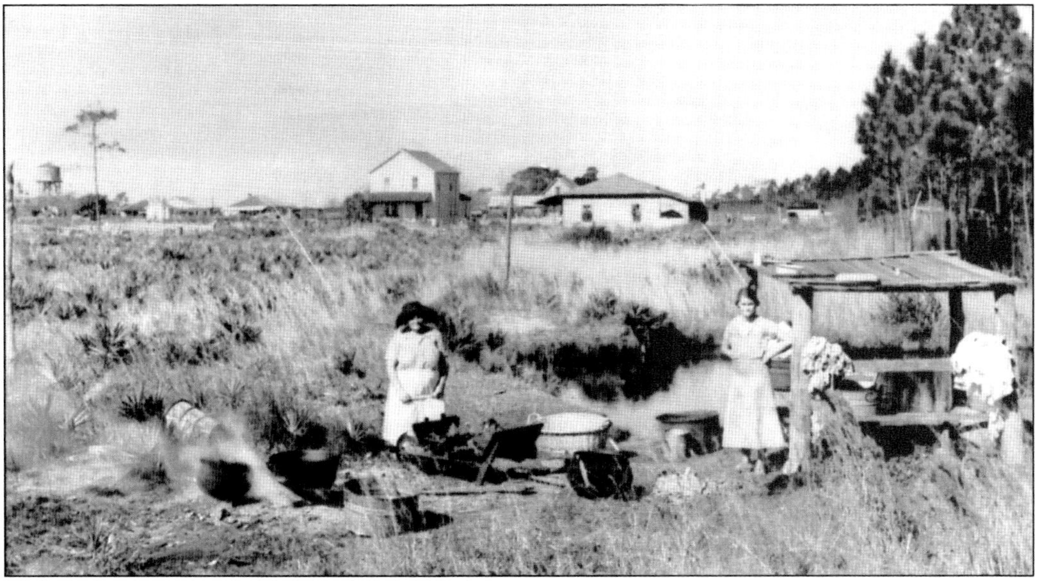

There was a small pond across the highway from the Parker house on Blossom Row. It had been dug by the state road department to supply fill dirt and water during road construction. Several families on the row used the water for washing clothes. There was a shed with washtubs and two cast-iron wash pots for boiling clothes. To all the locals this was the "Wash Hole." (TP and BH.)

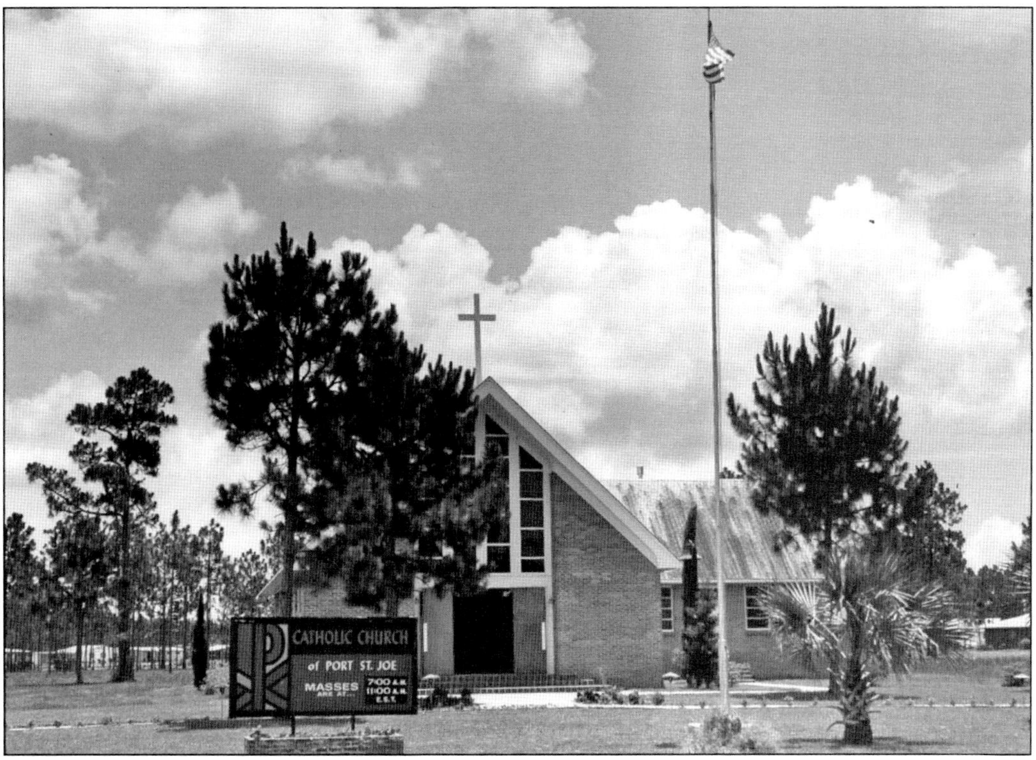

The present-day St. Joseph Catholic Church held a very special occasion in the life of their church. His Excellency Archbishop Toolen from Alabama dedicated this building on April 12, 1959. (Courtesy of the Gulf County Chamber of Commerce.)

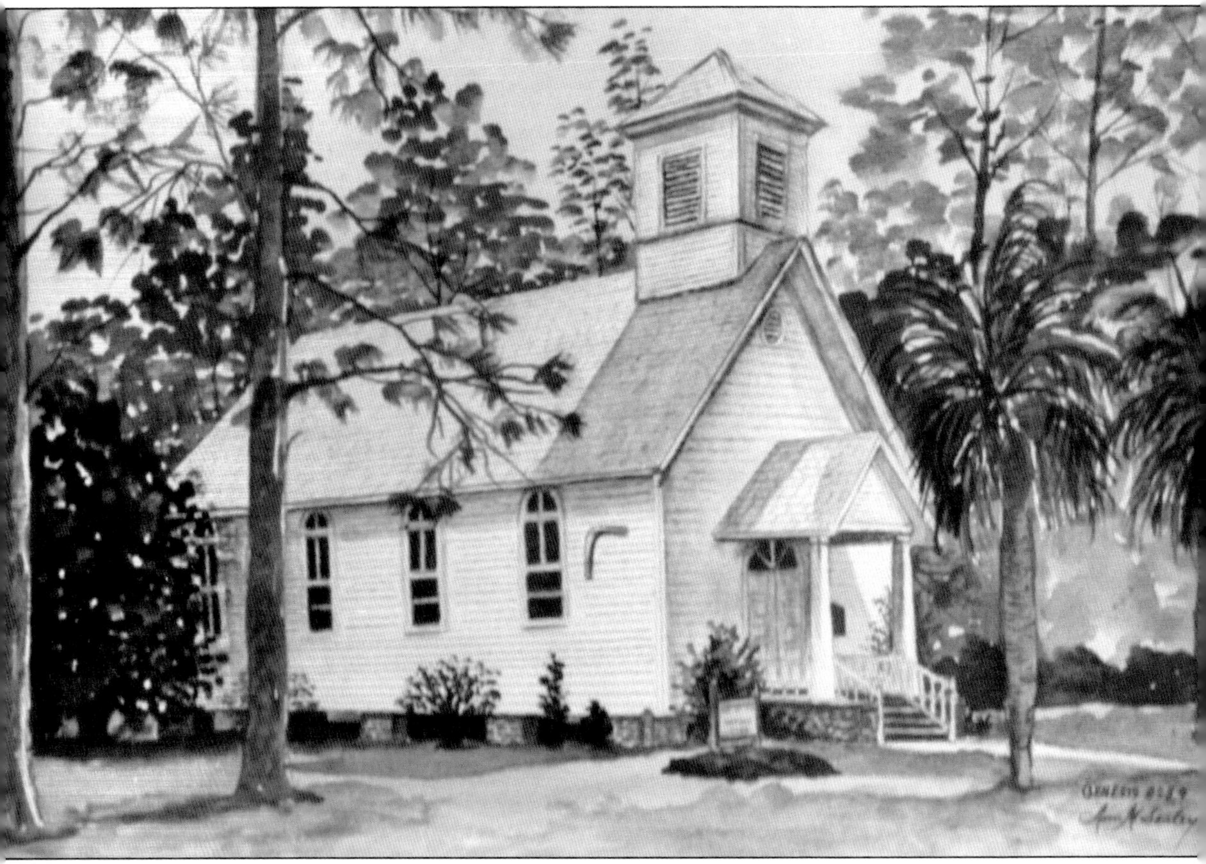

Before St. Joseph Church was established in Port St. Joe, priests came from Apalachicola in a Cadillac mounted on railroad wheels, chauffeured by Charles Mahon along the railroad tracks of Apalachicola Northern Railroad, where mass was celebrated in the home of Mr. and Mrs. Dennis Sullivan. In 1918, lots were purchased for a church, but because of the small number of Catholics, the building was postponed. In 1920, the Reverend Francis De Sales celebrated his first mass in Port St. Joe as a regular mission. This was in the home of Mr. and Mrs. Robert Tapper. The church was later erected in 1925 of milled lumber. It is an example of frame vernacular architecture and craftsmanship and is the oldest church in Port St. Joe. The building was deeded to the Port St. Joe Garden Club in 1969. (FHS and SJHS.)

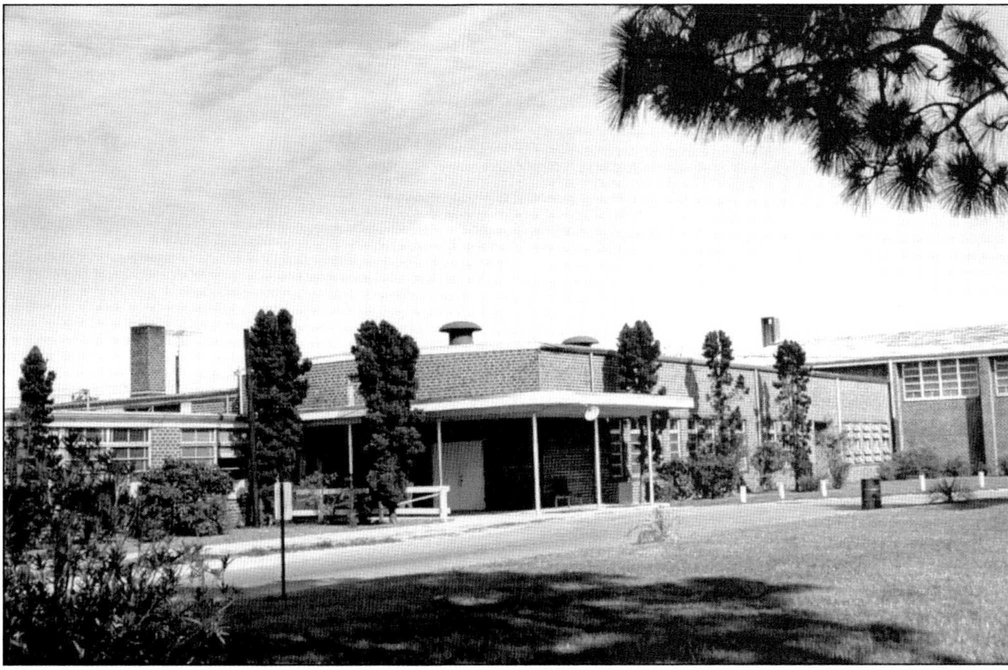

This building currently serves as the Port St. Joe Elementary School. It was previously the Port St. Joe High School, and the last graduating class was in 1970. (Courtesy of the Gulf County Chamber of Commerce and SJHS.)

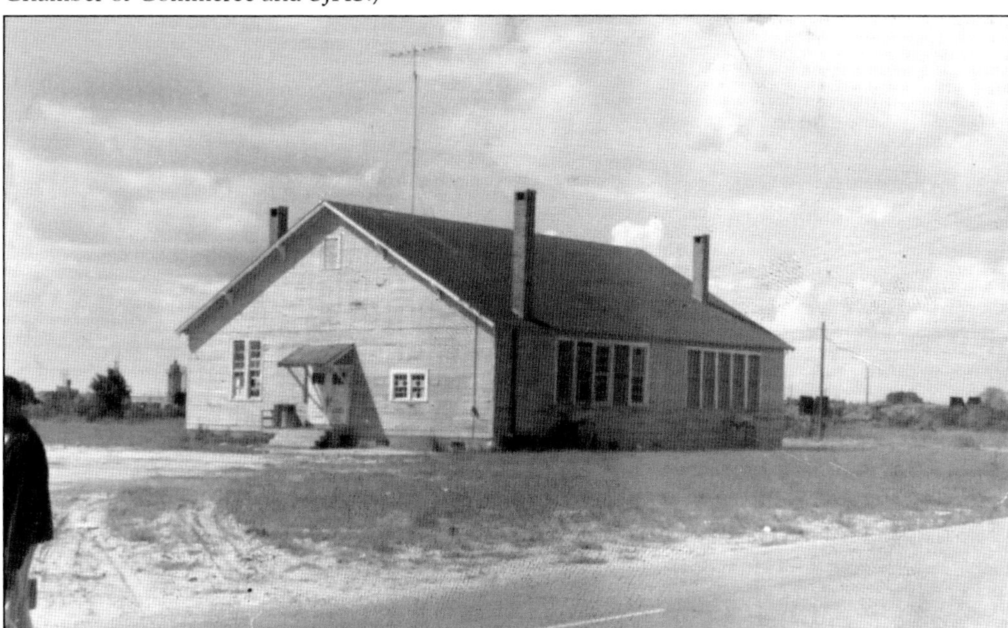

According to articles in the *Star*, the George Washington High School was built in 1929. It was in a wooden building that was later relocated to Martin Luther King Jr. Boulevard in 1939. A second, larger, L-shaped building was constructed in the early 1950s and faced Kenny Street. It housed students until Port St. Joe schools integrated in 1970. Emile Twine was its longest-serving principal; he served from 1946 to 1964. (CM.)

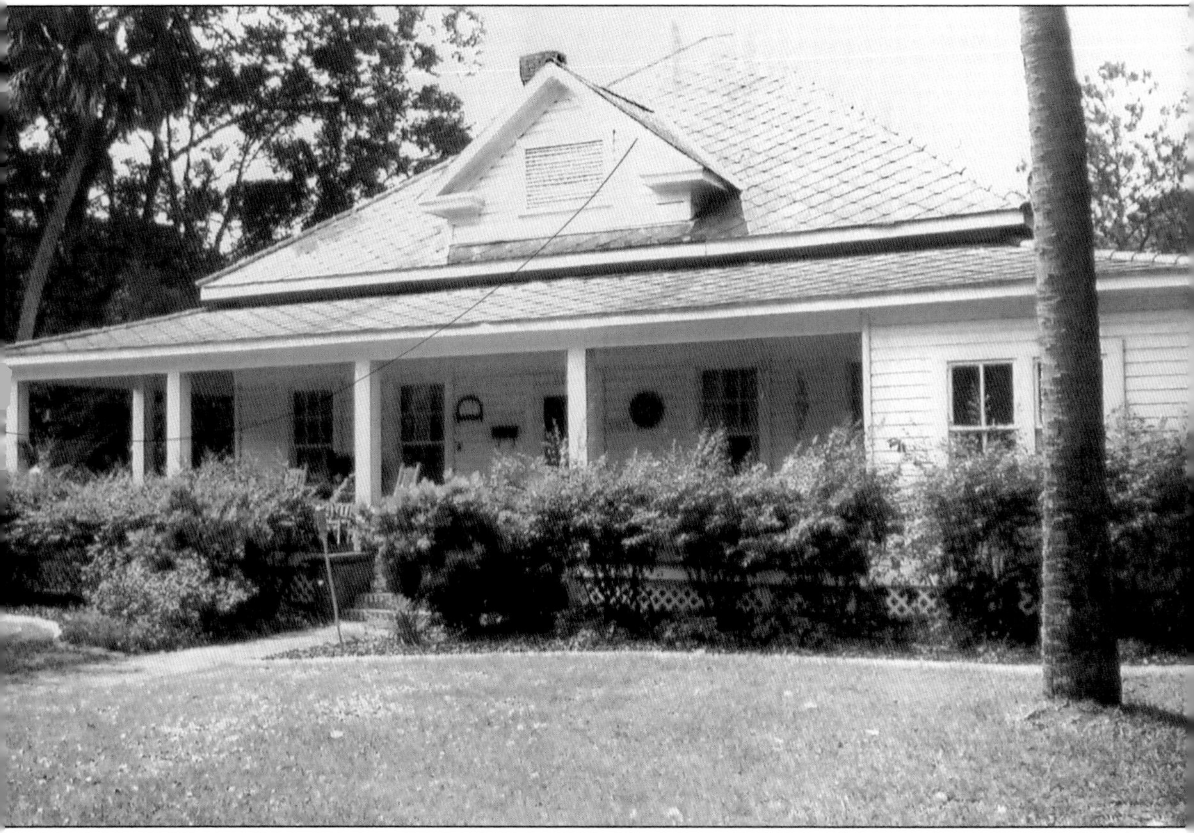

The Jones-Swatts House was one of the earliest homes built here. This largely unaltered, four-square frame vernacular home was built around 1912 for Asbury Morgan Jones and his family. He came to Port St. Joe with the arrival of the Apalachicola Northern Railroad. The home was sold to Ralph Swatts and his wife, Mabel (Stone) Swatts, and they raised their family here. The Durate family bought the home in 1996. (BMD.)

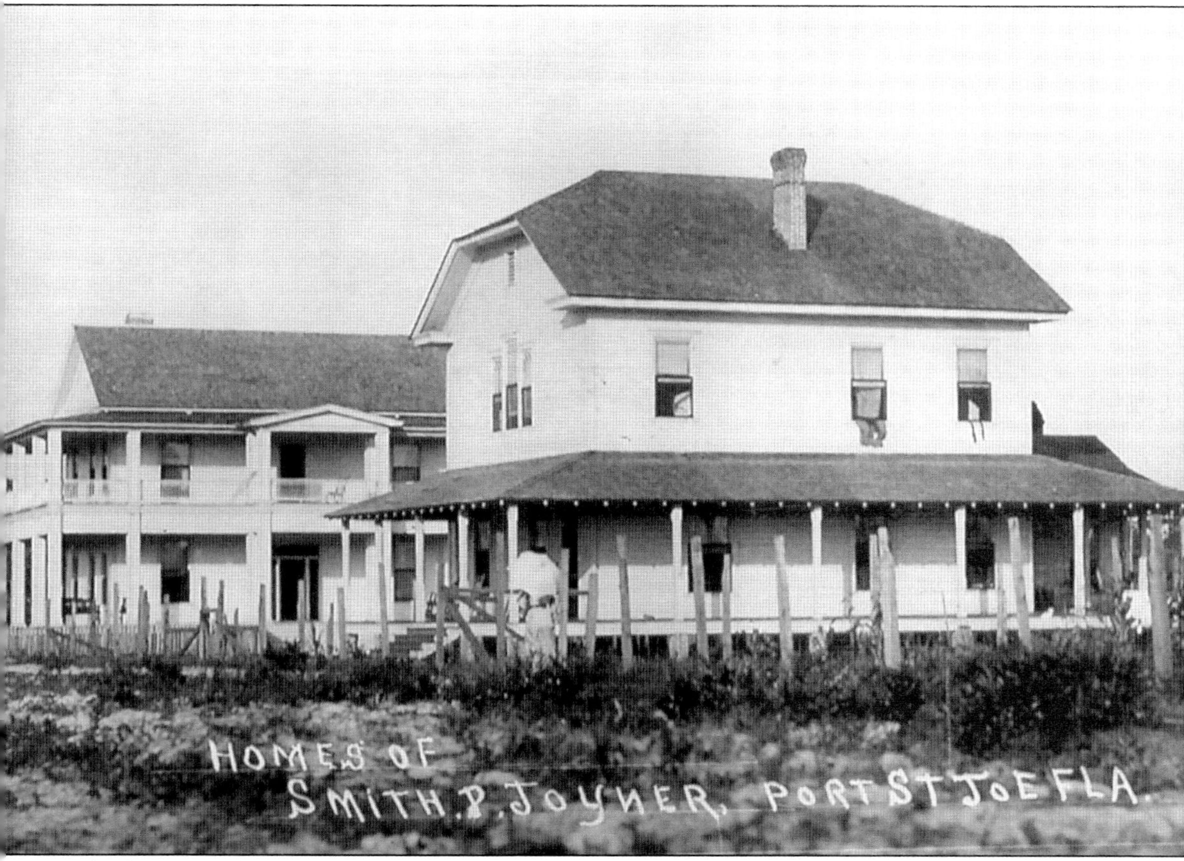

This home was built between 1907 and 1910 and was home for many years to George M. Johnson, engineer with the Apalachicola Northern Railroad, and his family. The house today has been restored and renovated by Reinhard and Delores Windolf and serves as the Windolf Construction Company offices. The house in the rear was the home of George M. Atkins, brother of Mrs. Gypsie A. McNeill. In 1920, the first Catholic mass in Port St. Joe was held here in the home of Mr. and Mrs. Robert Tapper. Later it was home for a short time to the Belin family. The building later was purchased by Pete Comforter in 1947 and is now owned and operated by Pete's son, Rocky Comforter, and is the office of the Comforter Funeral Home. (RC.)

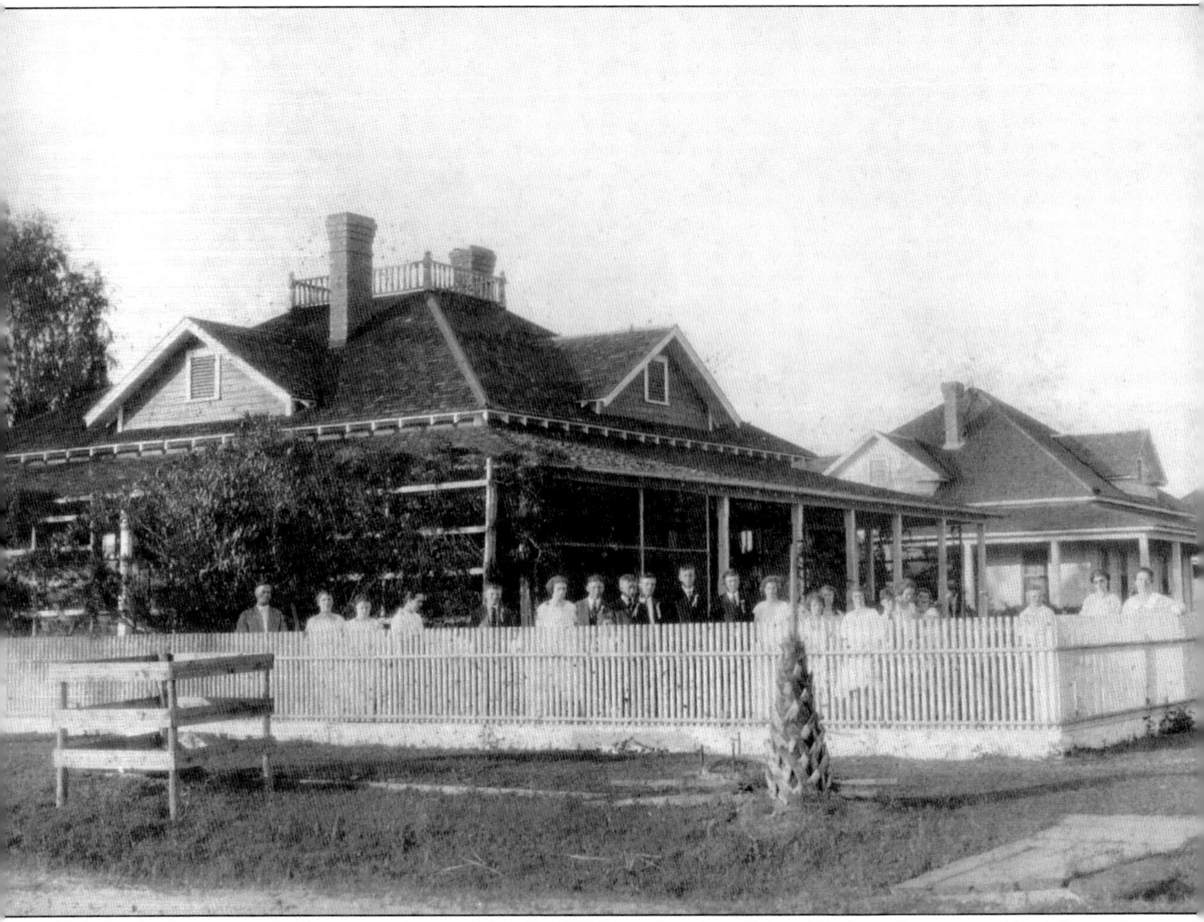

This home was built in 1918 or 1919 by the Walters family of New York and occupied by Mr. and Mrs. Max Kilbourn, owners of the ice plant and a fishing business. The Jake Belin family also lived here. The home was later purchased by Capt. Robert Tapper and his family in the early 1930s. Today it is the office of Dr. Owen Oksanen. Shown in this photograph is the eighth-grade graduating class of 1924; one of the girls is Ida Ethel Kilbourn, daughter of Max Kilbourn, former owner of the home. (VSH.)

New Bethel AME Church was organized in 1907 by the Rev. L. H. Brown. Services were held in an old frame house located in the Stone Quarters. The first church was built in 1910. In 1920, the church was destroyed by lightning. On May 18, 1947, the last day in the old church, the congregation sang "As the Saints Go Marching In" as they marched to the newly constructed church. (BP.)

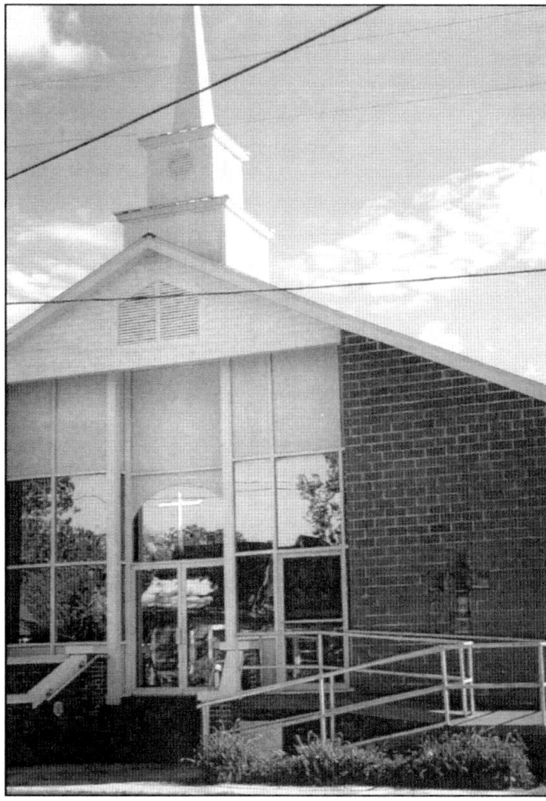

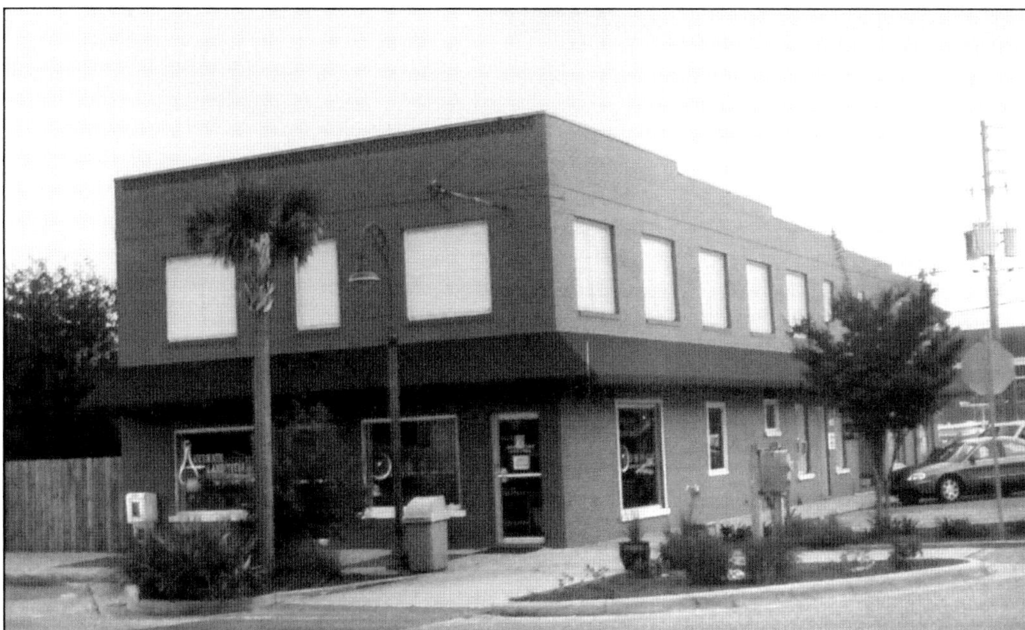

The Lawson Building was originally built around 1924; the old wooden structure burned in the early 1940s and was later rebuilt as a brick building. Mr. and Mrs. A. D. Lawson lived in the rear of the building and rented out rooms upstairs. (BMD.)

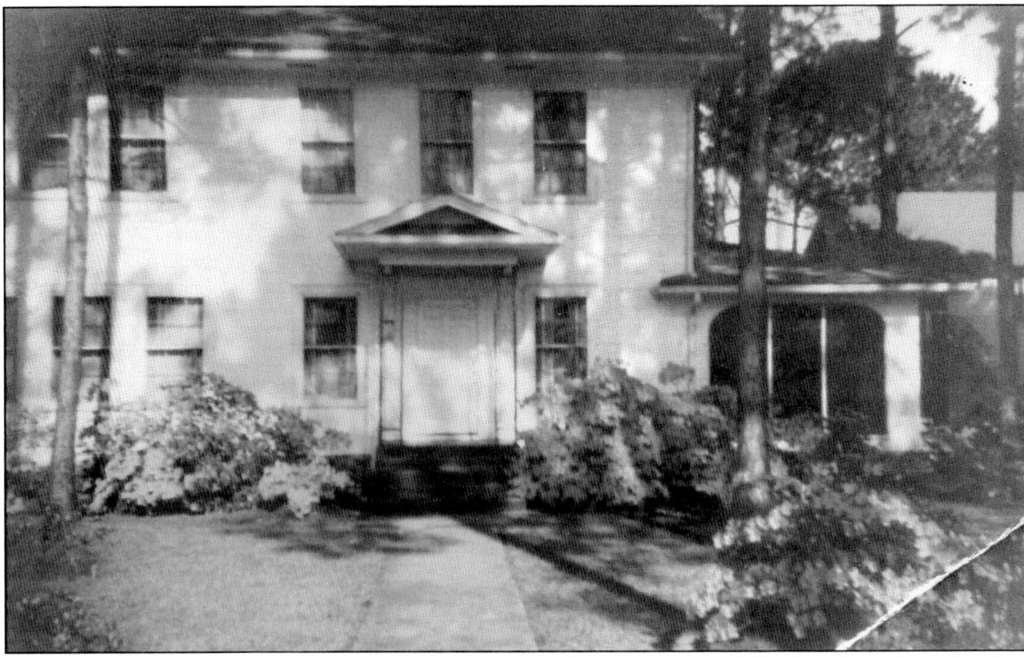

The Anderson-Smith Home was built for Otto Anderson, owner of the local Ford Dealership; they moved into the house in 1938. Otto and Emma Anderson raised two daughters, Dorothy and "Betty Otto," and lived there until Otto's death in 1975. At that time, Dorothy's daughter Frann and her husband, Roy Smith, moved in and raised their two boys. This home has been in the Anderson family for four generations. (PPL.)

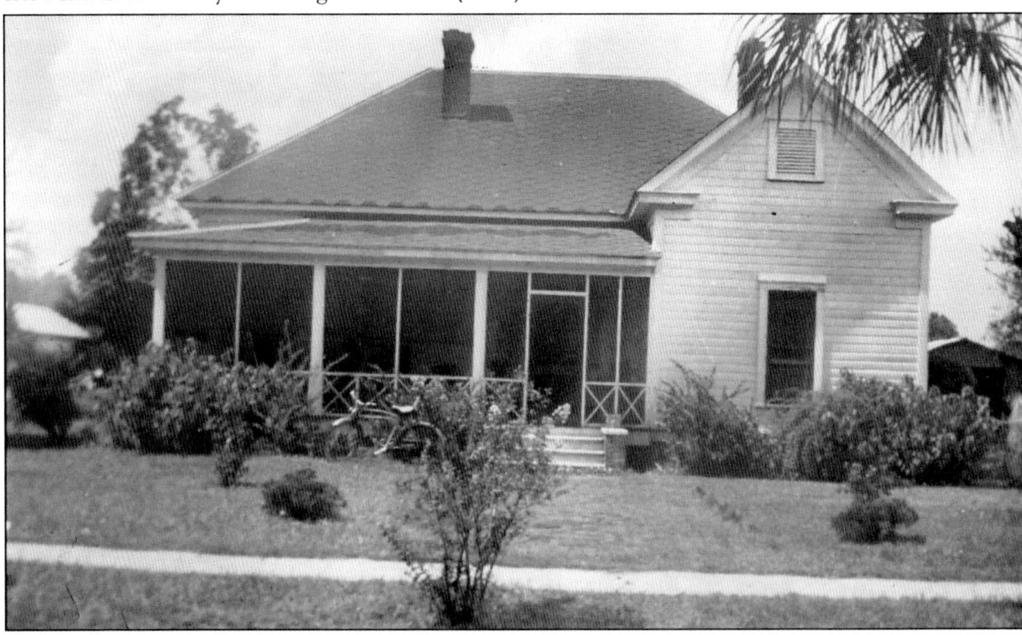

The Howell Home was built in 1915. The Howell family didn't move into the residence until 1932. Willie and Calla Howell raised their five children there. Willie died in 1969, and Calla lived there until she moved to the St. Joseph Care Center. The family owned the home until her death in 1996. (BH and PPL.)

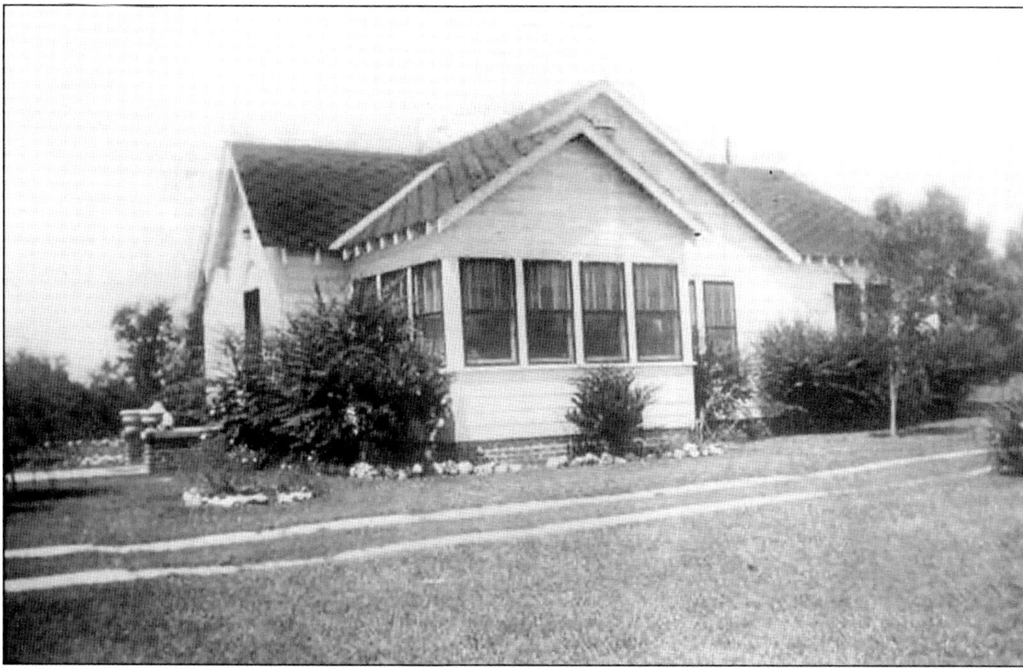

Henry A. Drake built this house in the early 1930s, while he and his wife, Minnie Ola, lived in their first home on the lot next door. They lived here until retiring and returning to Georgia. Today the building, owned by one of T. H. Stone's granddaughters, is known as Interiors Etc., a wonderful little gift shop. (GT.)

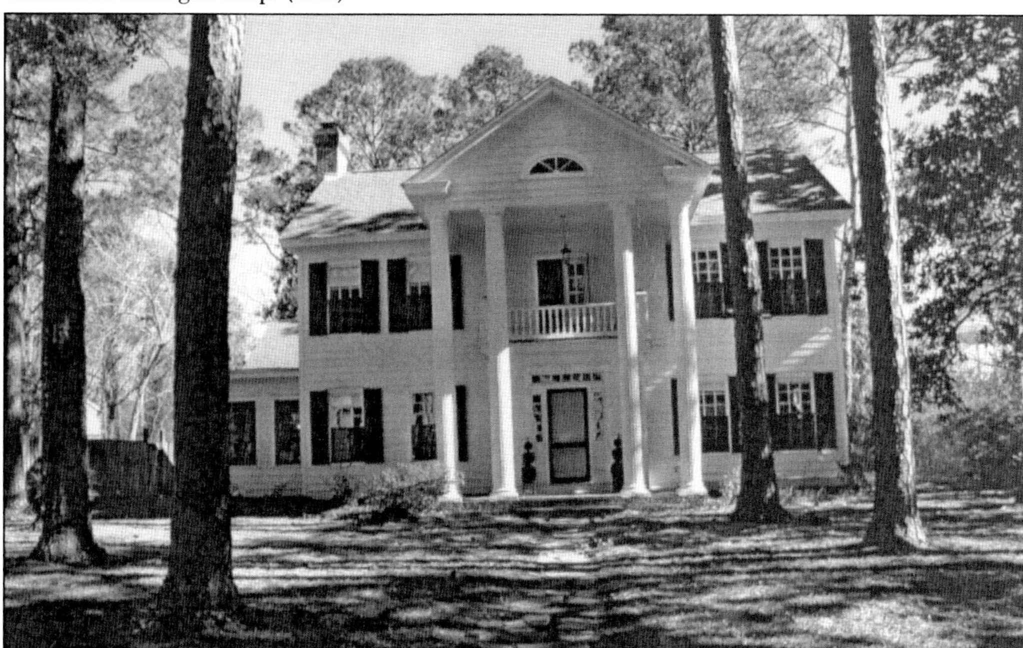

Byron W. Eells Sr. came to Port St. Joe in 1913 as vice president and general manager of the Apalachicola Northern Railroad Company. This Southern Colonial–style house was built in 1937 for the Eells family. (BP.)

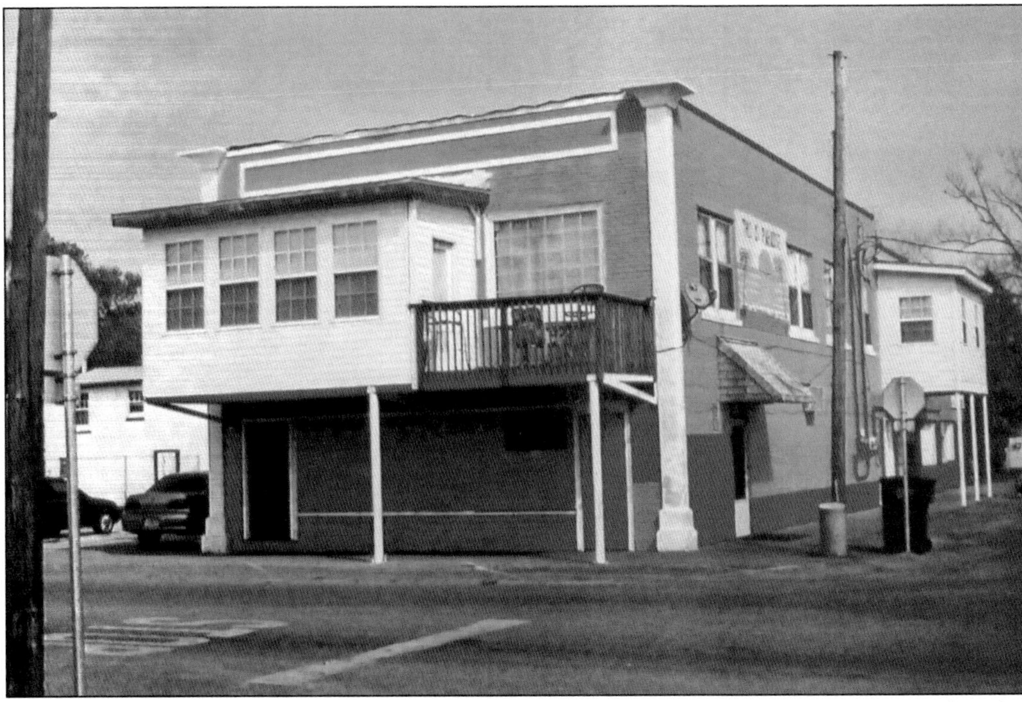

D. P. Peters' General Store was built in 1938 by Damon P. Peters Sr. as a general merchandise store; it is now owned by Nathan Peters Jr. and was remodeled in 2005. (BMD.)

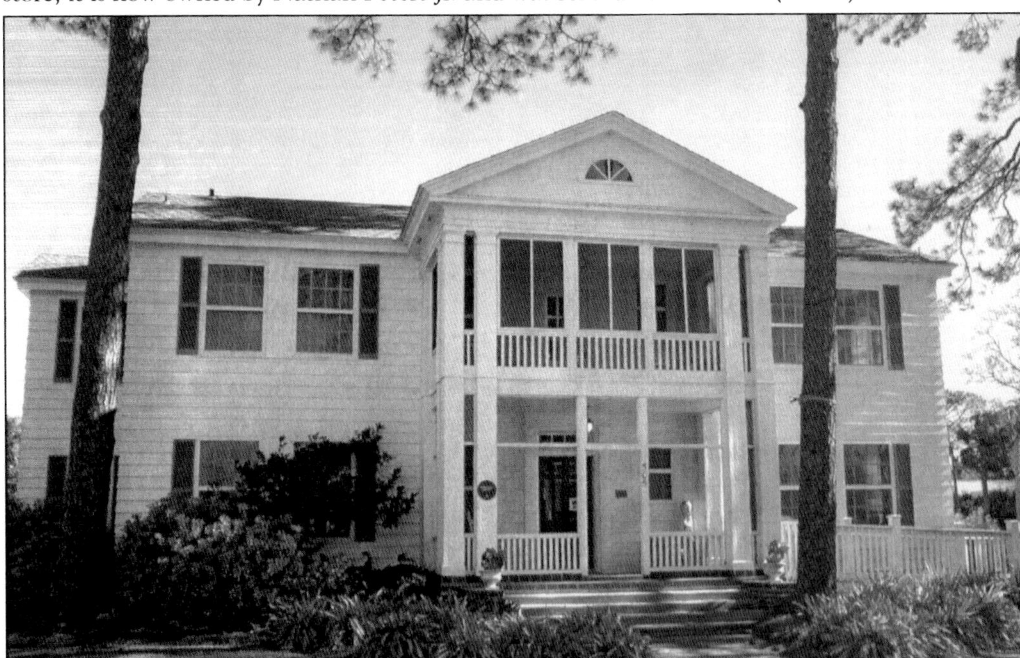

The Chateau was designed by architect Bryan Duncan and built in 1939 as the local residence for Jesse Ball duPont, the wife of Alfred I. duPont. The Chateau also provided lodging for St. Joe Company executives. Sold in 1998 as a bed-and-breakfast inn, the Chateau was later converted to the Coastal Community Bank. (BP.)

The City Council of Port St. Joe unanimously passed Resolution No. 320 on March 21, 1961, to name this park Patton Park in honor of Mrs. George Patton, whose life in Port St. Joe proved that she believed "a thing of beauty is a joy forever." Edna Mahon Patton, pictured with city councilman John Robert Smith, was fondly known to everyone as "Miss Ned," and to the town she contributed loving Christian leadership and able civic organization. (NP.)

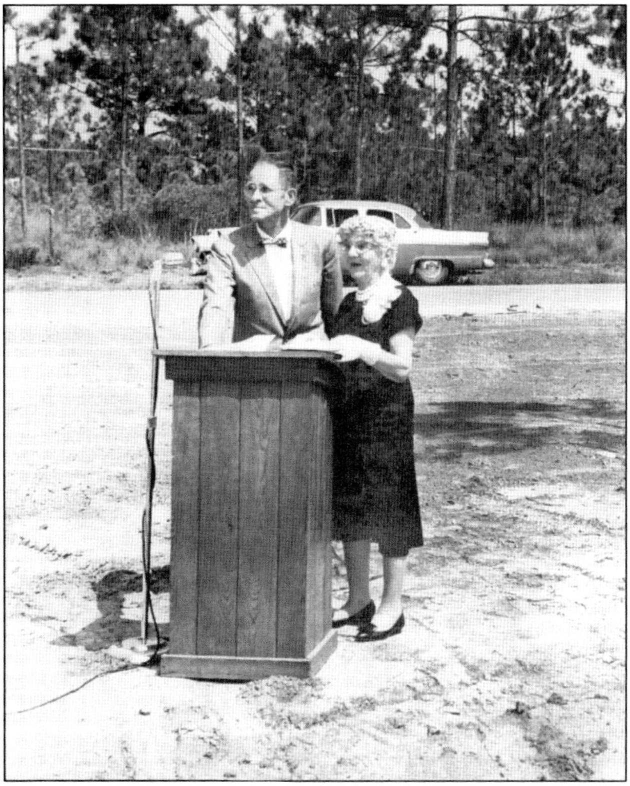

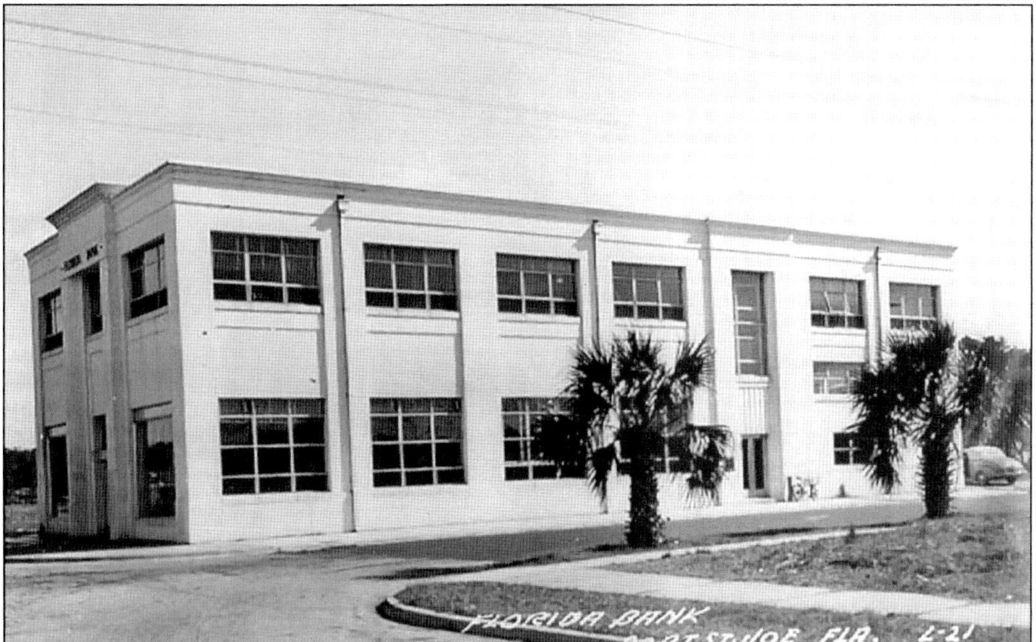

Built in early 1940, this building was home to Port St. Joe's first bank, the Florida Bank, before it later became the offices of the St. Joseph Telephone and Telegraph Company. Now it serves as the offices of the GT Com telephone company. (RC.)

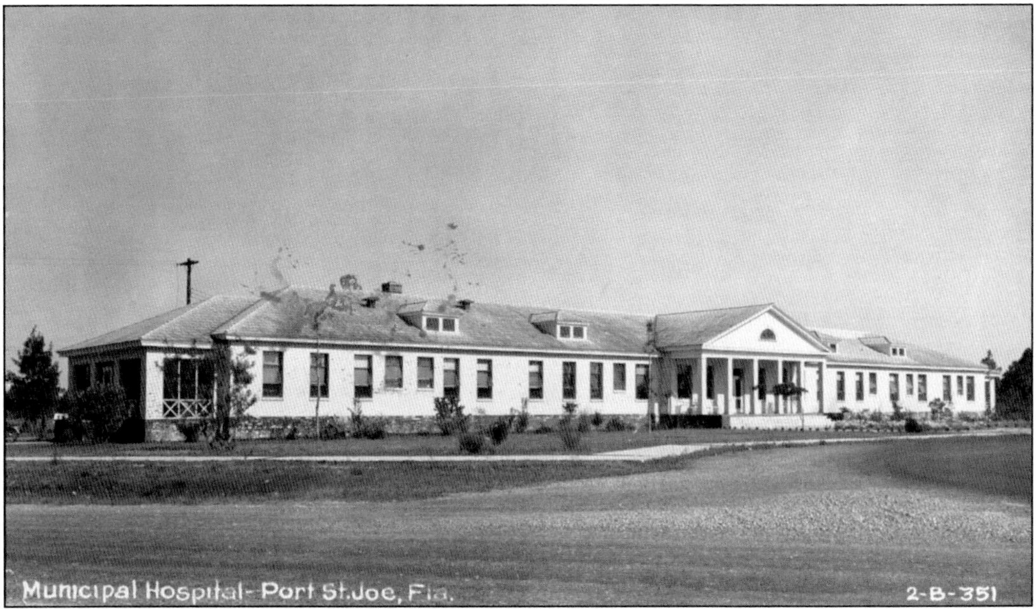

The *Star* reported that the Municipal Hospital in Port St. Joe opened November 16, 1943. The original land deed was signed on August 23, 1940. Ground breaking for the new wing was February 15, 1960, and the dedication was August 20, 1961. The longest years of service were Jean Atchison and Fannie Roberts. Physicians who served were J. R. Norton, Albert Ward, J. W. Hendix, J. P. Hendix, Conard Williams, Shirley Simpson, Bill Wager, John Edmiston, and Jorge San Pedro. (PPL.)

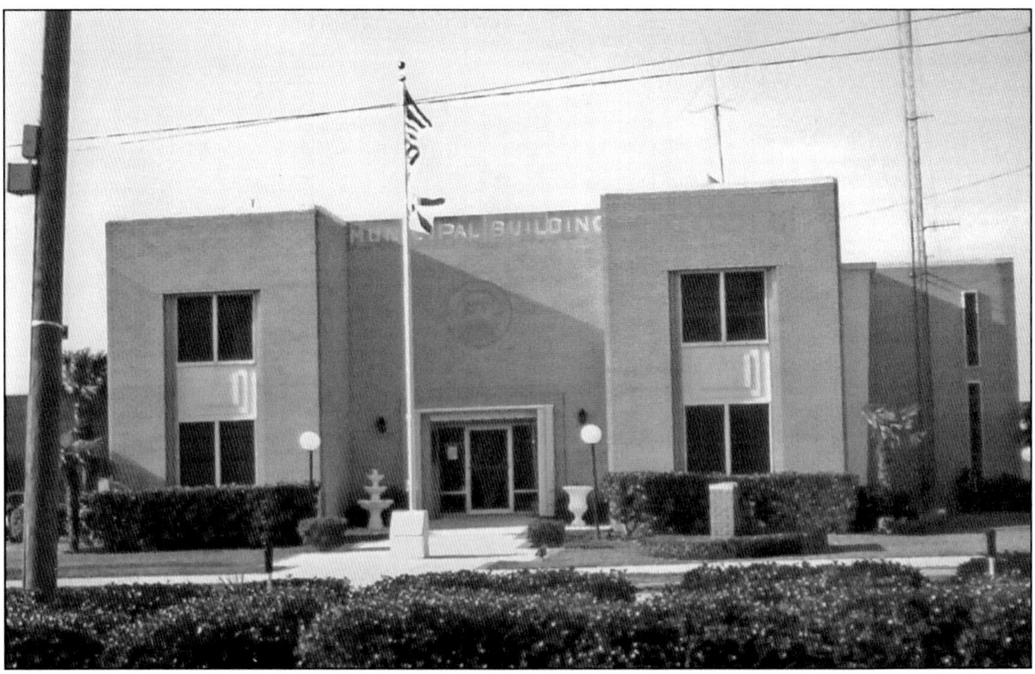

The Municipal Building was built in 1949 by an Alabama construction company. The architects were Norman P. Cross and Associates. In now serves as the Port St. Joe City Hall, Police Department, and Water Department and as a meeting place for the Port St. Joe city commissioners. (BMD.)

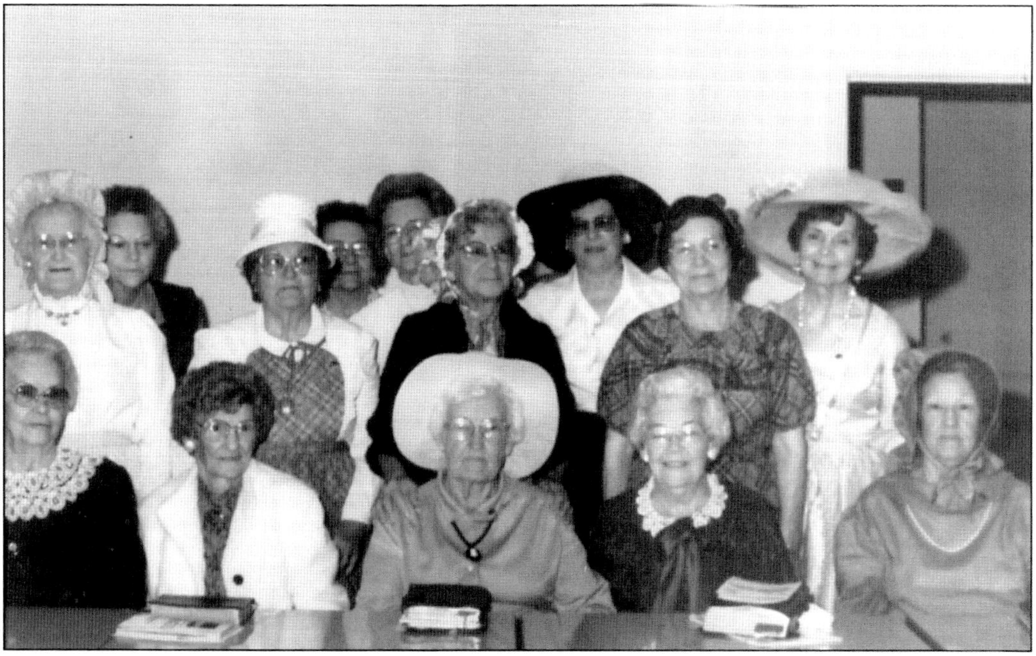

First Baptist Church celebrated Pioneer Day. Shown above is the 1988 Bethany Sunday school class. From left to right are (first row) Hatti Pierce, Leona Elliot, Myrtice "Mema" Wilder, Tiny Rich, Myron Davis; (second row) Mammie Lou Smith, Dessie Lee Parker, Malzie Baldwin, Bea Campbell, Frances Chafin; (third row) Lucille Sheffield, Fennie Raiford, Margaret Nichols, teacher Vedora Wilson. (PPL.)

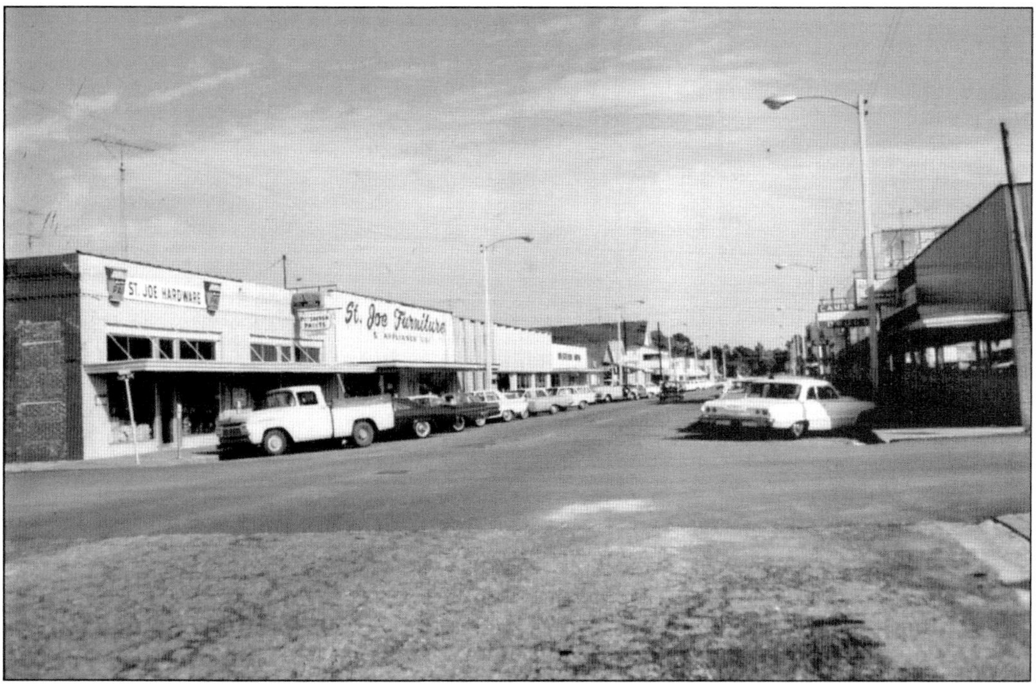

Looking down Reid Avenue in Port St. Joe during the 1960s, you would find parking meters and businesses of yesteryear. Take a trip down memory lane and look for the five-and-dime. (BH.)

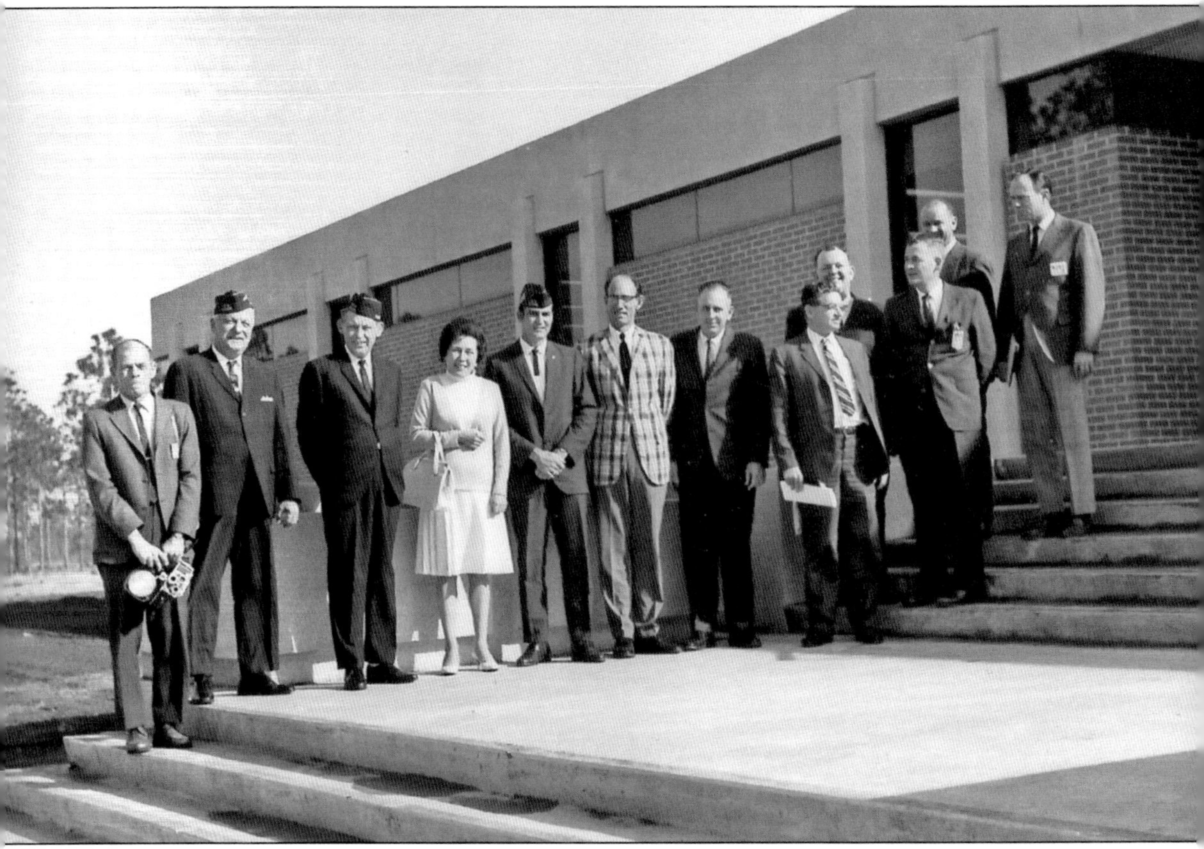

The Gulf County Courthouse was first located in Wewahitchka. In February 1968, it was moved to Port St. Joe. The center of the population in the county had steadily grown, and so it became necessary to moved the courthouse and provide larger quarters for the government. On the doorstep, those who attended the dedication included, from left to right, unidentified, Pete Comforter, Gannon Buzzett, Roberta Hardin, two unidentified, Frank Pate, Leo Kennedy, Bob Ellzey, unidentified, Gov. Claude Kirk, and Tom Hipps. (BH.)

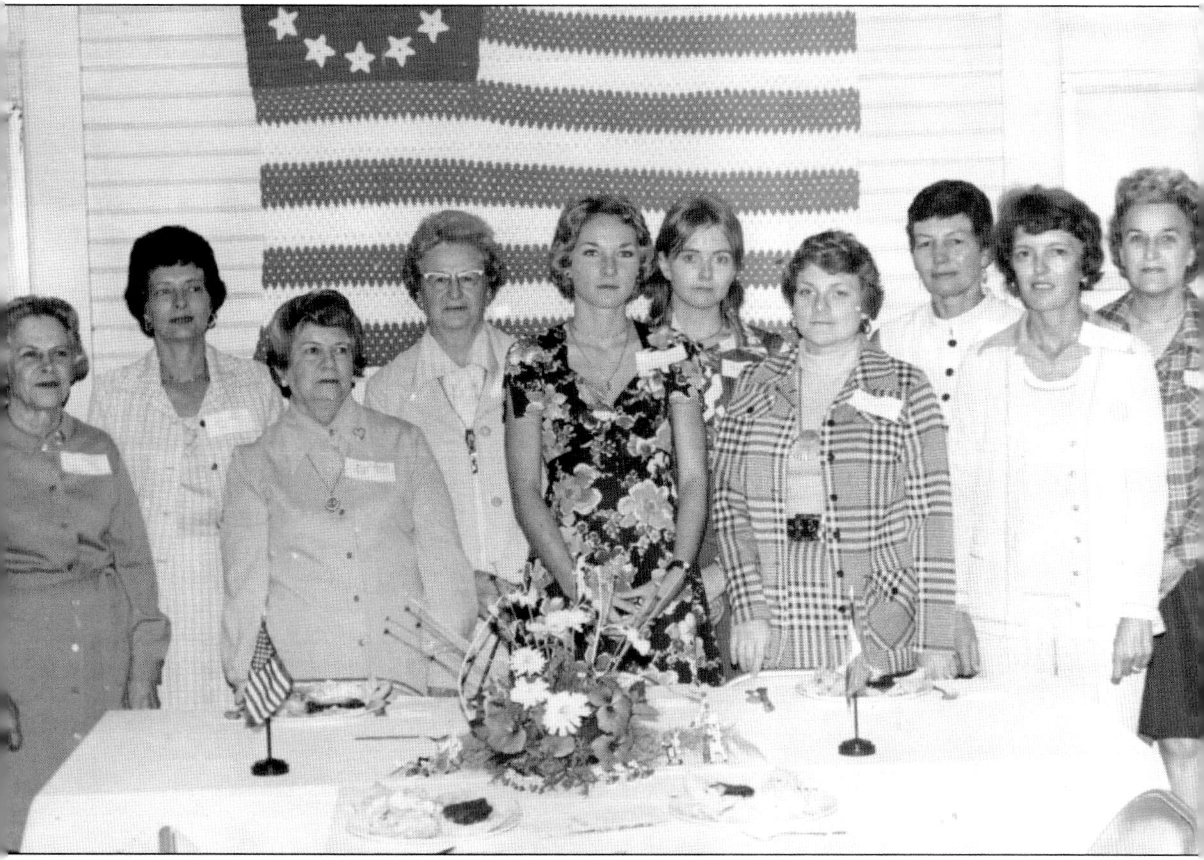

The Daughters of the American Revolution's Christmas Tea was held here in the Garden Club building during the late 1970s. Shown here are, from left to right, (first row) Elizabeth Tomlinson, Mabel Swatts, Midge Howell, Frann Smith, Eda Ruth Taylor; (second row) Nancy Howell, Eunice Brinson, Charlene Godfrey, Ida Ethel Smith, Alice Core. (DAR.)

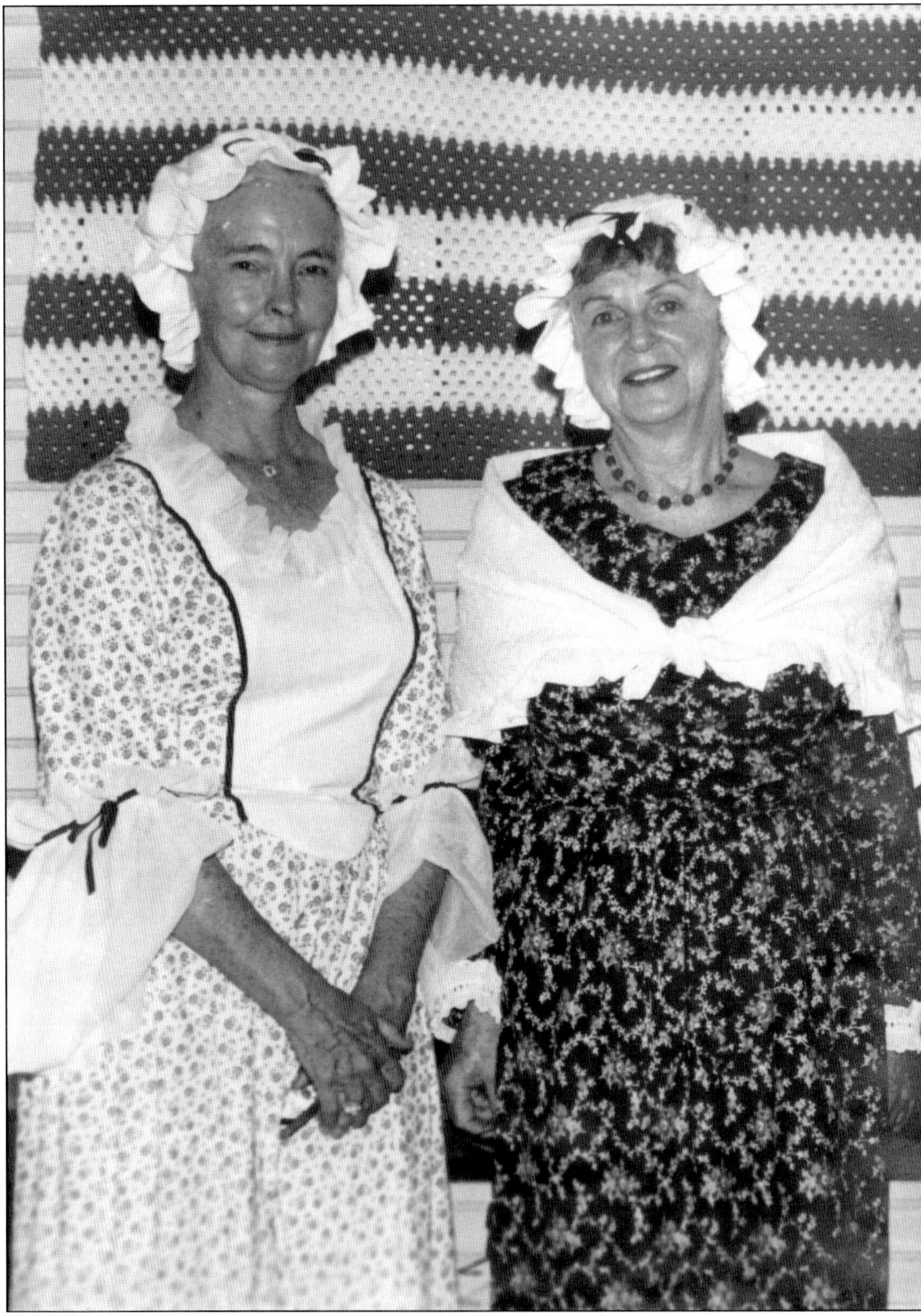

The DAR wore bicentennial costumes to represent the local chapter at the 74th annual state conference, held on March 1976 in Daytona Beach, Florida. Representing the chapter were members Betty Fensom (left) and Virginia Owens (right). (DAR)

Four

The Little City with a Big Heart

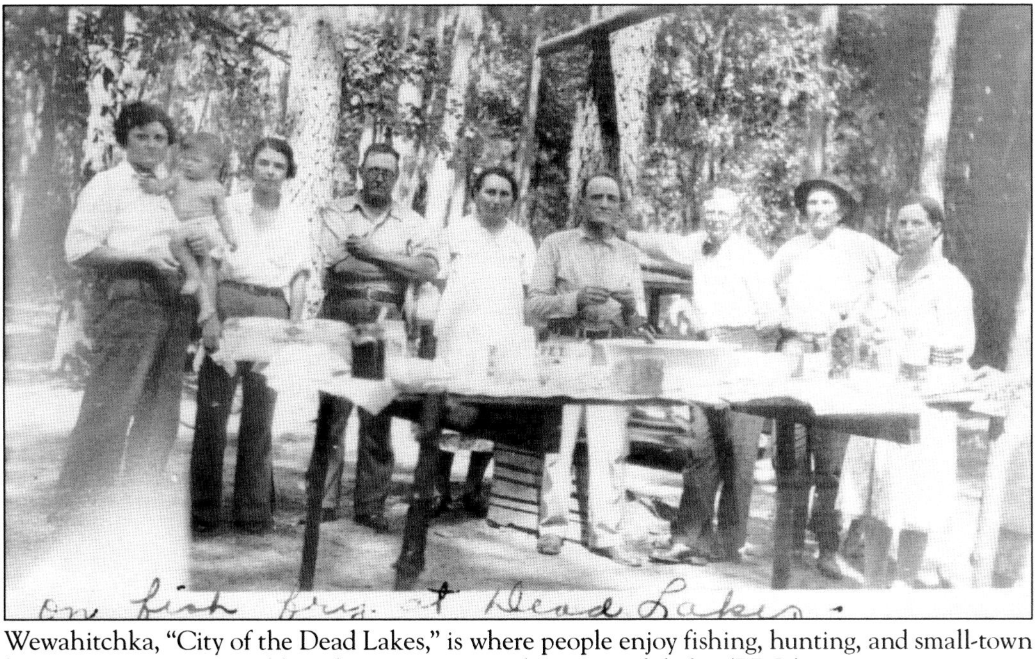

Wewahitchka, "City of the Dead Lakes," is where people enjoy fishing, hunting, and small-town living. Here is a group of friends enjoying a good time at a fish fry. (BBO.)

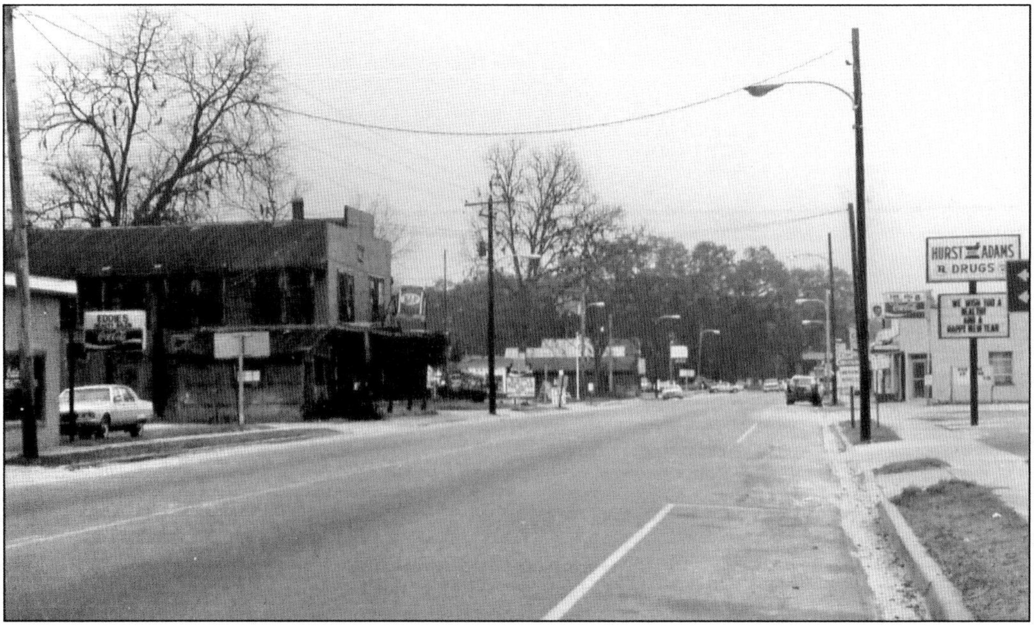

Wewahitchka, the original seat of Gulf County, is also the county's oldest permanent settlement and is located in the northeast section of Gulf County. "Wewa," the locals call it, is truly the "land of honey." Wewahitchka means "Water Eyes" in a Native American dialect. Two lakes in the heart of the city were thought by early residents to be eyes looking towards heaven. This town is the home of the Dead Lakes and the world-famous tupelo honey. (BH.)

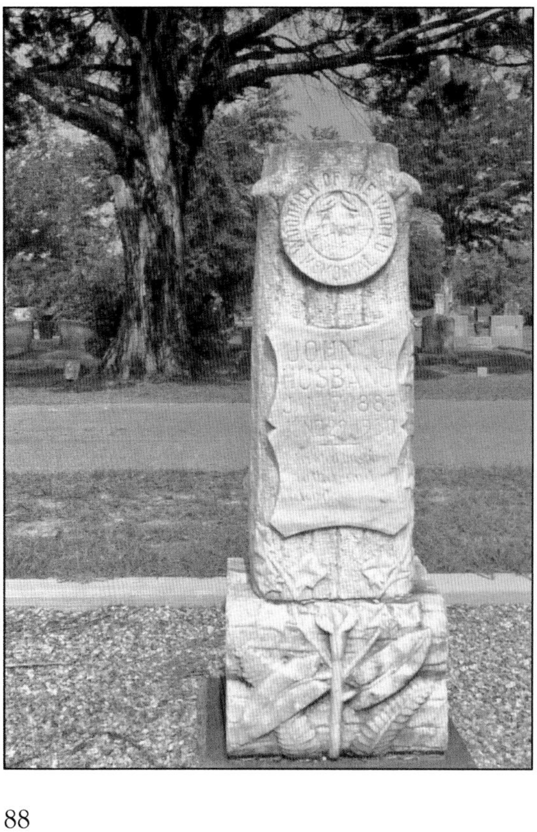

The Jehu Cemetery is named after Jehu Richards, a young boy who survived a Native American massacre in 1818. The Richardses were one of the most important families to settle in North Florida in the early 1800s. The cemetery has a number of massive headstones carved to look like tree trucks marking the spots where members of Woodmen of the World are buried. (BMD.)

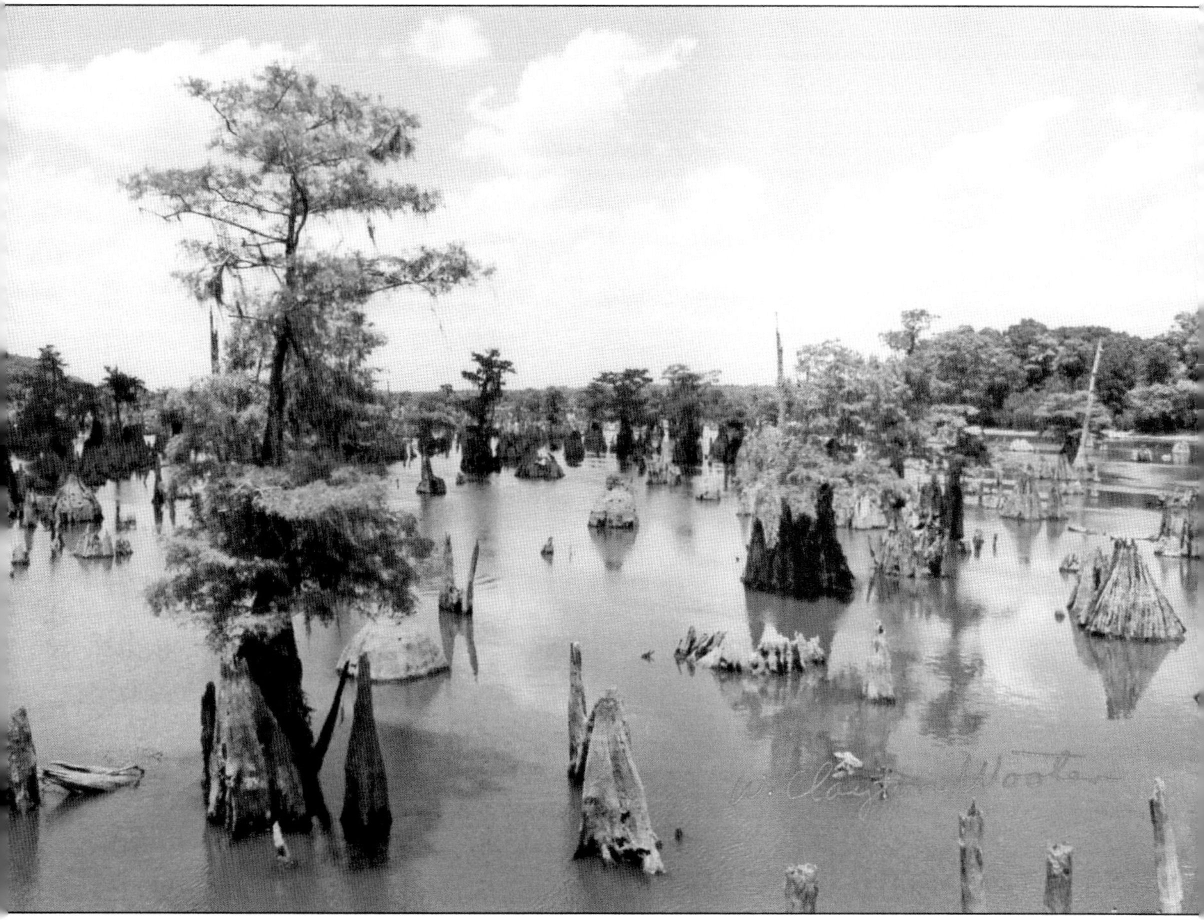

The Dead Lakes were filled with huge, majestic cypress trees, as were the entire swamps stretching from the Chattahoochee to Apalachicola, located 25 miles north of Port St. Joe. The Dead Lakes consist of 85 square miles of the finest bass and bream fishing in the state of Florida. Once known as Chipola Lake, the lakes were formed when the waters of the Apalachicola and the Chipola Rivers converged on a cypress swamp, flooding the low-lying area. Railroad pilings, remains of a St. Joseph and Iola Railroad trestle, considered an engineering marvel for its time and built by hundreds of slave laborers, are still visible. The lakes are bordered by some of the best hunting land in the state. (CW.)

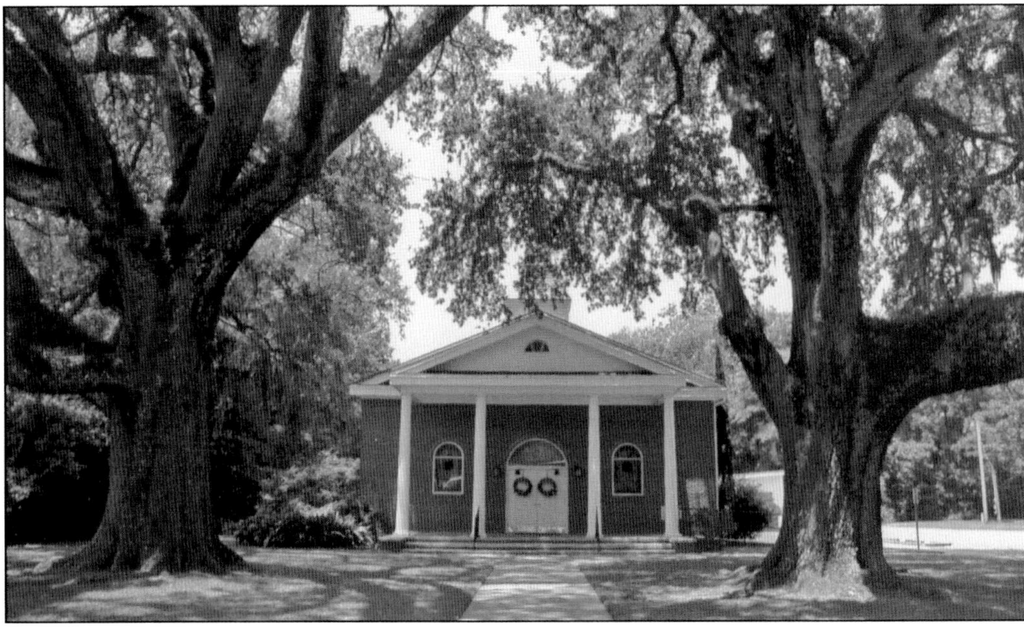

The First United Methodist Church of Wewahitchka was the first church established in Wewahitchka, although there had been a Baptist mission nearby. It was formally organized in 1876 by a member of the Richards family, John Wesley Richards, a Methodist minister and the father of Wewahitchka's John Norman Richards, the same John N. Richards who named the city and built the little log house that housed both the church and school for a time. (BMD.)

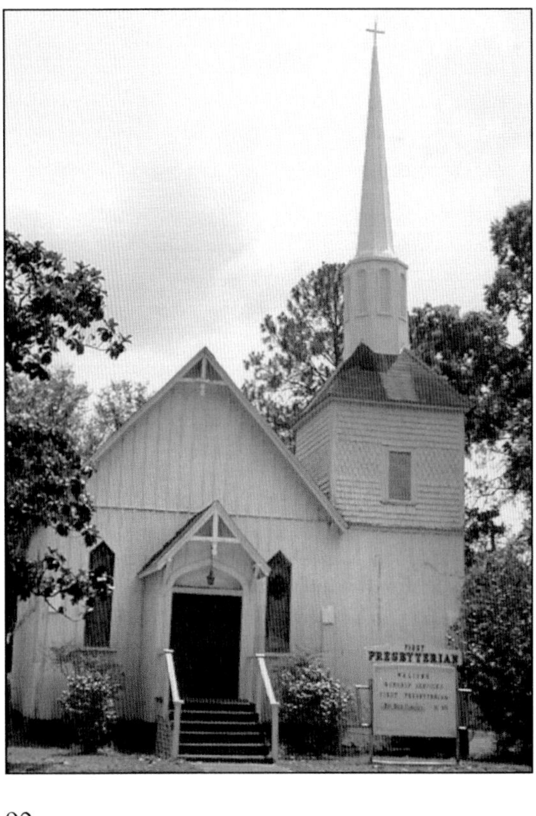

St. John's Episcopal Church was consecrated November 16, 1903. The church has survived hurricanes, lightning, fires, and car crashes and is one of the few buildings to have remained intact without serious structural alternations. The church was built by Francis C. Rommel, a carpenter and skilled craftsman. The old building owes its continued existence to the Presbyterians, who purchased it in 1943. (BP.)

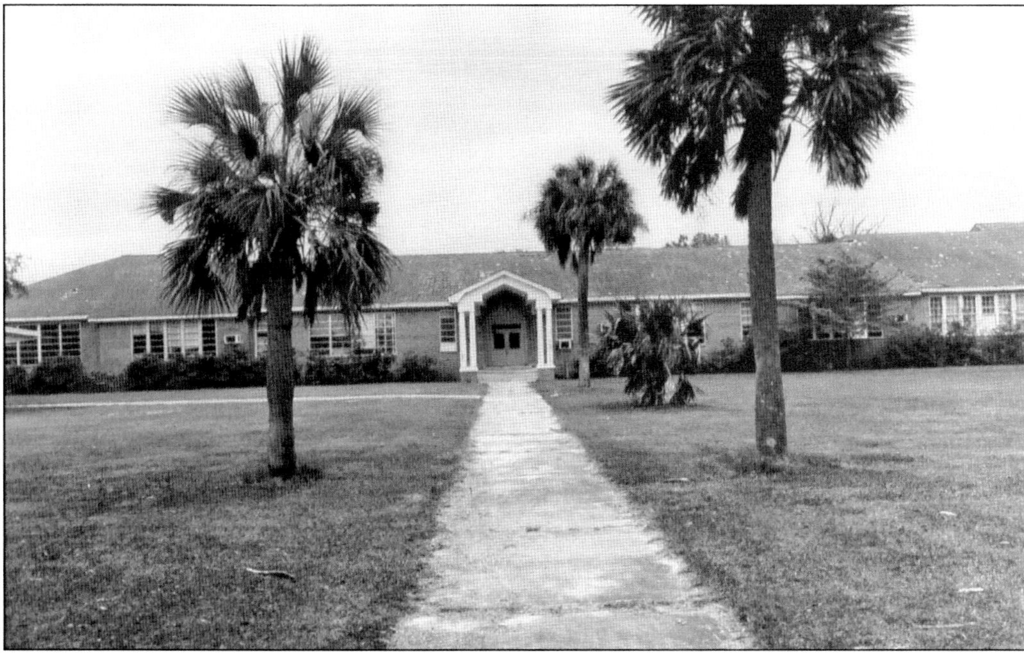

In 1925, a newly appointed school board began making plans for a new schoolhouse for Wewahitchka. The result was the beautiful red brick school that was located for many years just off Main Street south of town. The first graduating class was in 1938. This photograph was taken about 1932; the new gym was added in 1949; and in 1980, new classrooms were added. (AAW.)

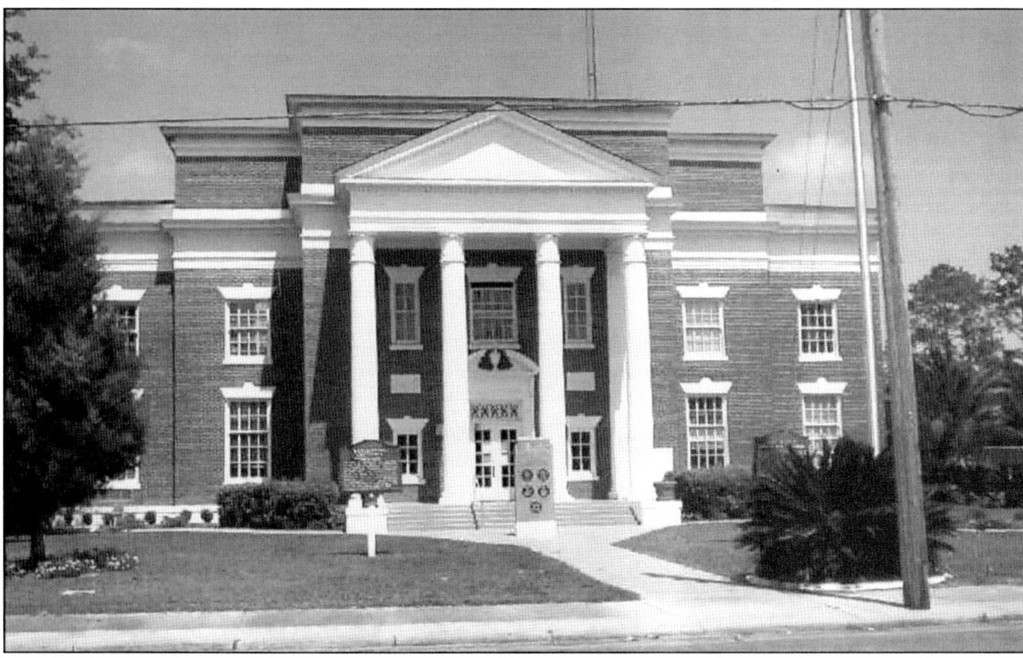

The Wewahitchka Court House, still a handsome building, was built by W. H. Taylor in 1927, two years after Gulf County was established from a portion of Calhoun County. It was the happy home of the county's business until the county seat was relocated to Port St. Joe in 1968; the building was renovated in 1991. (BMD.)

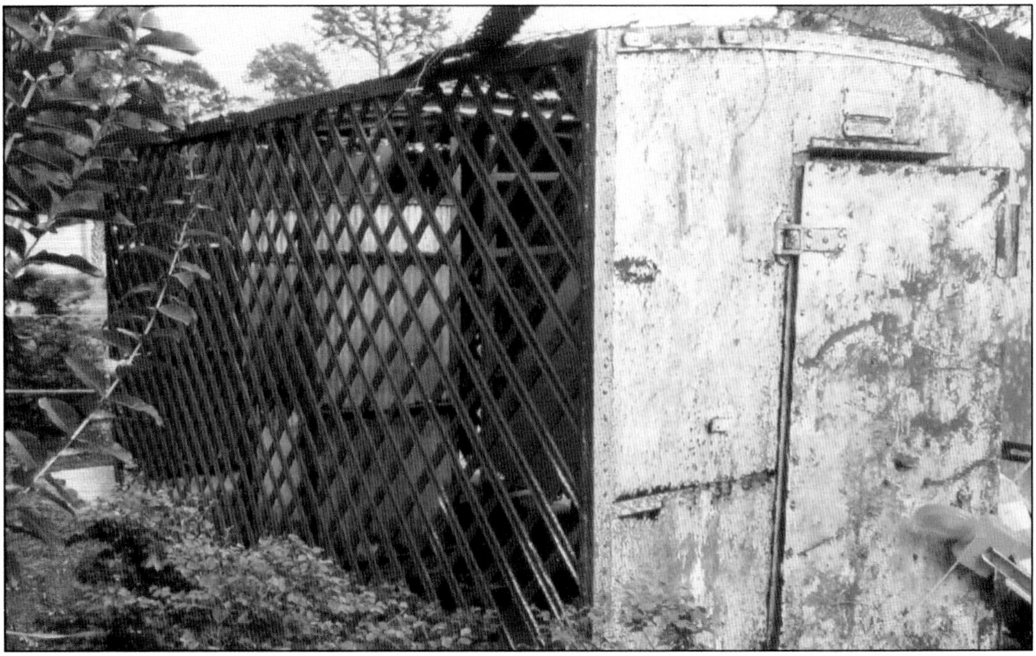

This metal cage served for a time as the Gulf County Jail. Longtime county clerk George Core recalls that it had a wooden roof and was set up across from the *Gulf County Breeze* office. Manly Jail Works of Dalton, Georgia, built this portable convict cage, which now rests in the Wewahitchka library parking lot. The jail temporarily housed James Ray, one of the FBI's 10 Most Wanted. (BMD.)

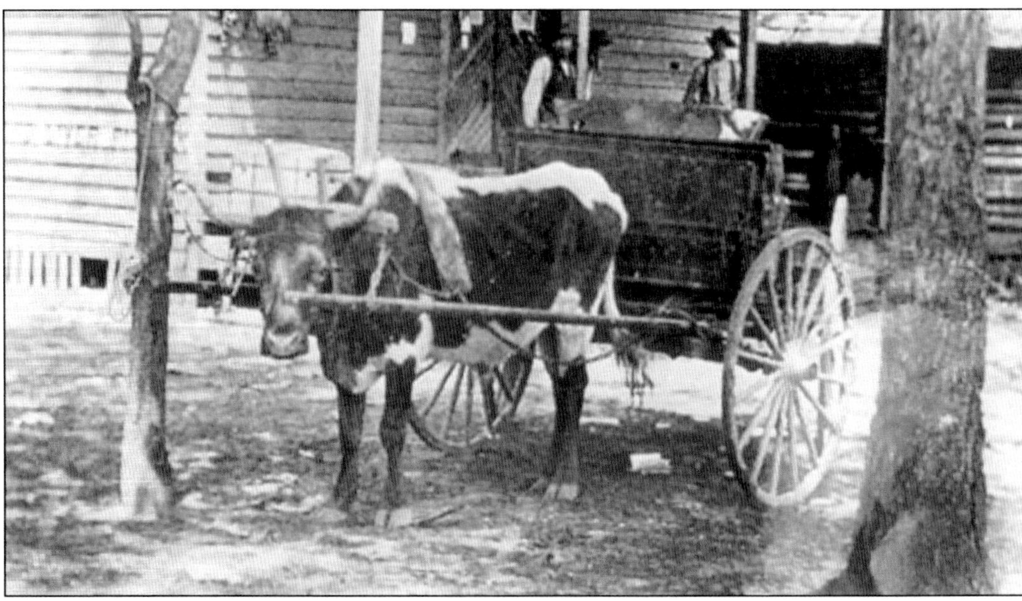

Iola, established in 1835 as the terminus of the St. Joseph and Iola Railroad, grew to be a bustling community with brick streets, several livery stables, five mercantile stores, and two gristmills. The town disappeared along with St. Joseph. Steamboats continued to ply the Apalachicola during the heyday of the "New" Iola (1904–1922). Shown here is Henry A. Rish, postmaster, and his mail wagon. (SJHS.)

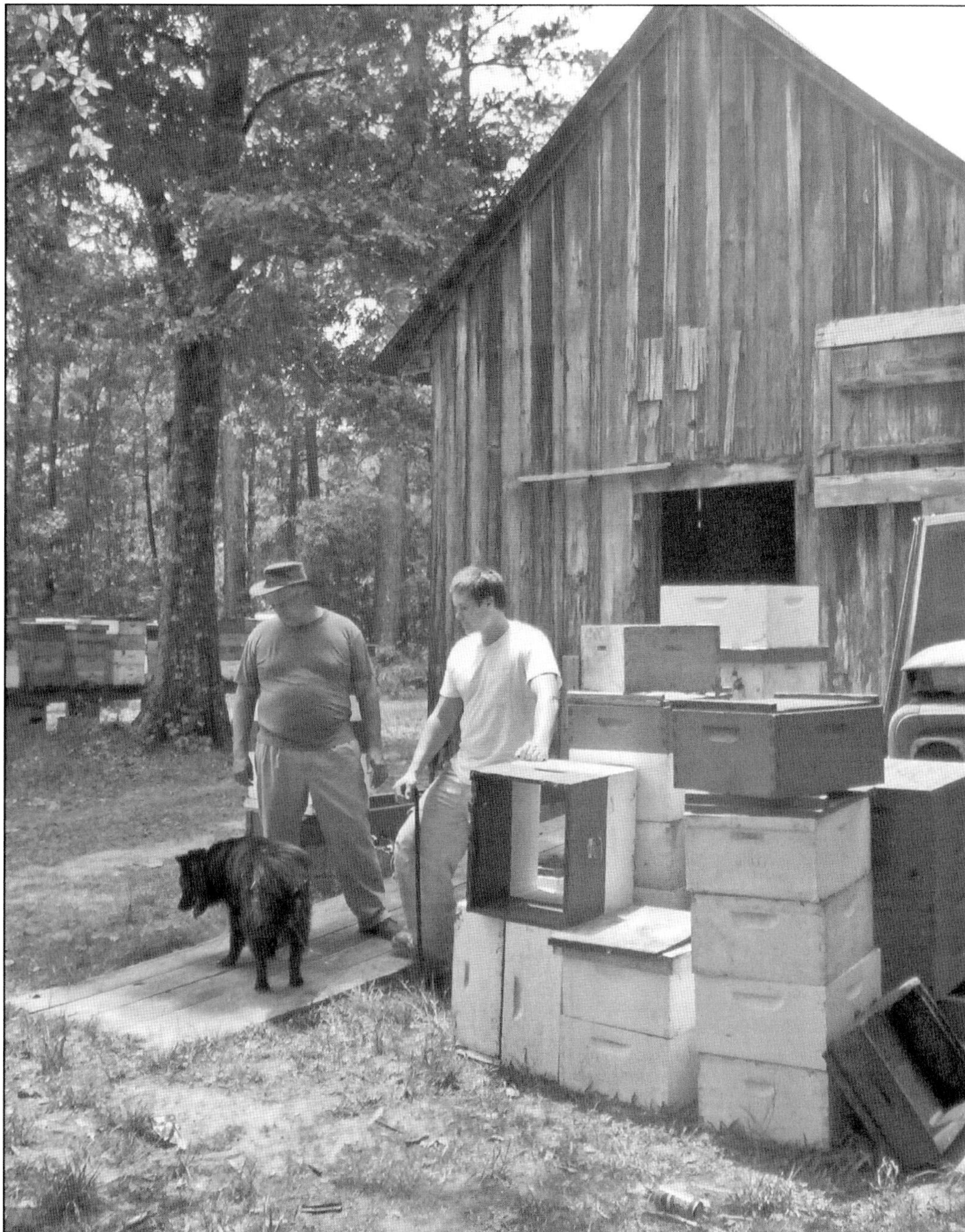

In what once was called the "New" Iola is Rish's Old Honey House. This building was built in 1902 by James Franklin Rish Sr. for the purpose of extracting honey and did without the use of electricity for over 100 years. Built of heart pine, the building has never been painted and has withstood floods and high winds from hurricanes. James's grandson James Ernest Rish and his son Nathan still keep their honeybees there. Three generations of the Rish family have worked at this location. Their new honey house is now located south of Wewahitchka at the home of James Earnest Rish. (BP and BMD.)

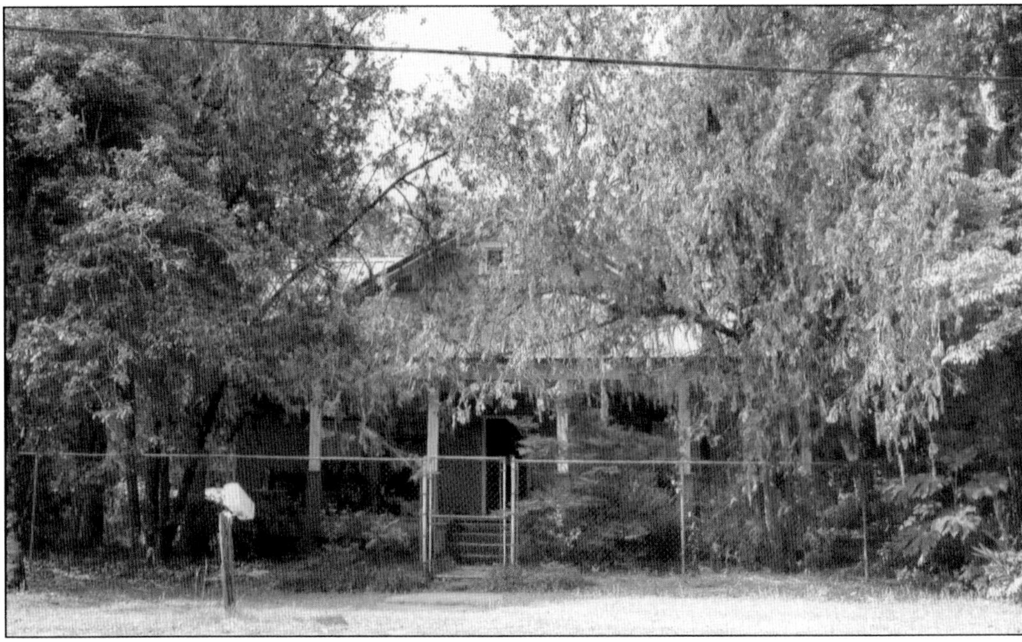

Lavernor Laveon Lanier Sr. was a pharmacist who tended his bee hives in a white shirt and bow tie. L. L. Lanier Jr. was born in this house, built in 1908 and occupied by three generations of Laniers, in 1923. He retired from the business in 1991 and turned it over to his son Ben and his wife, Glynnis. You can still buy tupelo honey from the nearly 100-year-old house in Wewahitchka. (BP.)

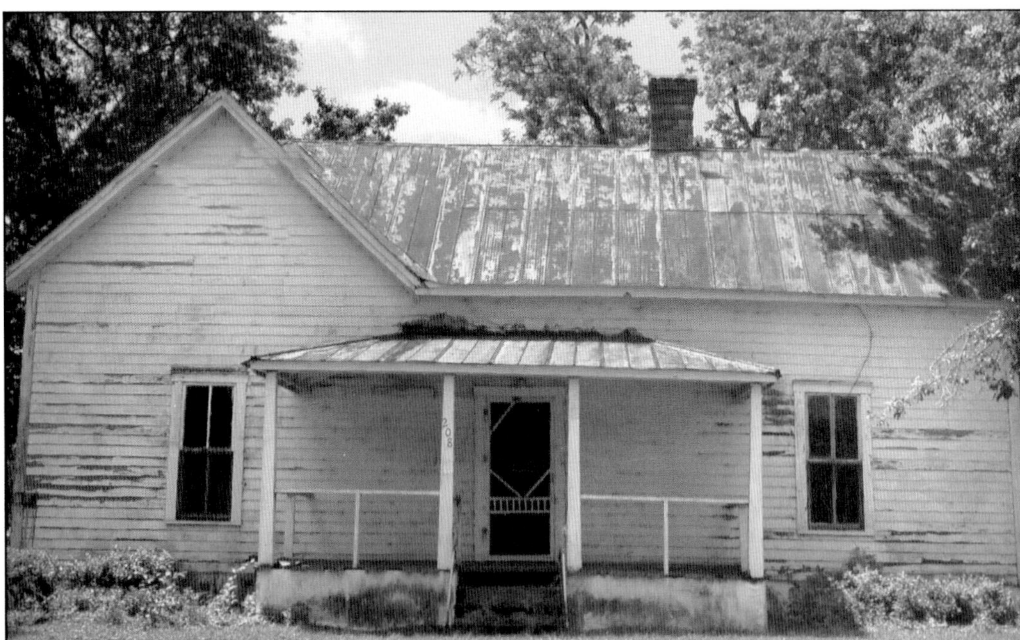

This house was built in 1916 by James Franklin Rish Sr. His father, Henry Alexander Rish, came to Iola in the 1880s, where he raised bees and owned and operated a hotel in the once-thriving fishing and hunting resort. James Ernest Rish recalls his grandmother sitting on the porch and selling honey to people stopped at the red light on the corner. (BP.)

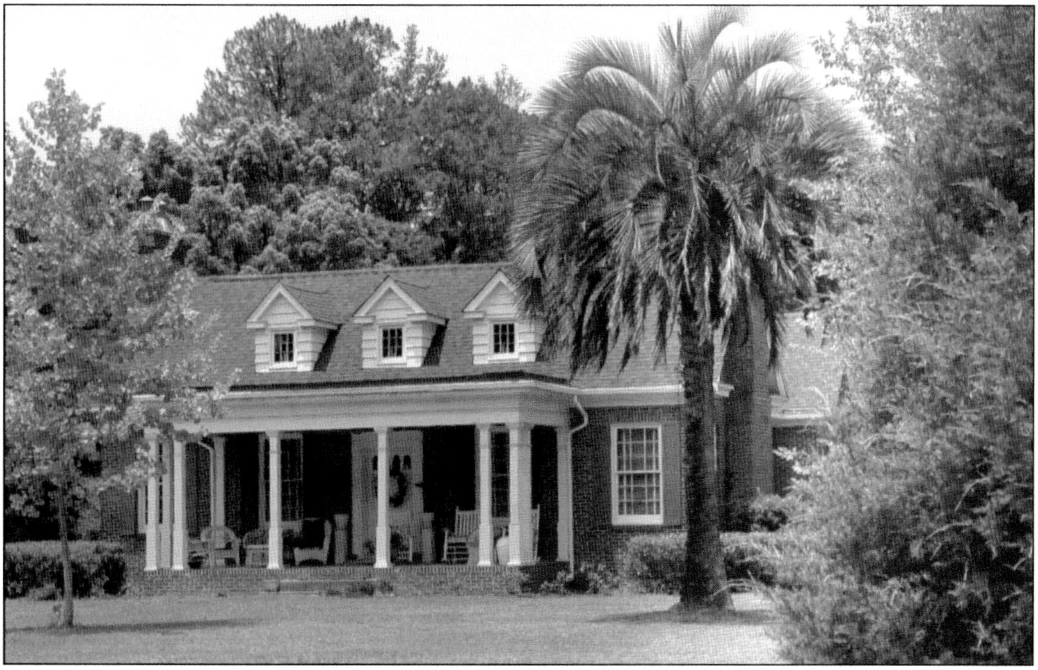

The Whitfield home was built between 1930 and 1935 in the Southern Georgian style by a man from Donaldson, Georgia. Folks in Wewahitchka say that this was "The House that Honey Built." It was the home of Joseph Alfred and Pearl J. Whitfield and their four children. They were the owners of the Whitfield Apiaries. It is now the home of Marlene and Alan McNair. (BMD.)

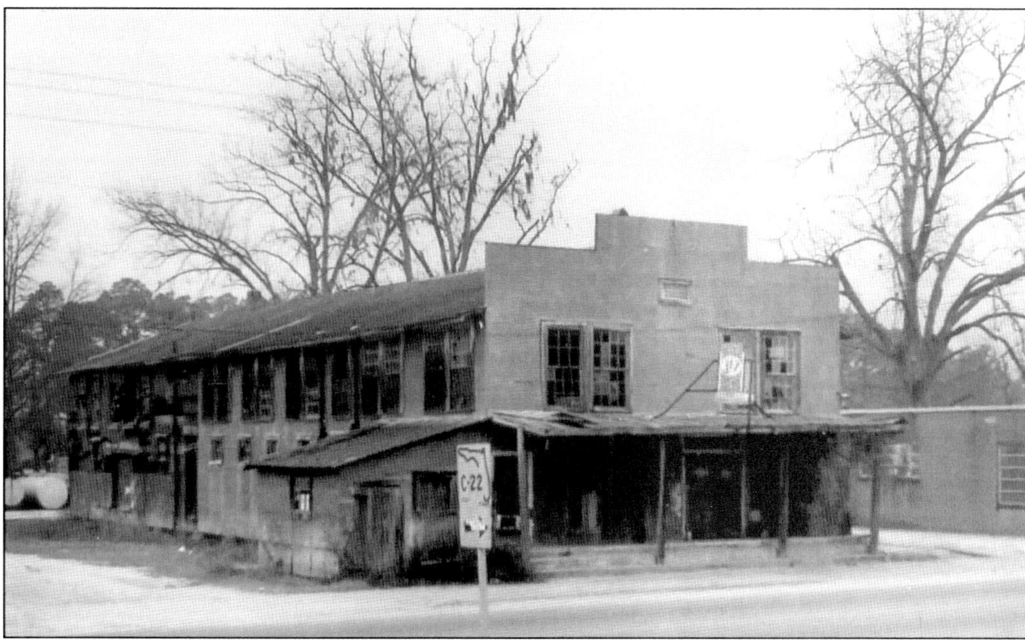

Wewahitchka Hardware Store, one of the oldest businesses in Wewahitchka, was built by H. C. Lister. The business was run by Lister's son Claude as the proprietor, and his brother R. D. Lister worked with him. The store was located in the middle of downtown Wewahitchka on Main Street. (AAW.)

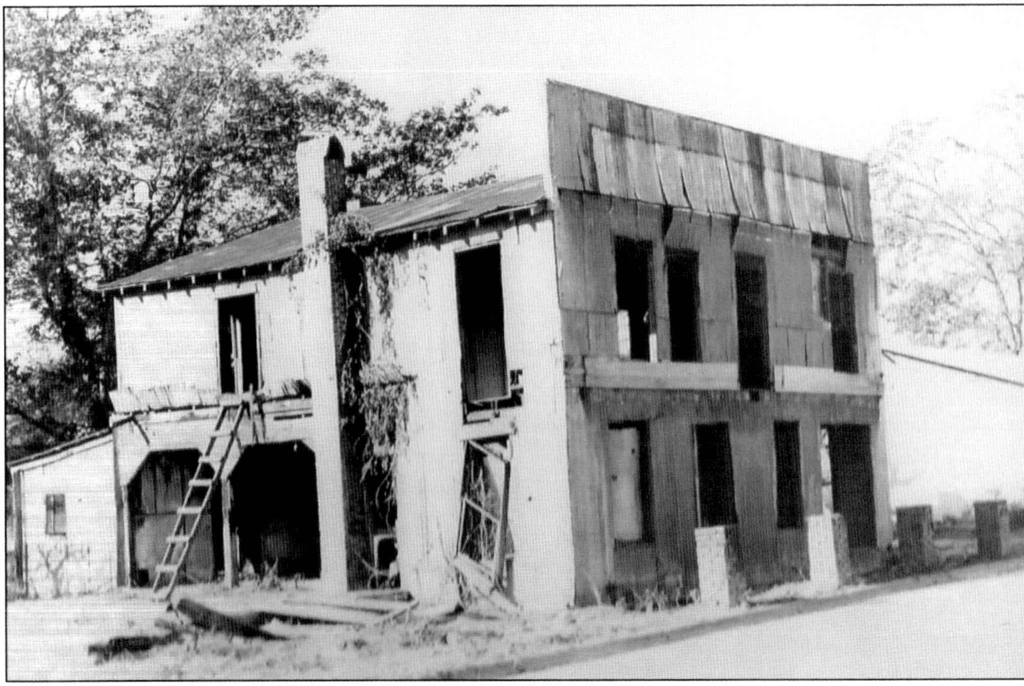

The old *Gulf County Breeze* office is shown just before being torn down. Claude Fogle Hanlon ran the *Breeze* in the early days. Edward "Ed" Banjough bought the *Breeze* and moved it next door to the garage of the Satsuma Hotel. There were several other publishers between Hanlon and Banjough, but all worked out of this building. L. E. Evans of Fairhope, Alabama, bought the *Breeze* and the *Port St. Joe Sentinel* from Hanlon in 1939. (AAW.)

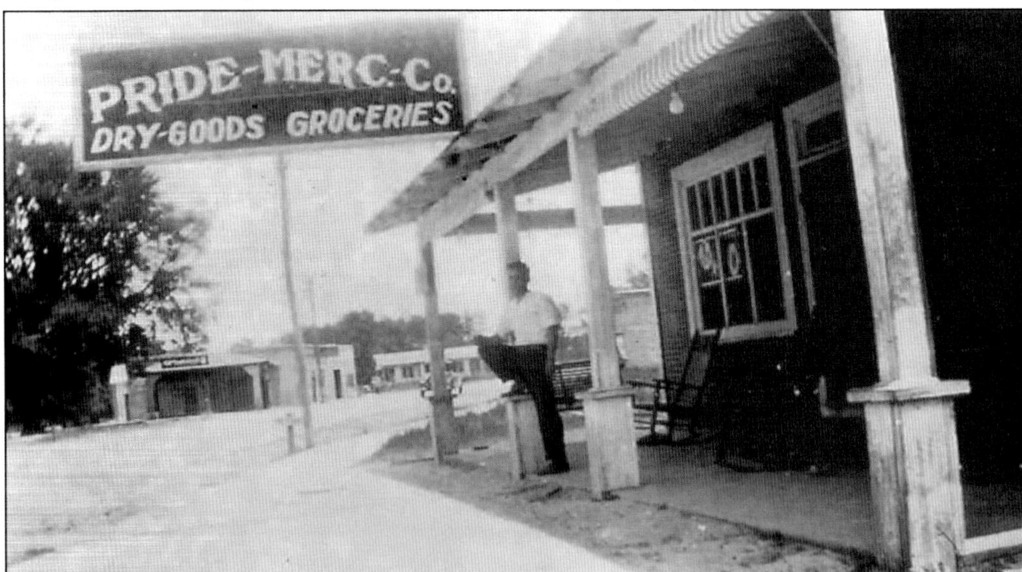

This store, owned by Joe Whitfield in the early 1930s, was located a couple of doors from the intersection of Highway 22 and State Road 71. Sammy Dorsey and Claude Teat had a garage in back. There was a restaurant near the front of the building owned by Irene Britt and Sally Lewis. The building in the far background was where Sammy Patrick lived. (AAW.)

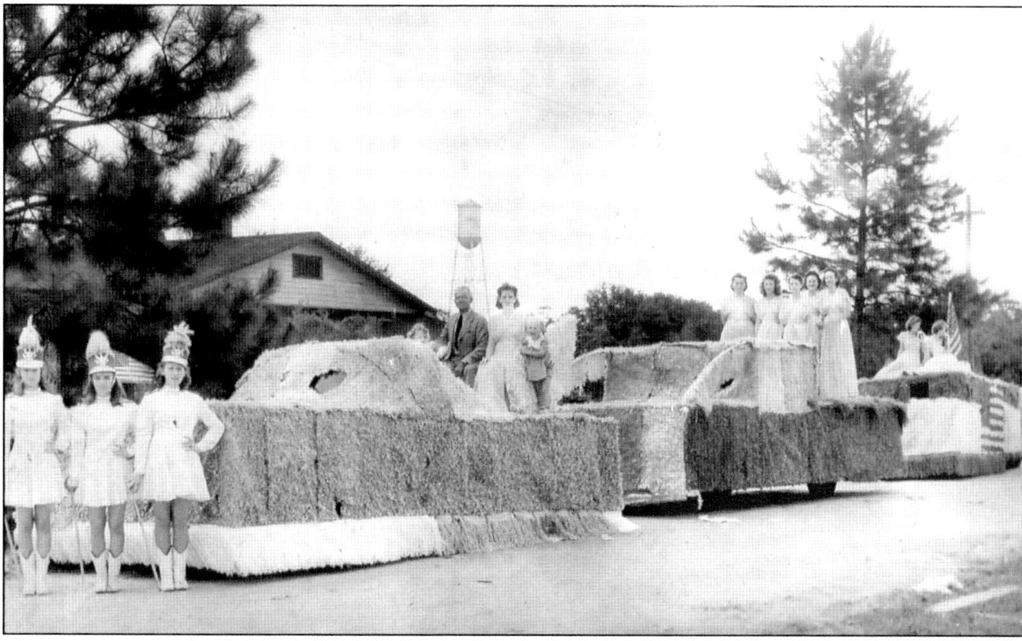

The Tupelo Honey Festival is held every May in Wewahitchka. Shown here is the first parade, held in 1941, with Honey Queen Janie Redfearn. The little girl at her side is the first maid, Sue Gaskin, at the age of five. (SGD.)

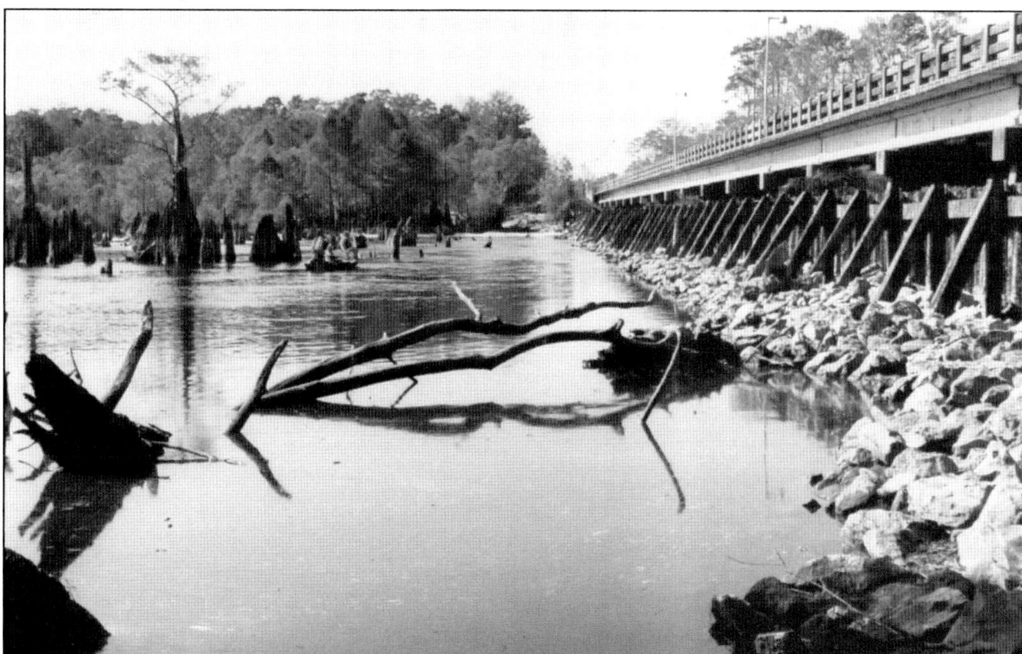

The Wewahitchka dam was built at the bottom of the lake near the Chipola Cutoff, where some of the water from the Chipola River flows into the mighty Apalachicola. From the bridge where the dam used to be, hundreds of cypress trees, knees, and stumps can be seen poking through the slow-moving water. The dam at Dead Lakes was removed in 1987 after vegetation began choking life in the impounded waters. (CW.)

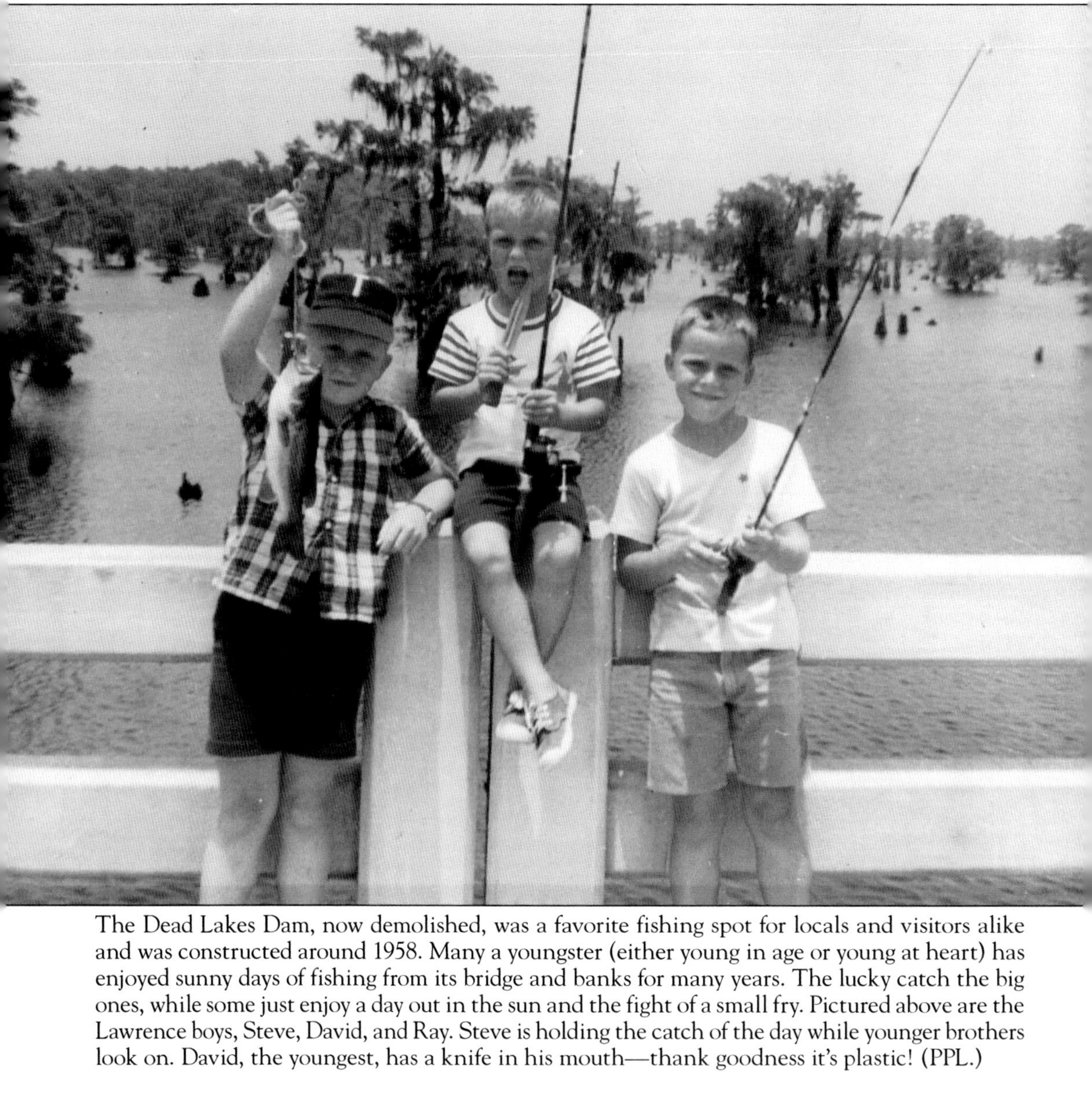

The Dead Lakes Dam, now demolished, was a favorite fishing spot for locals and visitors alike and was constructed around 1958. Many a youngster (either young in age or young at heart) has enjoyed sunny days of fishing from its bridge and banks for many years. The lucky catch the big ones, while some just enjoy a day out in the sun and the fight of a small fry. Pictured above are the Lawrence boys, Steve, David, and Ray. Steve is holding the catch of the day while younger brothers look on. David, the youngest, has a knife in his mouth—thank goodness it's plastic! (PPL.)

Five

OUTSIDE THE CITY LIMITS

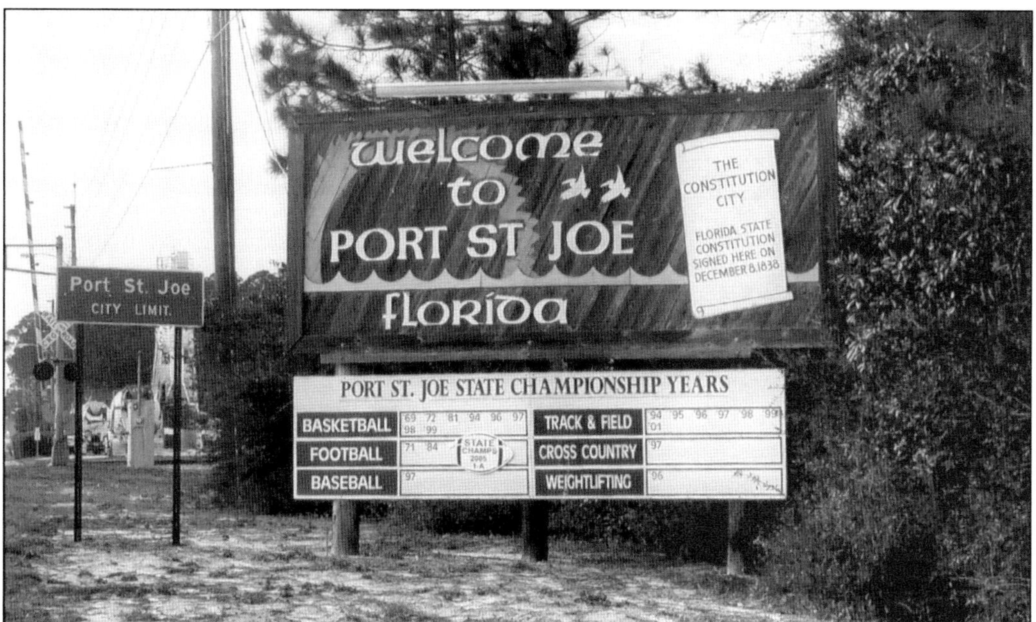

Welcome to Port St. Joe, Florida. (PPL.)

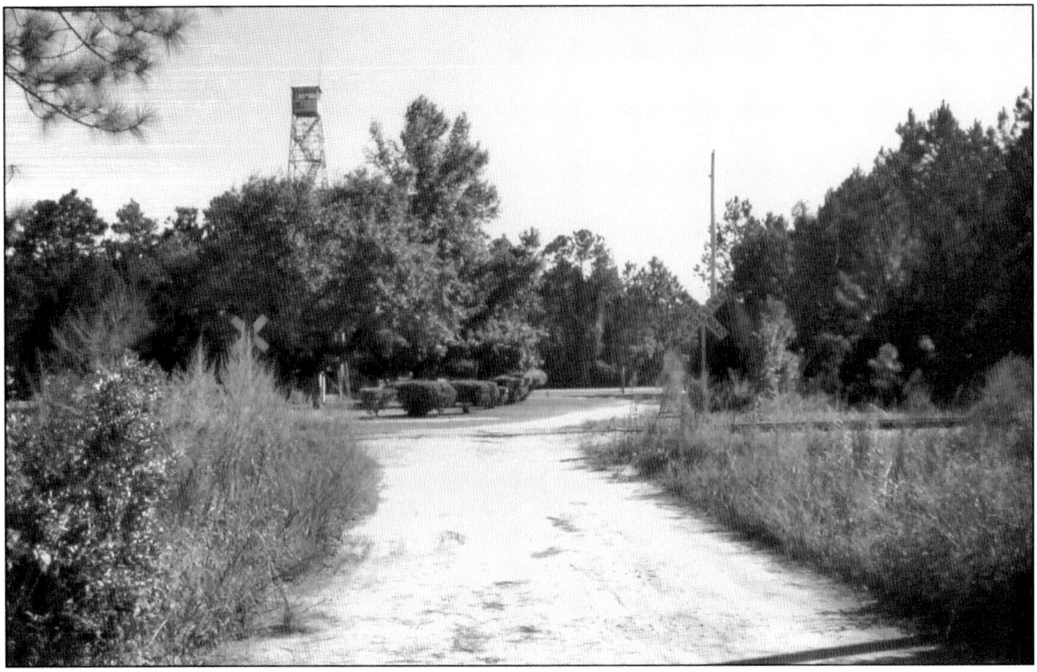

This is the terminus, or end of the line, of the short-lived (1836–1839), nine-mile St. Joseph and Lake Wimico Railroad, the first steam-operated railroad in Florida. In 1909, the Apalachicola Northern Railroad named the site Odena and built a side track station to pick up turpentine from local stills. The Odena fire tower stands on U.S. 98 between Port St. Joe and Apalachicola. In 1947, Florida listed 122 fire towers scattered around the state. (BMD.)

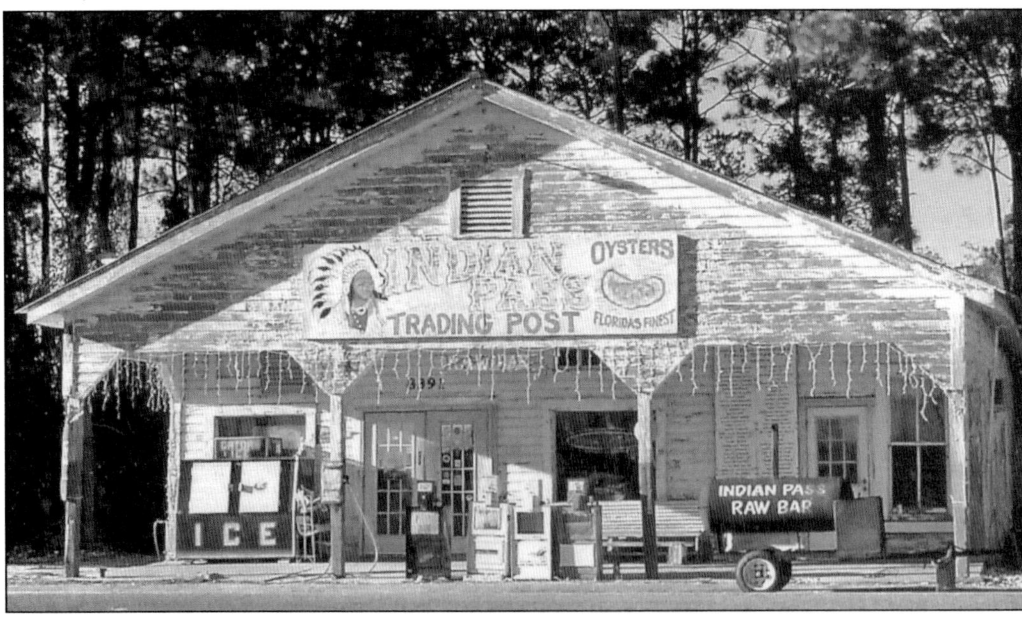

In 1903, James T. McNeill came to Indian Pass, then known as the Lagoon, from Wewahitchka to turpentine a track of 13,000 acres. The general store, established in 1929, began as a commissary for turpentine workers. In 1985, McNeill's grandson James T. McNeill III began the Indian Pass Raw Bar in the same building. It is popular with celebrities as well as with locals. (BH.)

For the first time, black families are now able to enjoy the beach without intimidation from whites. Washington High School students are enjoying a "Class Day" at Money Bayou in May 1968; here are Mary Thomas (left) and Patricia Dawson enjoying the water and their watermelon. (CM.)

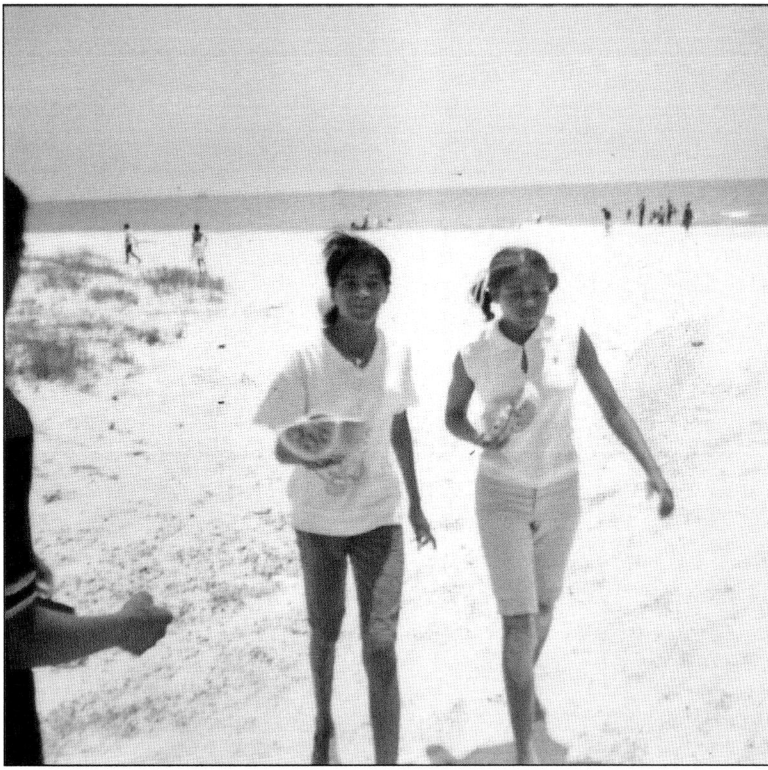

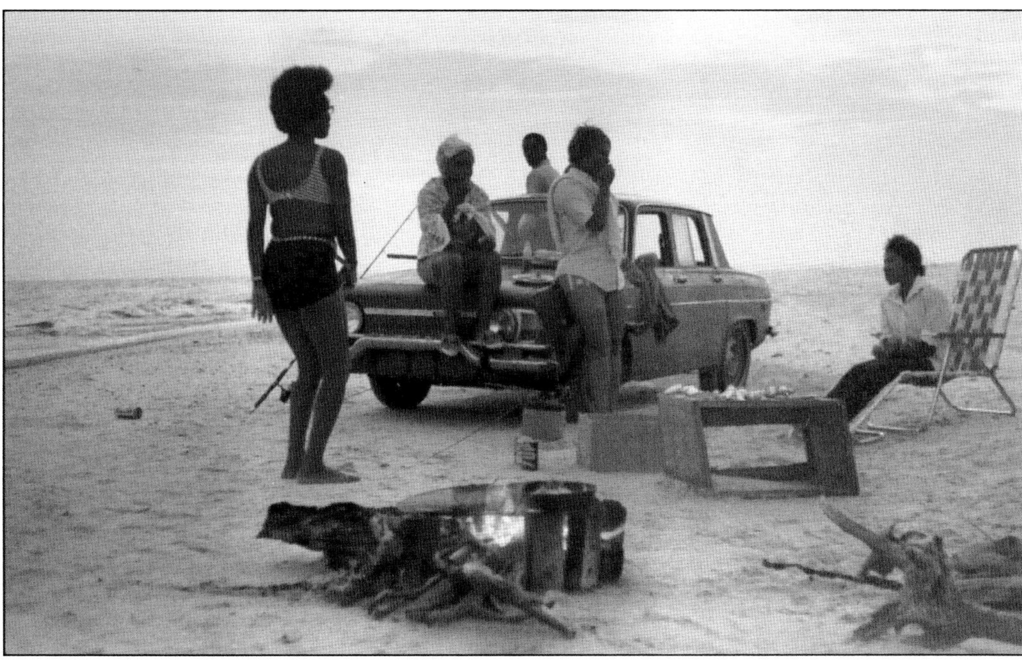

Maxine (Cain) Gant, Audrey ?, Willie Otis Smith, Rebecca Smith, and Minnie Likely are enjoying the waters at Money Bayou Beach. At that time, in 1968, black residents or tourists could not visit white beaches. This was the second beach established in the state of Florida for African Americans. (CM.)

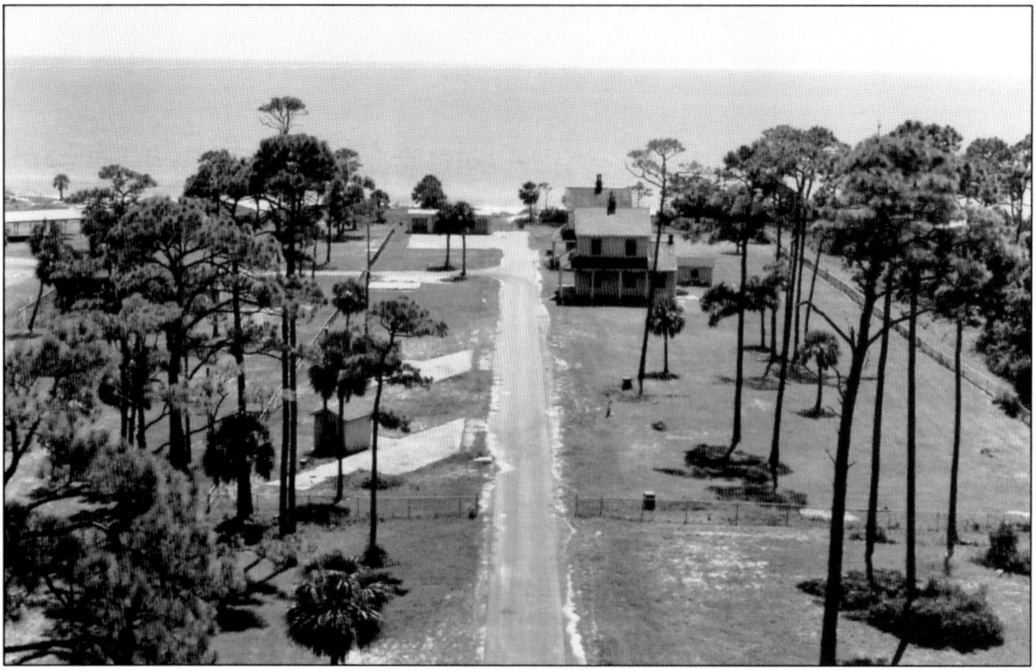

An aerial view of the Cape San Blas Lighthouse looks down toward the keeper's cottages. The cottage closest to the water is in danger because of encroaching tides. The two buildings were once home to the lighthouse keepers and are nearly identical, except that one is closer to the water and thus more vulnerable in a storm. (BH.)

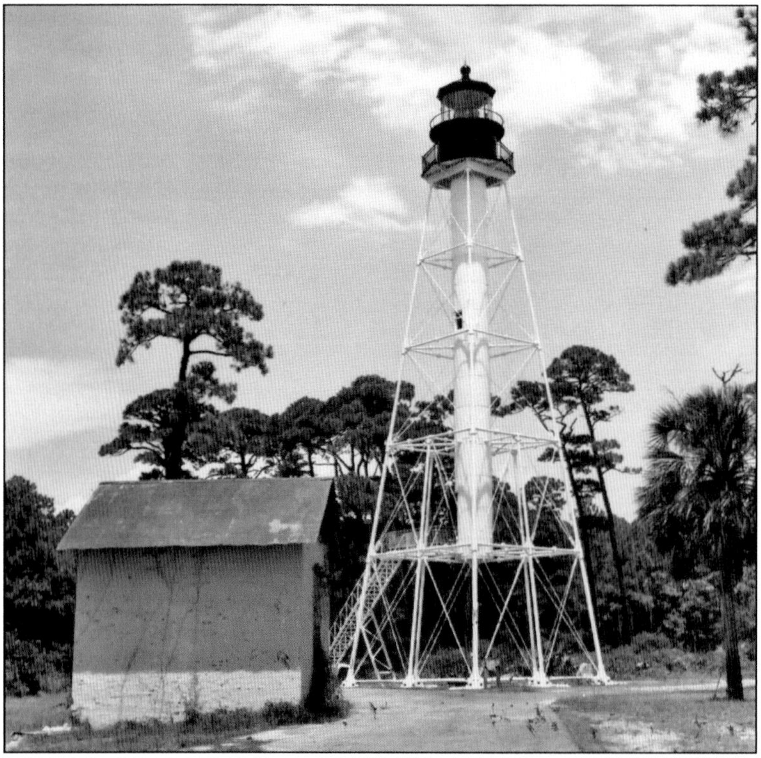

In 1918, the 1885 lighthouse—a 98-foot-tall iron skeleton tower—was moved to its present location. In 2002, one of the two keepers' quarters was restored. Severely deteriorated and tilting to one side, the second house, affectionately known as "Sleeping Beauty," was restored in 2005. (BH.)

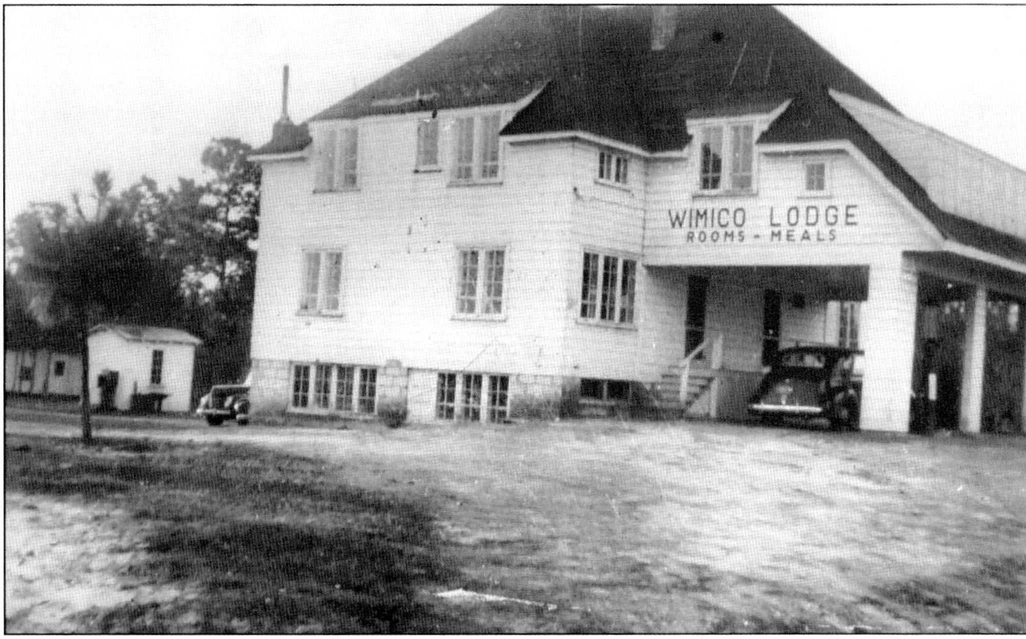

Wimico Lodge, on the northeast side of the Eglin F. Bayless Bridge, is located just off the Intracoastal Waterway. Charles and Joe Sebel, two early White City residents, constructed the building around 1930 as a hunting and fishing lodge. The lodge operated until the late 1970s and is now restored as a private residence. This building also served as a boardinghouse during the construction of the St. Joe Paper Company in 1937–1938. (BS.)

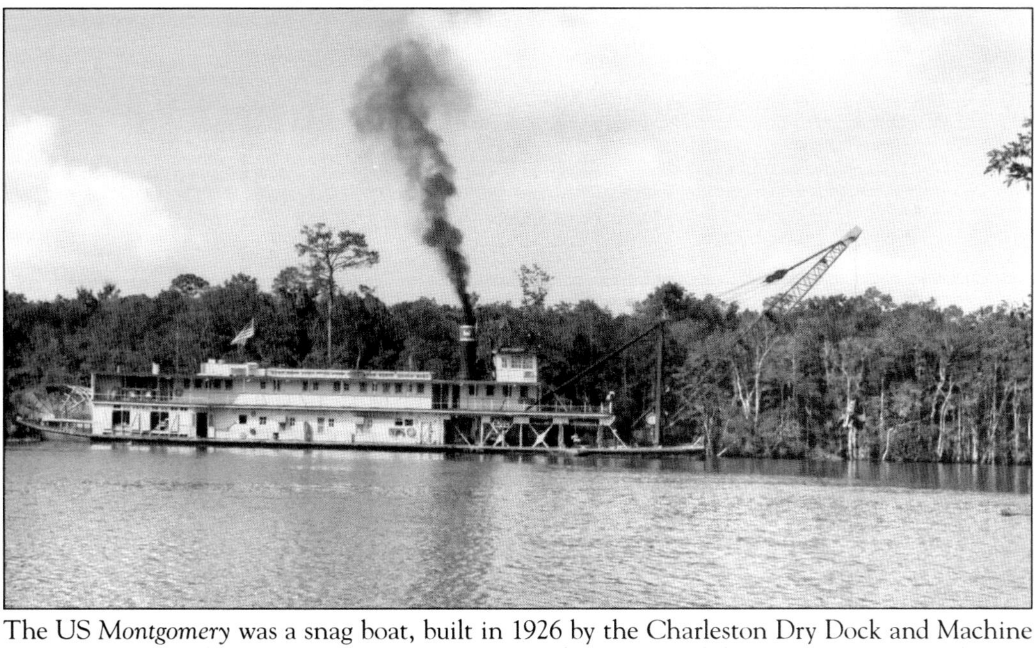

The US *Montgomery* was a snag boat, built in 1926 by the Charleston Dry Dock and Machine Company of Charleston, South Carolina. It served on seven of the South's rivers until 1982. Many times, you could see her pulling snags from up and down the Apalachicola River. Here it was tided up at White City, Florida. In 2003, it was fully restored and now serves as a National Historic Landmark. (CW.)

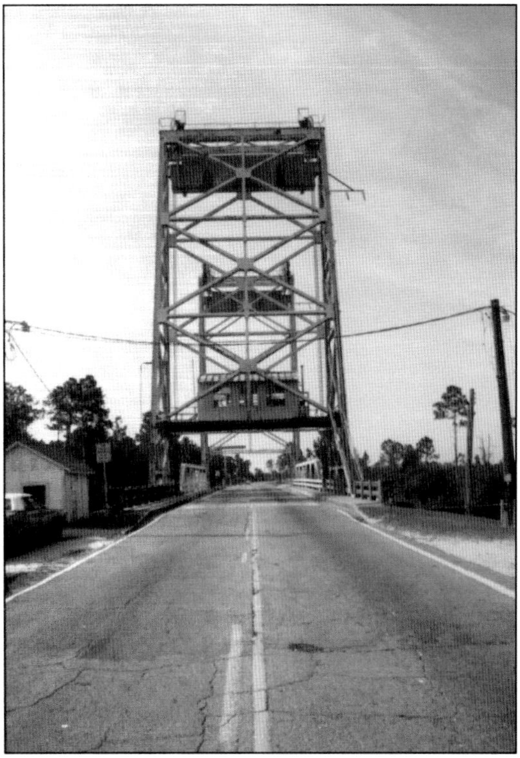

F. Elgin Bayless Bridge is located at White City, Florida, north of Port St. Joe, or 17 miles south of Wewahitchka on State Road 71. The bridge crosses the Intercoastal Canal, a waterway running from Texas to St. Marks, Florida. It was dedicated on August 24, 1948, and named for F. Elgin Bayless, chairman of the state road department. (AAW.)

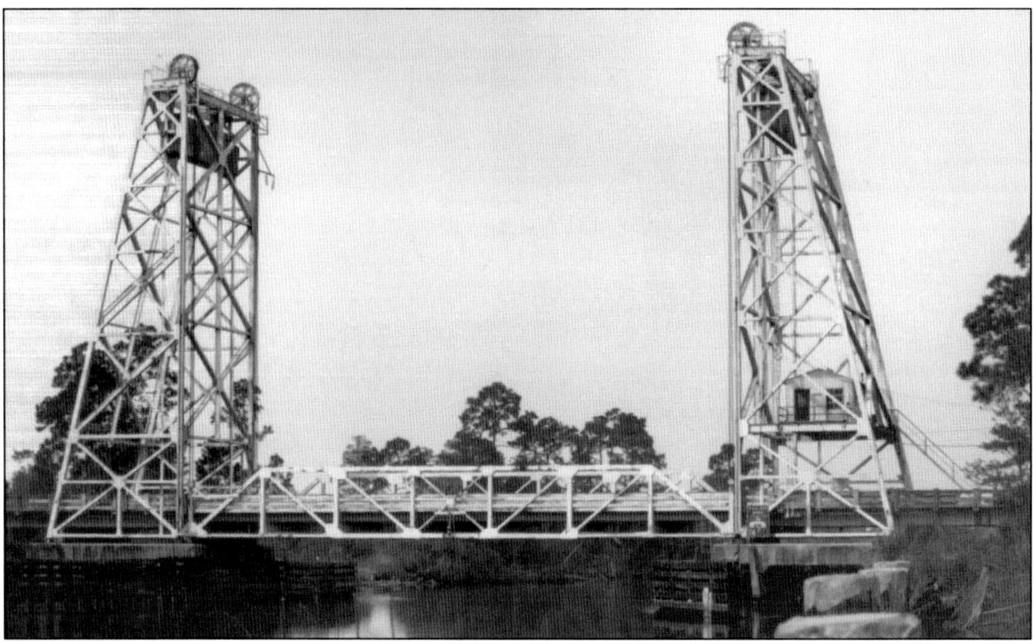

The F. Elgin Bayless Bridge is 236 feet long, built of steel and concrete, and is a vertical-lift type bridge that has an 86-foot horizontal structure and a 90-foot vertical clearance. It was built by the Cleary Brothers Construction Company. Construction started December 4, 1945, and the bridge was open to traffic September 1947. Final completion was August 4, 1948, when automatic electrical equipment was installed. The bridge cost $300,000. (AAW.)

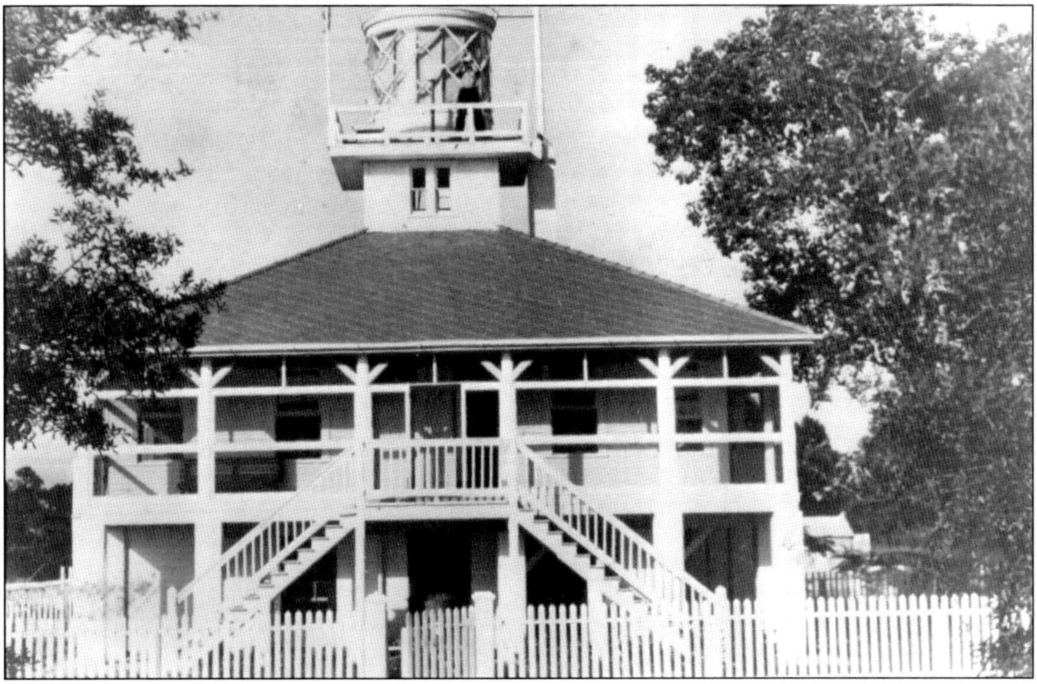

This was established in 1902 as the St. Joseph Light Range Station. Mr. and Mrs. Charles A. Lupton were the first lighthouse keepers. It was constructed from heart pine that was transported by barge from New Orleans to Beacon Hill. The lighthouse was replaced in 1960 with a skeletal steel structure. The house was sold in 1978 to Danny Raffield and has been meticulously restored. (BH.)

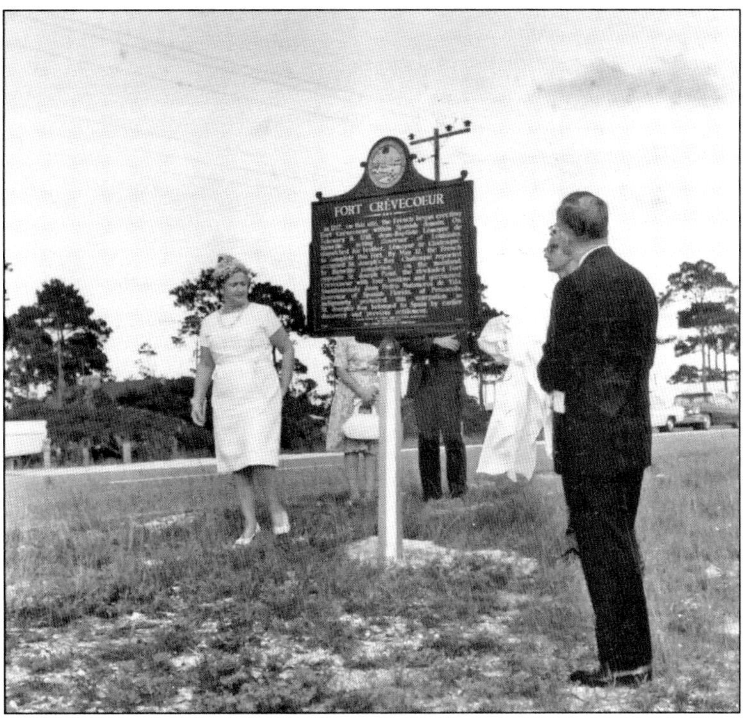

Constructed in 1718 by Lemoyne de Chateaugue, younger brother of Bienville, the founder of New Orleans and Mobile, Fort Crevecoeur consisted of four bastions enclosed within a stockade. After protest by the Spanish, the French burned and abandoned the fort. The exact location of Fort Crevecoeur is unknown. The St. Joseph Historical Society erected a marker in July 1964 to perpetuate the site. (SJHS.)

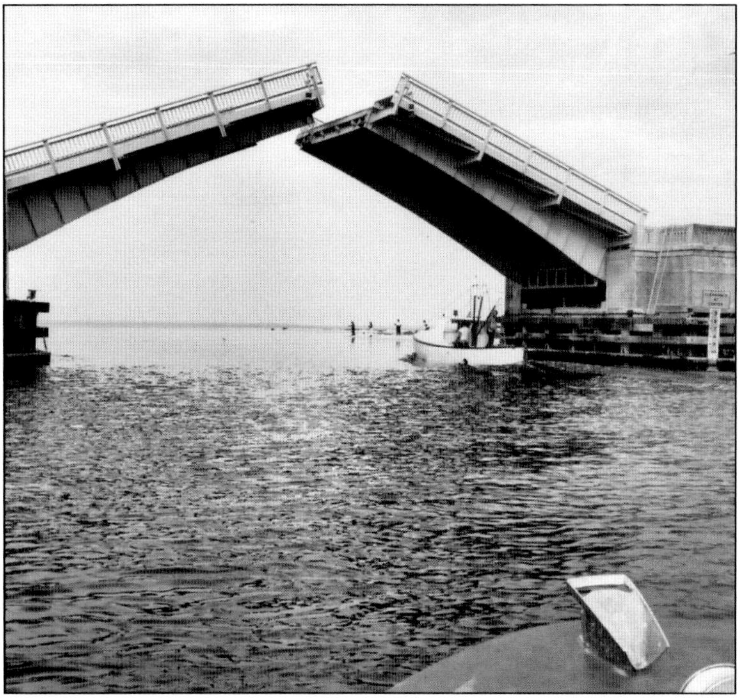

The Highland View drawbridge that served as a link over the Intracoastal Canal west of Port St. Joe was thrown open to traffic March 1939, and the old wooden bridge was torn down. The bridge, costing $133,575, was built by the Cleary Brothers Construction Company of West Palm Beach and is approximately one-third of a mile long. In June 1993, the bridge was dismantled and made into a fishing reef. (BH.)

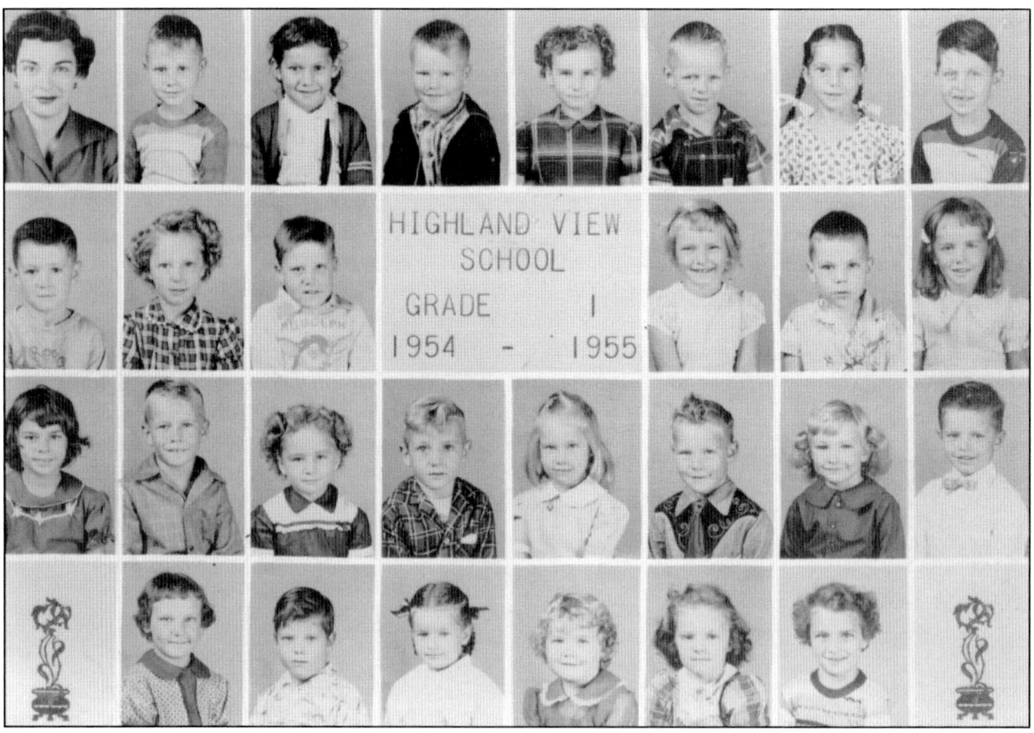

Highland View School opened in 1952 and remained open for more than 50 years. After flooding from many hurricanes, the school was closed and all the students transferred to school in Port St. Joe. Today the school houses a Head-Start Program. Shown here is the first-grade class of 1954–1955. (MC.)

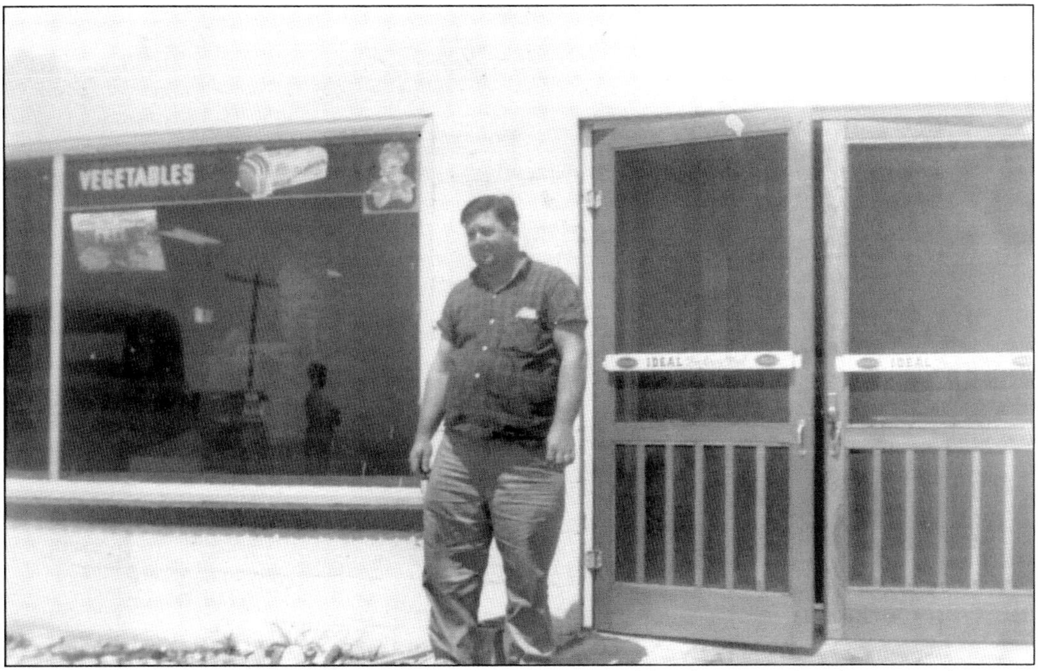

Player's Super Market was located off of Highway 98 in Highland View. Silas Player ran this store for more than 50 years. Silas was a member of the Highland View Men's Club and served as a county commissioner from 1963 to 1965 and again from 1969 to 1974. (JPB.)

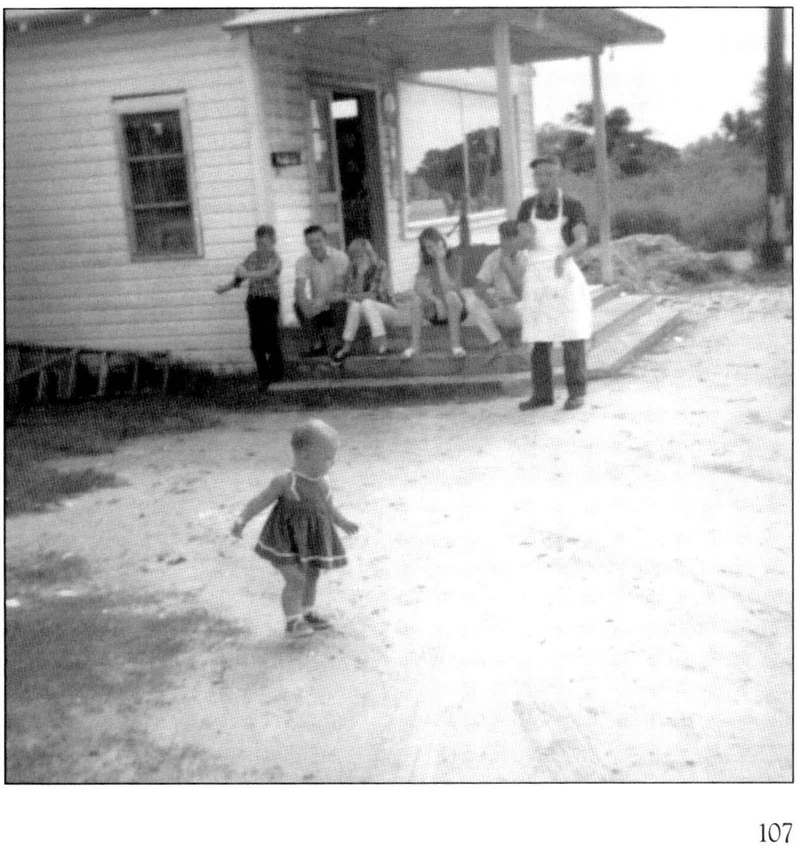

Highland View was a small community across the canal from Port St. Joe. The families were poor but good and honest folks; many were fishermen, shrimpers, and mill workers. Grover Clark and his wife, Mae, raised a family of five, while he ran a grocery store, worked at the nearby fish house, and operated the local drawbridge. Grover was a member of the local men's club. (MC.)

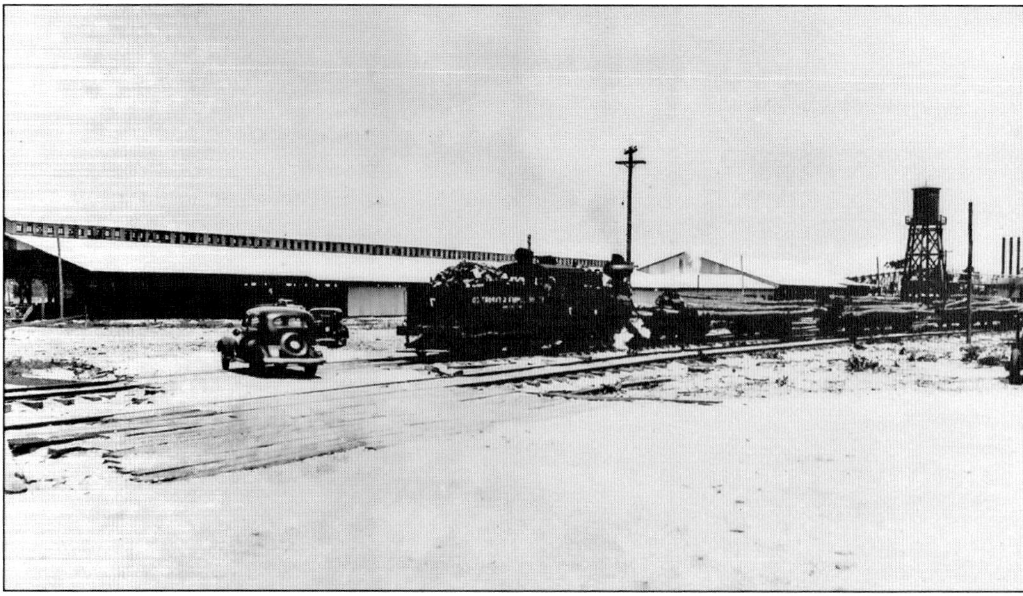

M. L. Fleishel and Basil E. Kenney Sr. were the two principal owners of the St. Joe Lumber and Export Company. The Kenneys acquired complete control of the sawmill and plant, and thus it has been known as Kenney's Mill. This new sawmill plant was located on the northwest side of Port St. Joe. The mill ran on two eight-hour shifts daily and produced about 120,000 feet of lumber a day. (BH.)

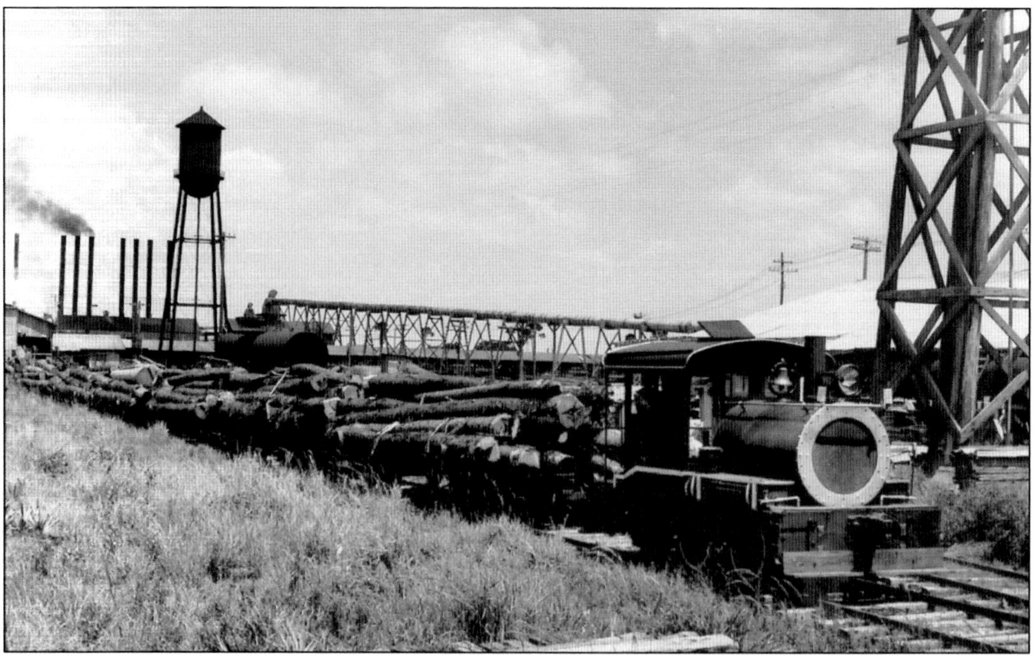

Locomotives, log loaders, log skidders, steam pile drivers, track laying machines, and log cars were never bought new. They could be found scattered all over Florida by the end of the 1930s, so the St. Joe Lumber Company took advantage of any surplus railroad equipment they could find available for sale. The No. 1 was a small engine perfect for a work train but useless at pulling logs. (BH.)

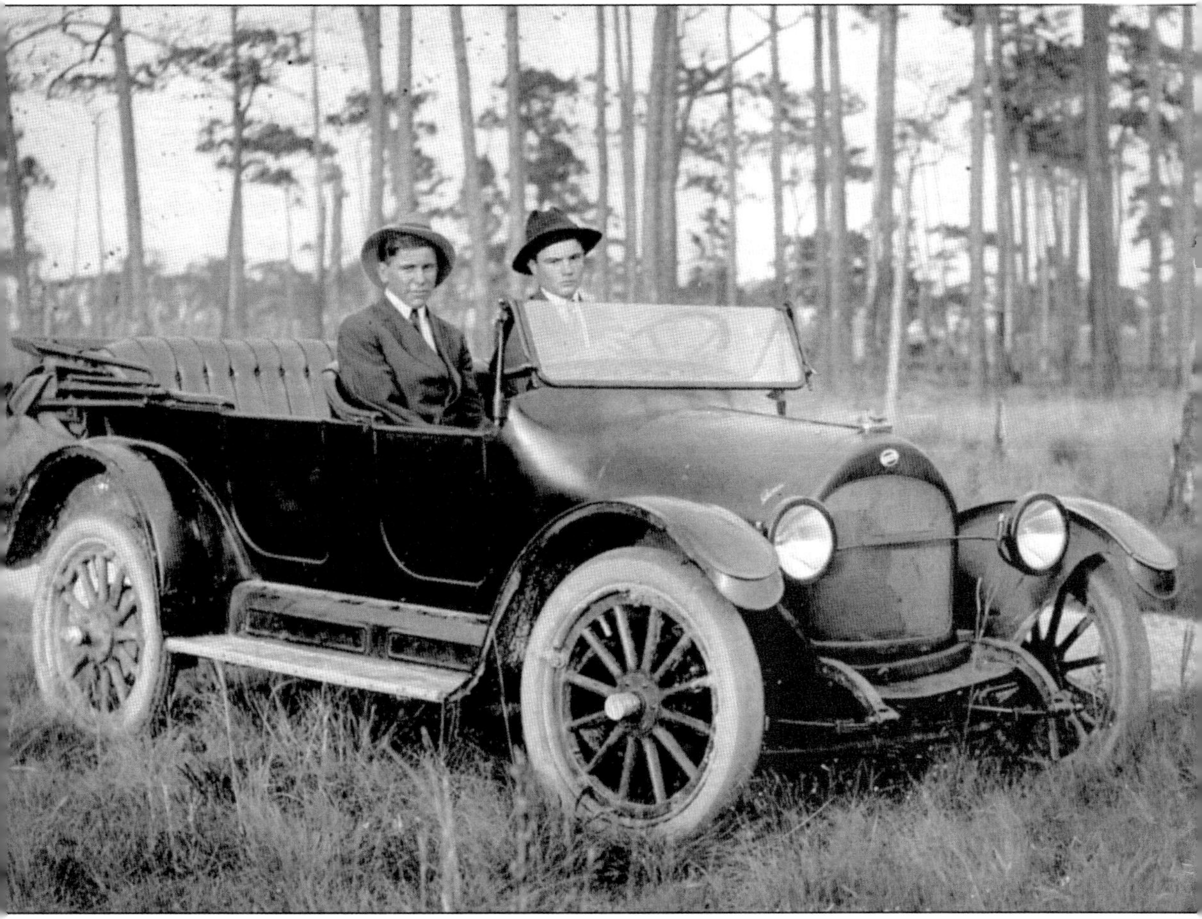

Mrs. Early was a midwife who lived on Wetappo Creek. Will Whitfield named his son after her. Mrs. Early was highly respected and admired by the community. Needing a post office, the government agreed to locate one in the Whitfields' country store, but first the community needed a name so that letters could properly be addressed. Will was instructed to send in three names. The government would choose one for the community and the new post office. He submitted one name, and the newest mailing address in the United States became Early, Florida. This is a photograph of Early Whitfield and his cousin Clarence Whitfield. (LBS.)

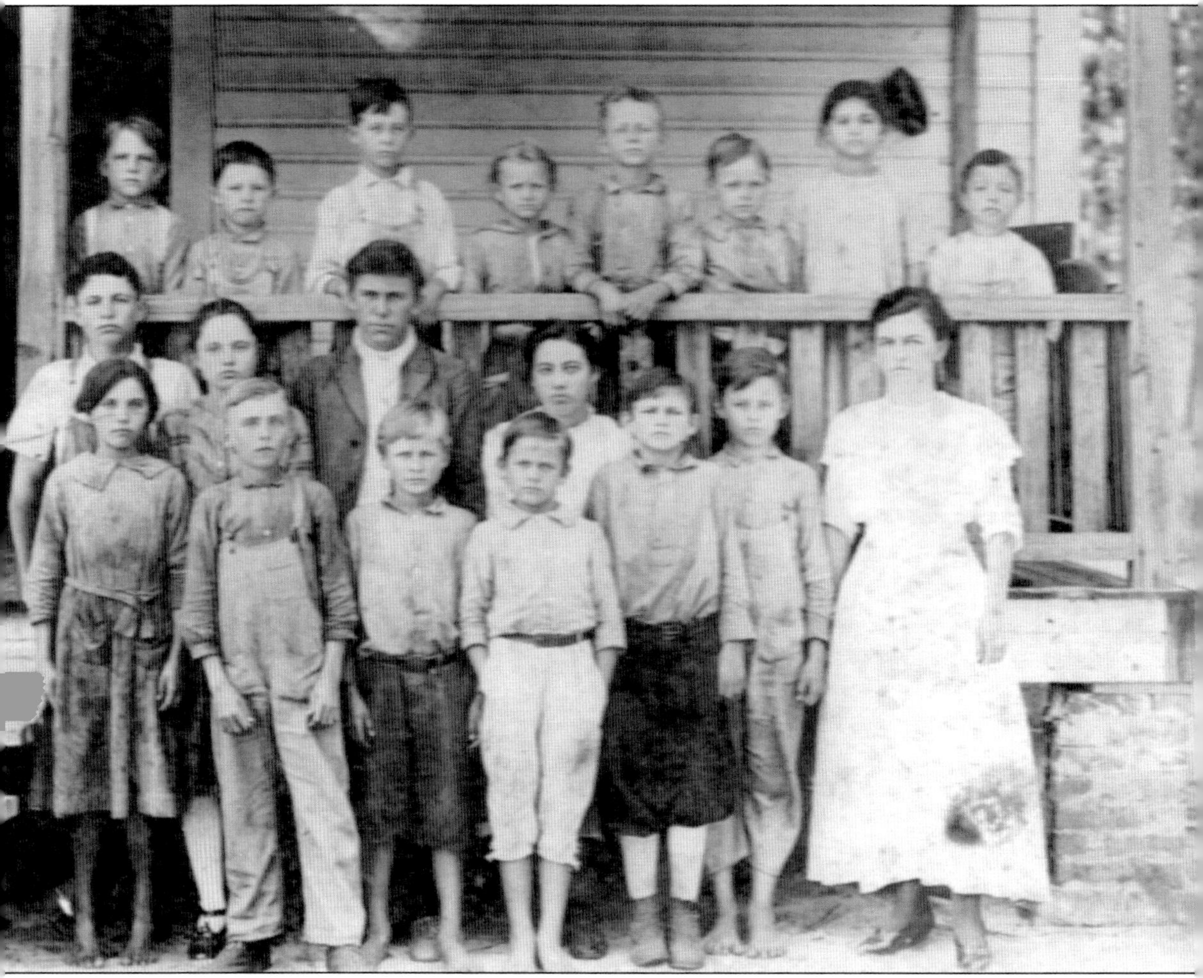

The Early school was built on land donated to the Calhoun County School Board by Lee Daniels. Grades 1 through 12 were all taught in one room by a single teacher. Students pictured here from left to right are (first row) Ethel Moses, Walter Moses, Jim Daniels, Jarrott Daniels, Charles Daniels, James Laurimore, Hattie Yon (teacher); (second row) Lonnie Whitfield, Lula Whitfield, Early Whitfield, Josephine Buttner; (third row) General Kinard, Harry Laurimore, George Laurimore, Erie Daniels, Joe Daniels, Roy Whitfield, Lilla Whitfield, Ted Whitfield. (LBS.)

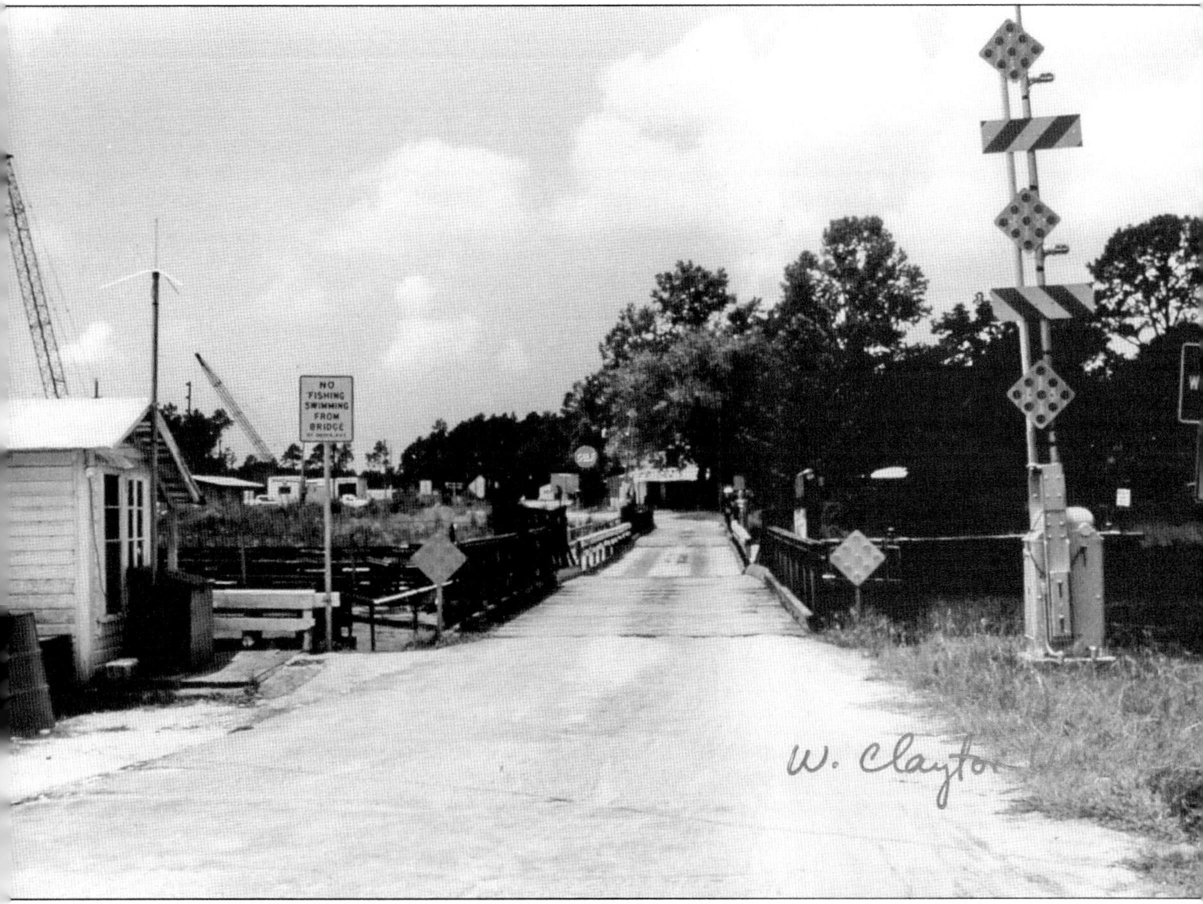

Overstreet is a small community on State Road 386, between Wewahitchka and Mexico Beach. Thomas Patrick first opened a store located on the banks of the Intercoastal Waterway on May 1, 1916. The U.S. postal inspector, summoned by George Overstreet two years earlier, arrived at the small settlement. The inspector established a post office in "Miss Lillie Scott's corncrib," and Miss Lillie became the first postmistress. The new post office was called Overstreet, and thus the community was officially named. A few months later, the office was moved across the canal to Patrick's Store, and Thomas Patrick became postmaster. What you see in front of the store is a barge that locals called the "Overstreet flooding bridge." Before the barge, there was a ferry to get folks across the canal. (CW.)

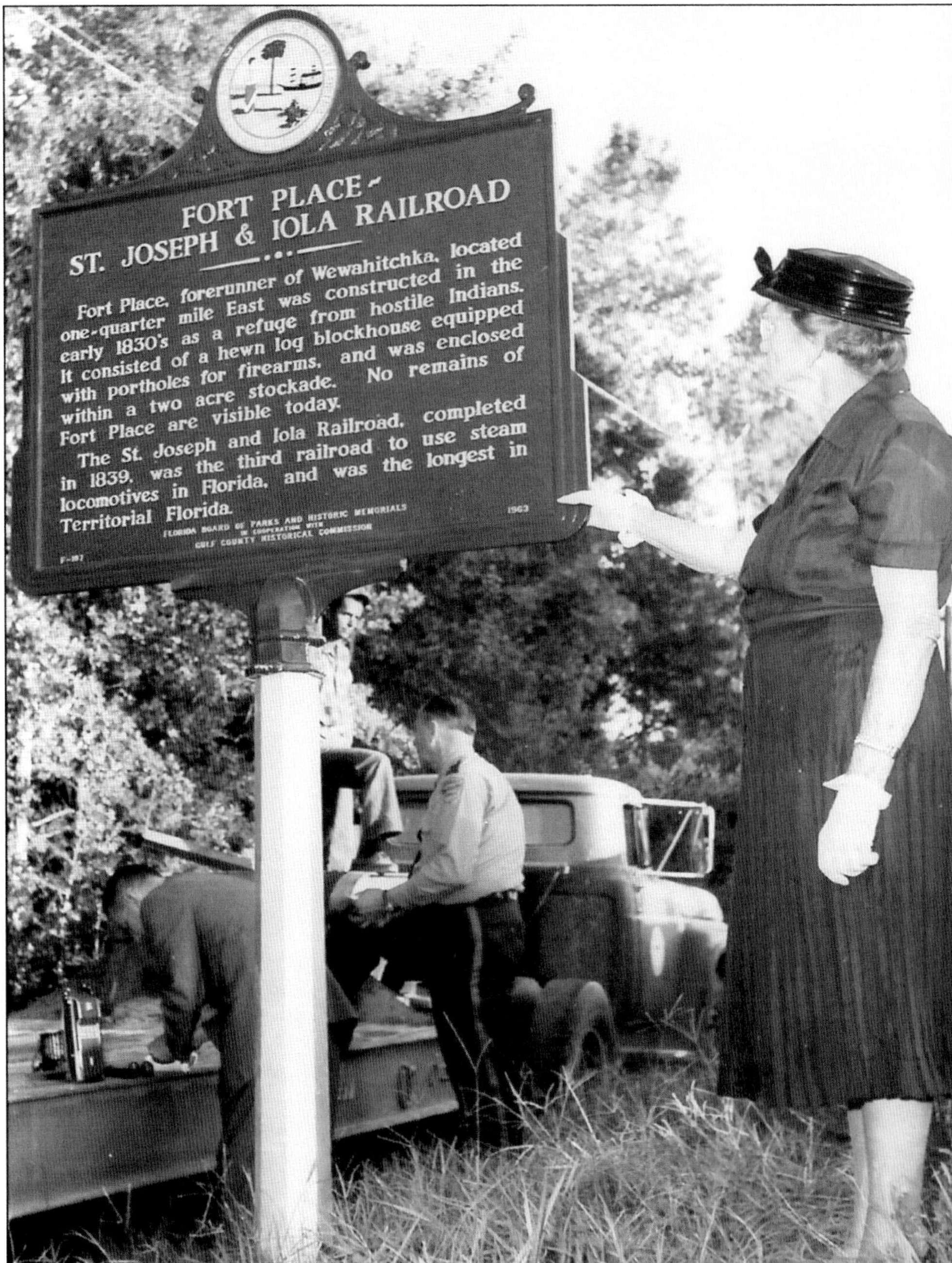

Fort Place was constructed in 1833 as a refuge from hostile Native Americans. It was a blockhouse-type fort enclosed within a two-acre stockade formed by vertically placed logs. Portholes were built into the heavy, hewn log walls, admitting light and serving for the use of firearms. Pioneers of Wewahitchka remember seeing the fort intact around 1900. It was dismantled about 1930 for its timber, and no remains are visible today. The St. Joseph Historical Society erected a marker, which stands near the site of the old log fort south of Wewahitchka on State 71. It's a reminder of pioneer days along the Apalachicola River. Zola Maddox is holding on to the marker. (BH.)

Six

Fun in the Sun

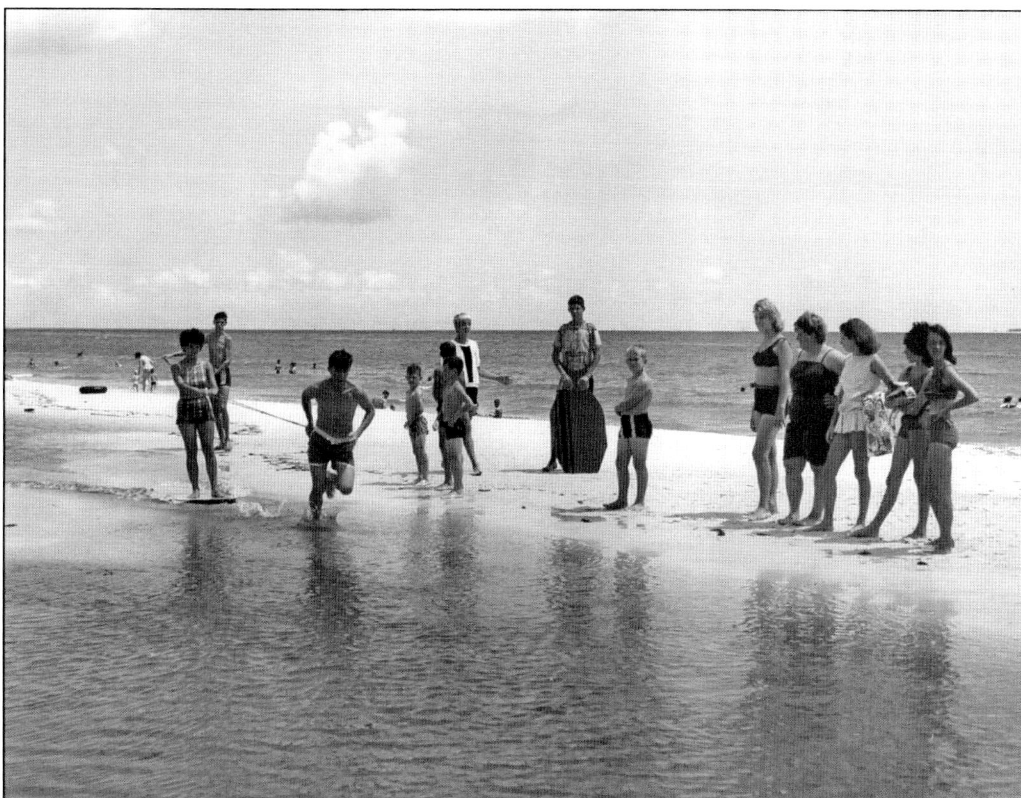

Gulf County has a great deal to offer the vacationer and tourist. Located in the Florida Panhandle and along the Gulf Coast, it offers miles of beautiful white beaches, surf fishing, motorboating, waterskiing, swimming, and skin diving, all much safer activities here because there is no undertow. (Gulf County Chamber of Commerce.)

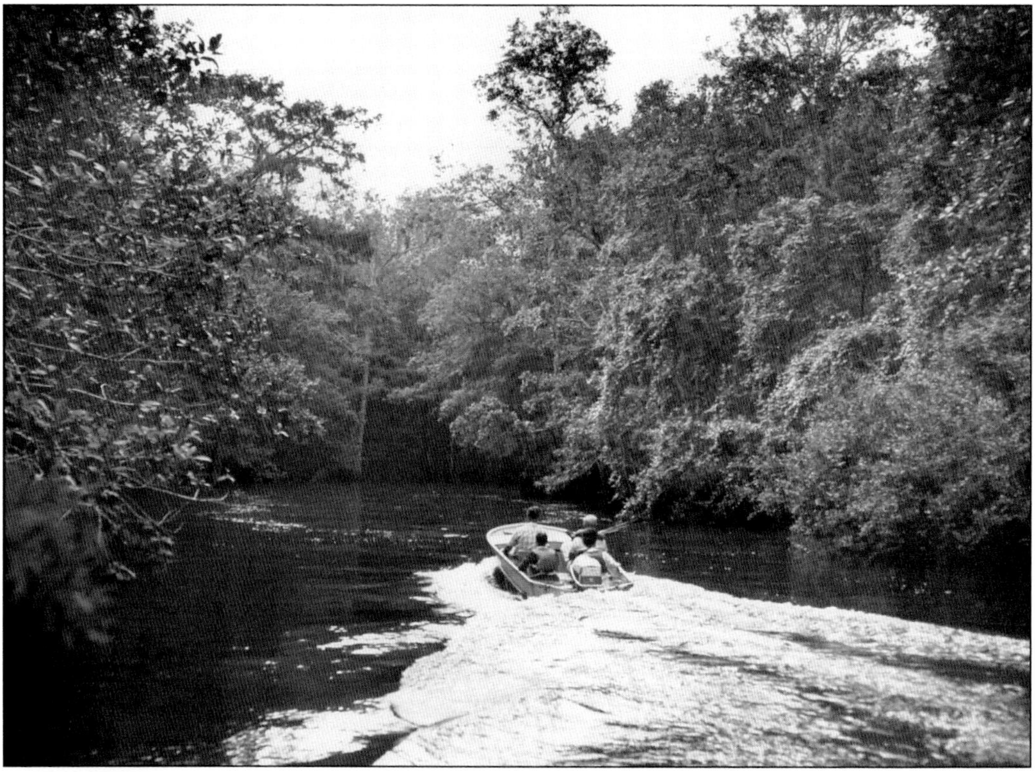

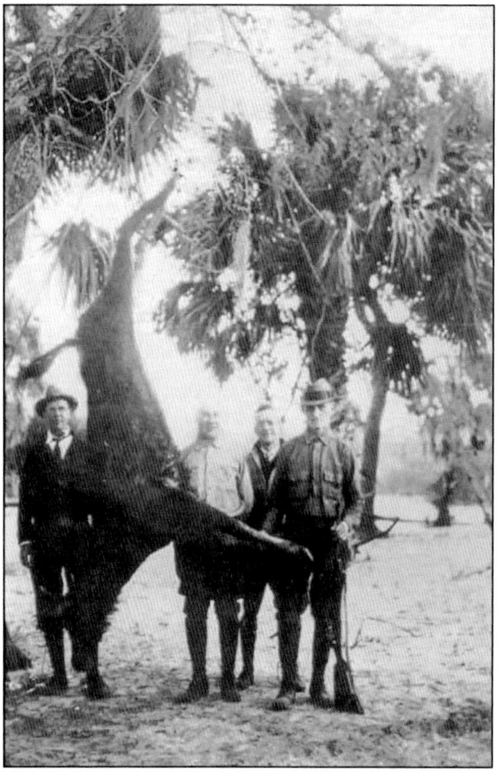

Good hunting and fishing can be found in the woods, swamps, and endless waterways of Gulf County—fresh, salt, and brackish waters beneath the surface of which the sportsman's finny friends lie waiting. Largemouth black bass, bream, and shellcracker court the angler's further acquaintance in the Dead Lakes, Lake Wimico, and the county's various canals and smaller lakes and streams. (Gulf County Chamber of Commerce.)

Hunting was good out at St. Vincent Island years ago. Many hunters had good luck with sambar bucks like this one in the late 1920s and in the early 1930s. From left to right are Frank Sharit, unidentified, DeWitt Marks, and George Patton. (NP.)

This is a photograph taken around November 1954 of Ed Ramsey and Clyde "Skinny" Fite during hunting season. The deer was killed off the river in Gulf County. (TTW.)

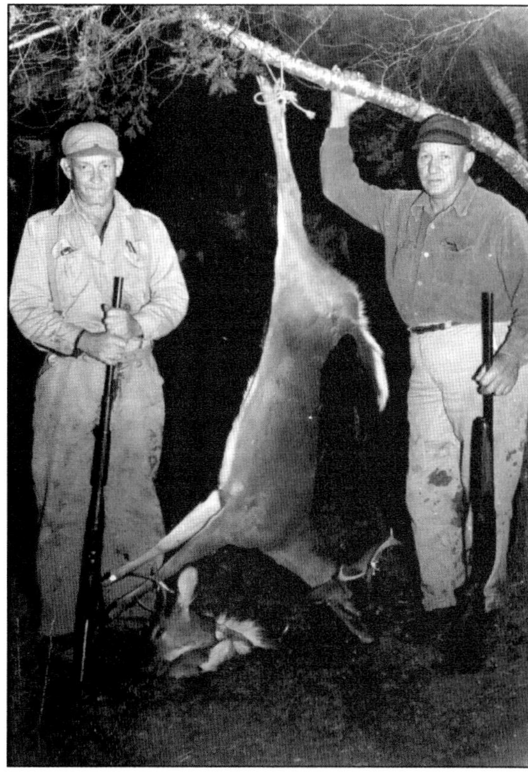

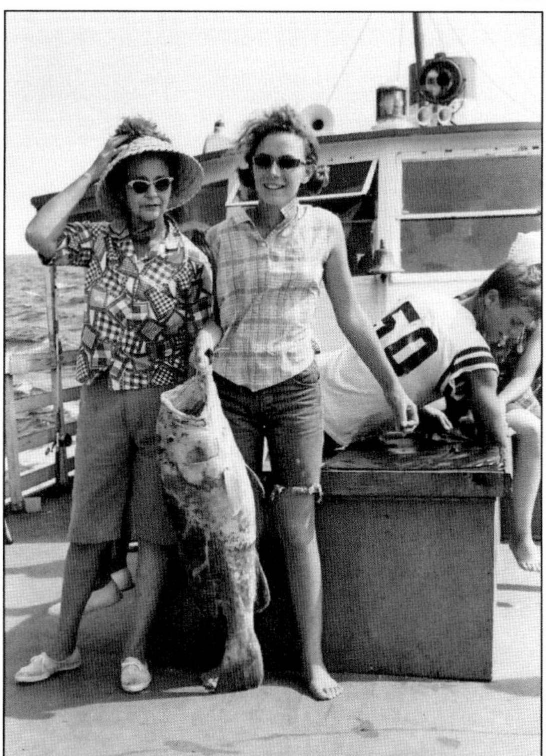

Midge Howell Stevens and her grandmother Callie Smith are on the *Azalea Queen* holding up a large grouper caught in the waters near the St. Joe Peninsula. (BH.)

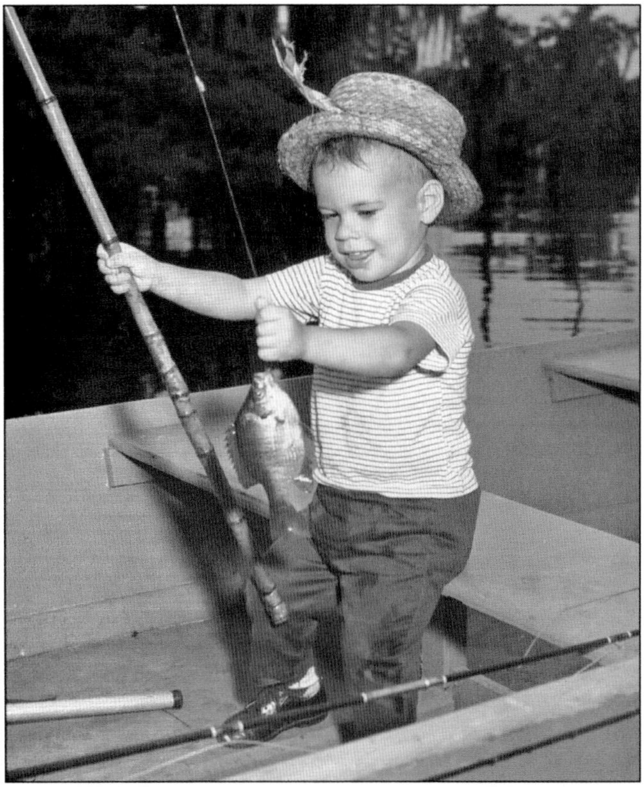

This little man is young Otis Skipper Jr. fishing in Wewahitchka, Florida. Taken about 1965, the photograph goes to show that you are never too young to enjoy fishing here on the lakes. (Gulf County Chamber of Commerce.)

Many locals and people from out-of-state have fish camps and houseboats all up and down the rivers, like the Big 10 Retreat. This fish camp was bought in the 1960s by 10 local citizens; today their descendants are enjoying it. (Gulf County Chamber of Commerce.)

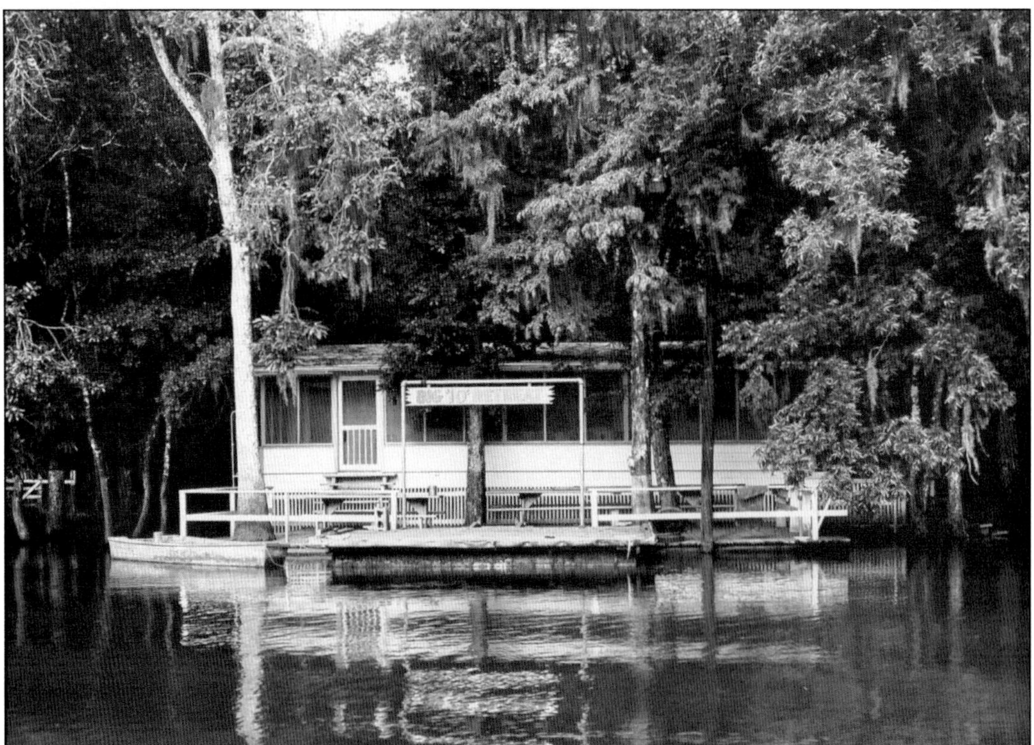

Gulf County provides some of the best hunting in the state. This deer came out of Gaskin Wildlife Management Area. At the top left is E. C. Hardin Jr., and at the top right is Grady "Paw" Booth. On the bottom left is BoBo Owens, who killed the deer in November 1964. At the bottom right is an unidentified man. (BBO.)

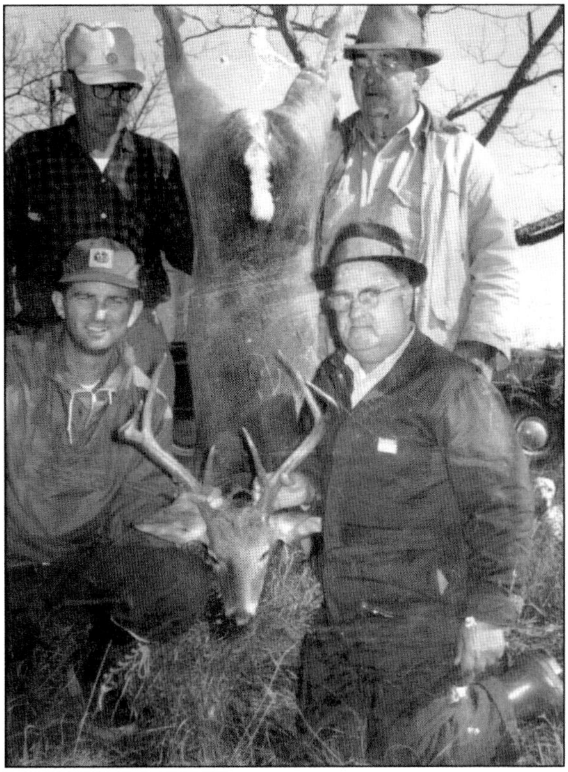

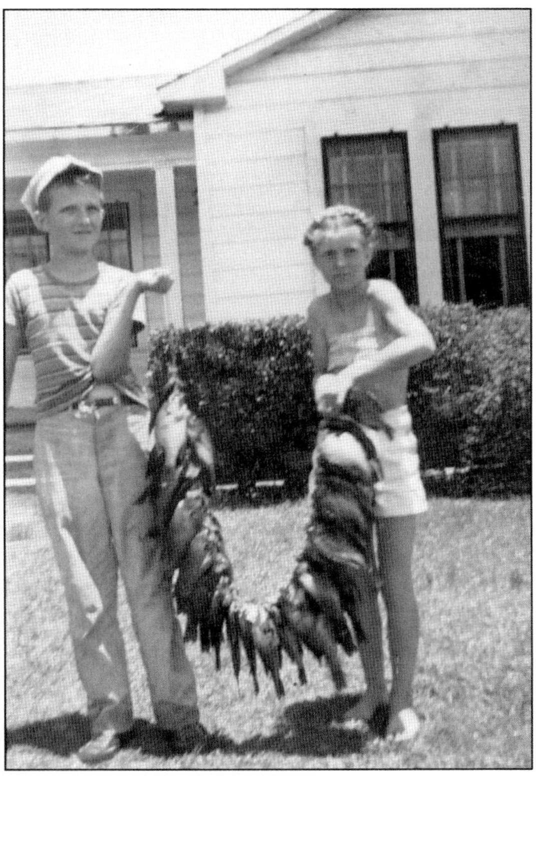

Children in Wewahitchka spent most of their time sharing in the fishing as well. Sometimes they catch more fish than the grown-ups do. Here during the mid- to late 1940s, little Sue Gaskin and Don Rester hold up their string of fish. (BBO.)

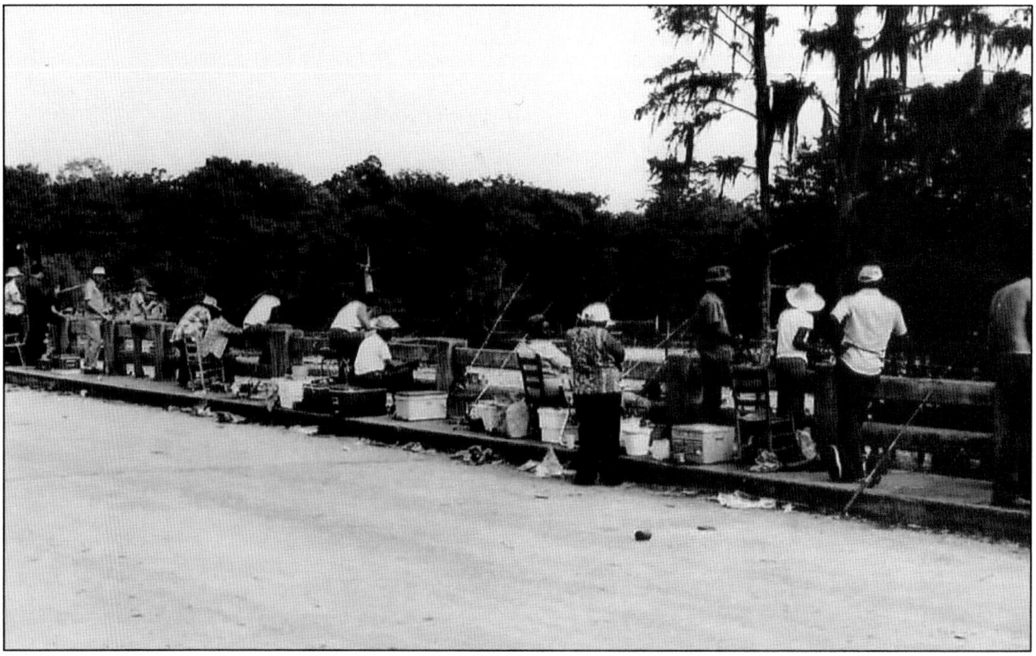

Roadside fishing was fishing fun, a chance to socialize, and a refreshing roadside stop from sunup to sundown atop the low-level spillway at Dead Lakes, Wewahitchka. The top catch is panfish and catfish, but bass and striped bass are taken occasionally. A few dozen others are present along the raceway below. The total is fascinating. The best thing about it is that they were catching fish. (AW.)

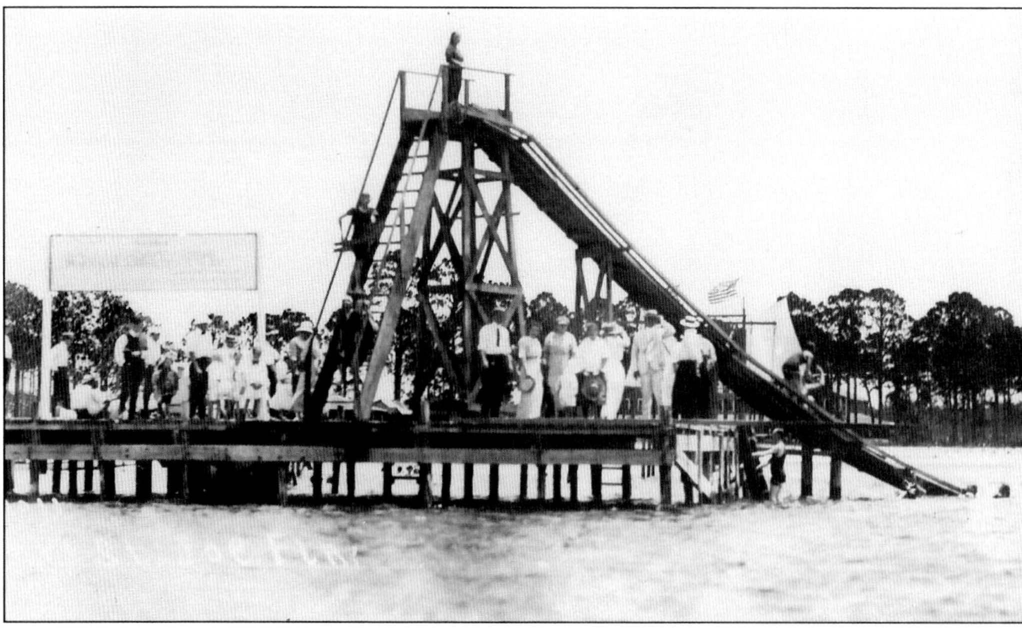

Waterslides and windmills are shown near the bathing pier at Port St. Joe in 1915. Mermaids and mermen disported themselves in the warm waters of St. Joseph's Bay at this time. This elaborate bathing pier was destroyed some years ago by a heavy storm. Notice the "cover-all" bathing suits on both the men and women. (BH.)

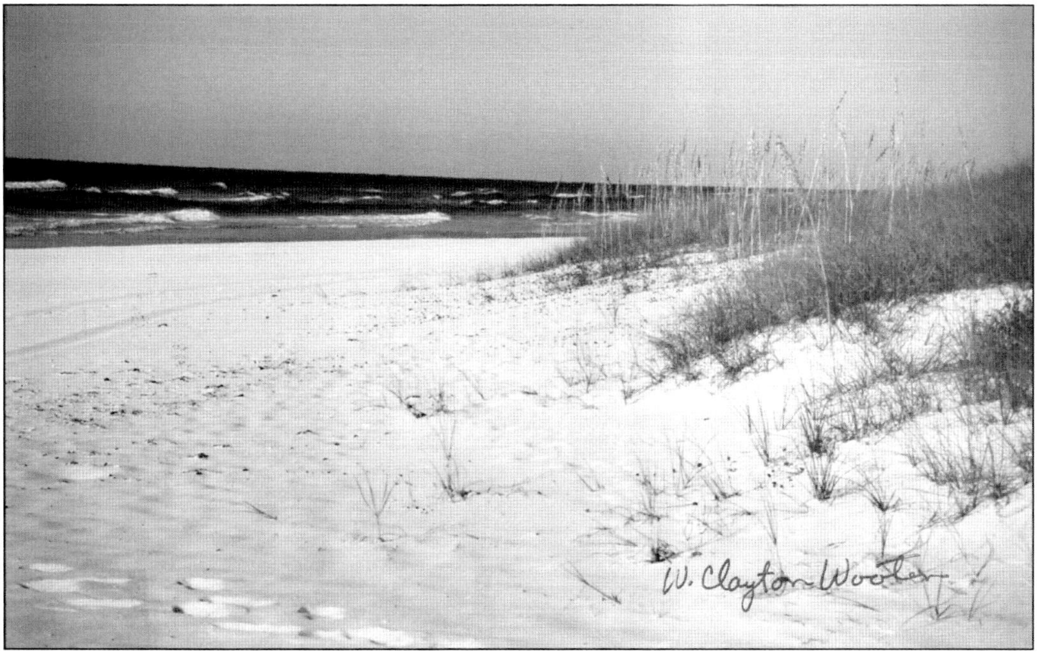

There may be whiter sands somewhere else, but none are more secluded or more serene than those of Gulf County. Protected by the St. Joseph Peninsula, which extends into the gulf like a barrier island, beaches here are some of the safest in the world. Gulf County beaches were also chosen as the No. 1 beaches in the continental United States by Dr. Stephen P. Leatherman, known as "Dr. Beach." (Gulf County Chamber of Commerce.)

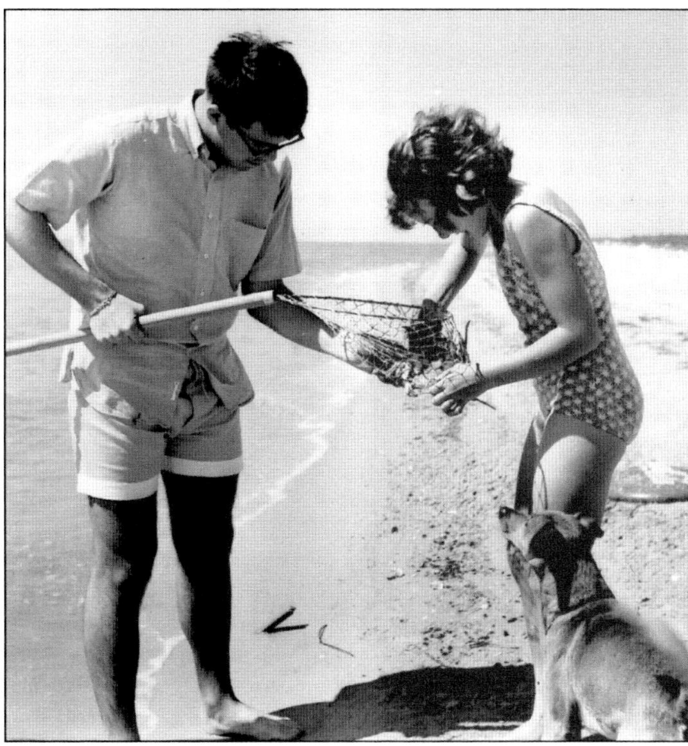

Beachgoers enjoy swimming nearly year-round. Walking and shelling, scalloping, and crabbing are enjoyed the most. Here you see that Ronnie Cox and Julie Allen with their dog Jip enjoying a little crabbing. (BH.)

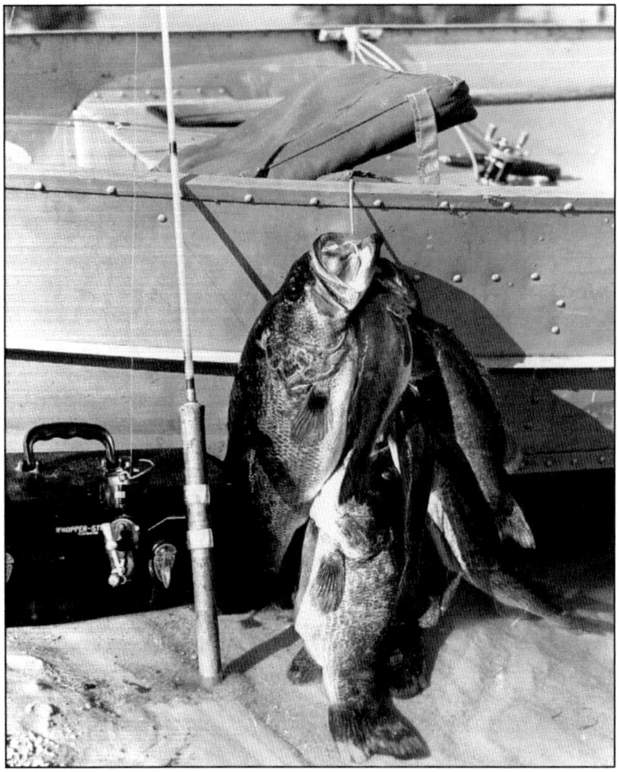

These black bass were caught here in Gulf County, whose numerous lakes and streams are teeming with finned beauties like these. Freshwater varieties include bream, shellcracker, speckled perch, catfish, mullet, and several varieties of bass. Some of the state's biggest largemouth bass are caught at Dead Lakes and in creeks and rivers throughout the area. Several fish camps are located along the banks of the rivers and Dead Lakes. (Gulf County Chamber of Commerce.)

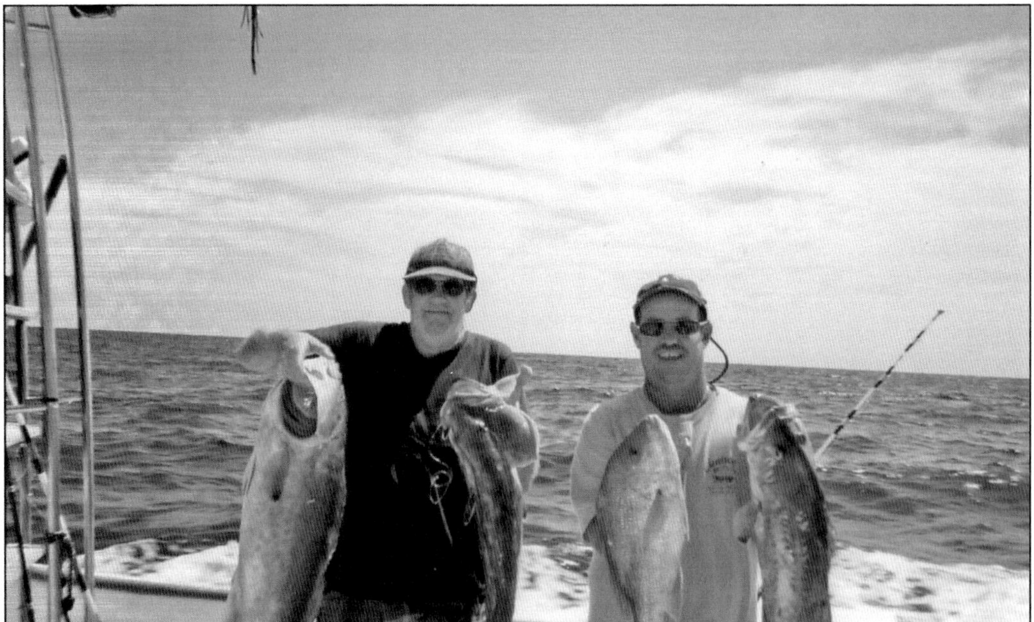

Try your luck at deep-sea trolling; there are charter boats leaving the Port St. Joe marina every day. Photographed are Ronnie Brake (left) holding a couple of nice grouper and Mark Moore holding a red snapper and a grouper. These beauties were caught off of Dog House Charters, owned and operated by Kenny and Karen Lemieux, and right out of the Gulf of Mexico. (BMD.)

Seven

Tigers, Sharks, and Gators

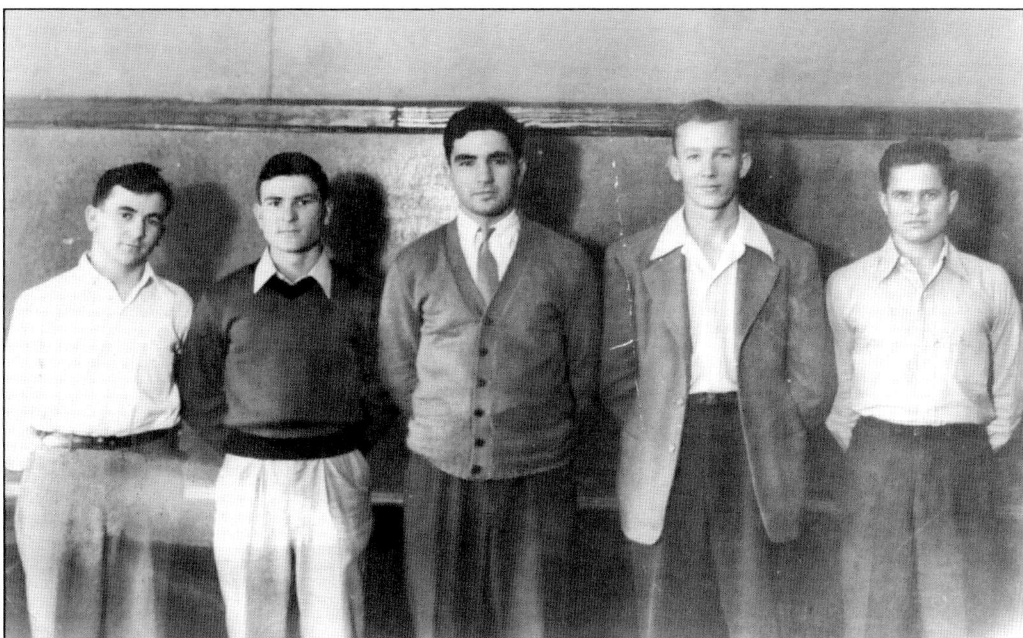

The 1945 Mens Key Club of Port St. Joe High School was, from left to right, Punk Stephens, Dooder Parker, Ralph Silva, Alfred Rhames, and G. W. Parrish. (PPL.)

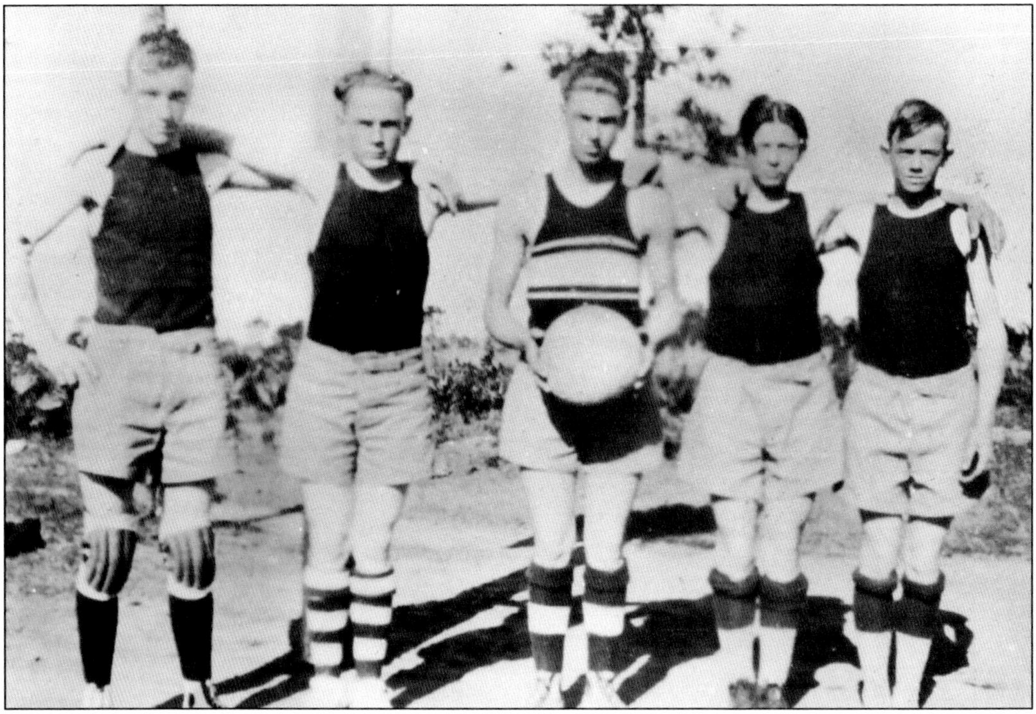

The Port St. Joe Sharks of 1926 were, from left to right, Jack Griffin, Jimmy Dean, Joe Aralti, Buster Owens, and John Dendy. (CM.)

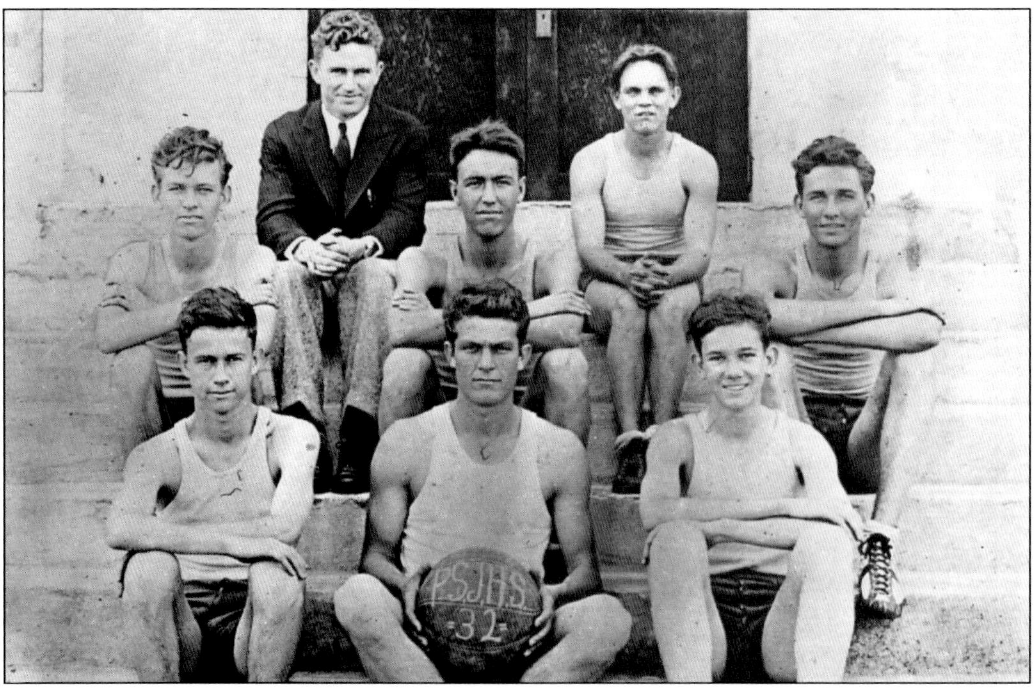

This photograph of the Port St. Joe Sharks basketball team was taken in March 1932. Seated here from left to right are (first row) Alton Dendy, Joe Ferrell, George Tapper; (second row) Harold Smith, Mayo Johnson, Jake Belin; (third row) coach J. Lewis Hall and Morty Mahon. (CM.)

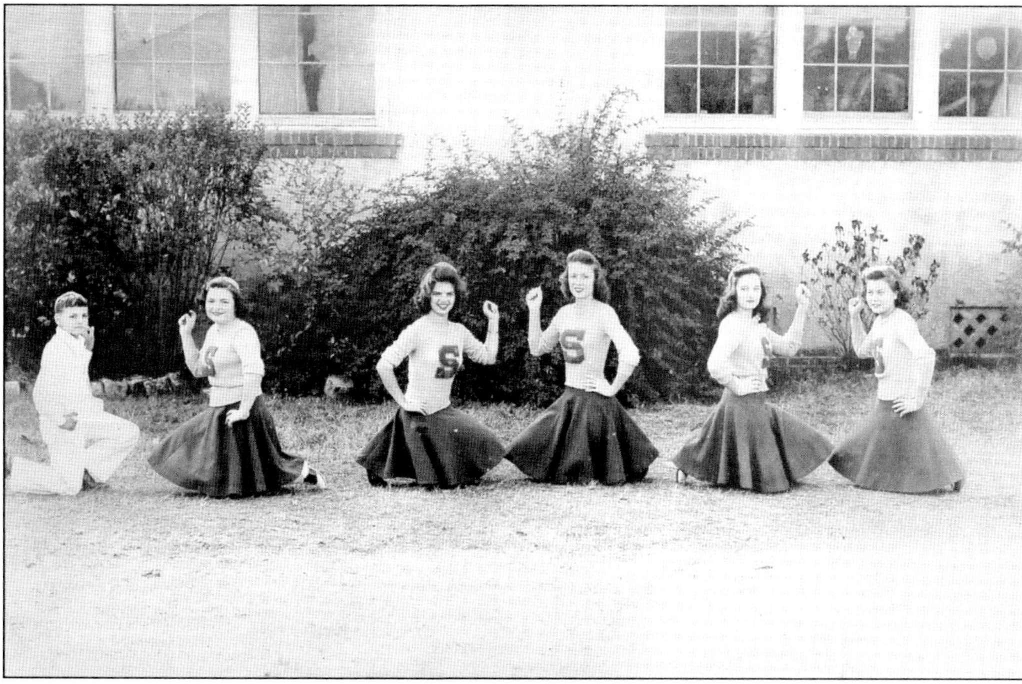

The Port St. Joe Sharks cheerleaders in the year 1946 were, from left to right, Bruce Parker, Gerry Parker, Mary Lidea Dees, Teresa Edwards, Hazel Burnett, and J. Edwards. (CM.)

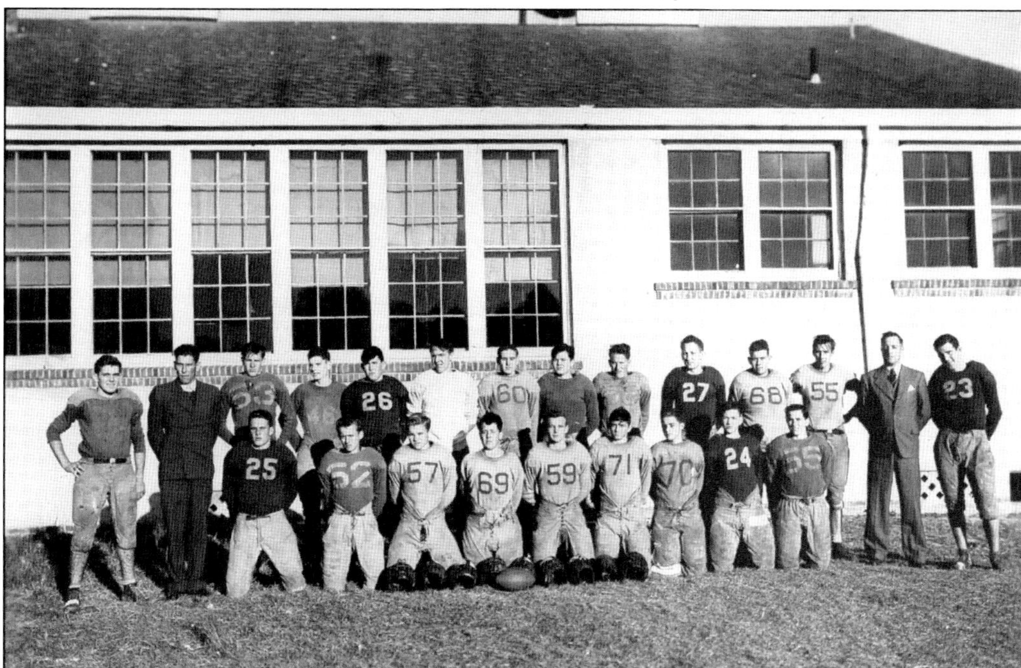

The Port St. Joe Sharks football team from around 1946, pictured, included Carl Guilford, Randall Brady, Billy Joe Jones, Grady Plair, Buster Owens, P. B. Fairley, Bill Traxler, Gale Traxler, W. A. Beggart (principal), J. D. Shealey, Jack Mahon, Chuck Gibson, Dan Coleman, Tommy Owens, Nowland Rawls, Will Ramsey, coach E. M. Bailey, Donald Linton, and Claude Cowart. (CM.)

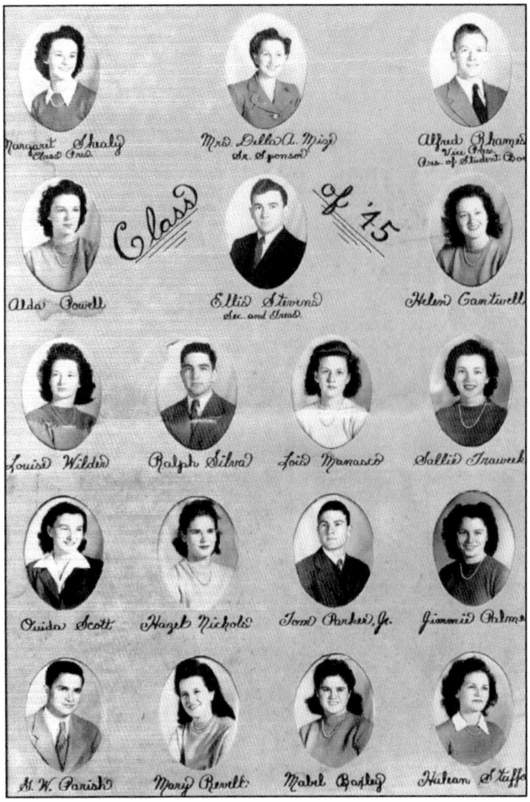

Donated by Mr. and Mrs. Tom Parker, this photograph of the Port St. Joe High School graduating class of 1945 is located in the history case in the Port St. Joe Library. (PPL.)

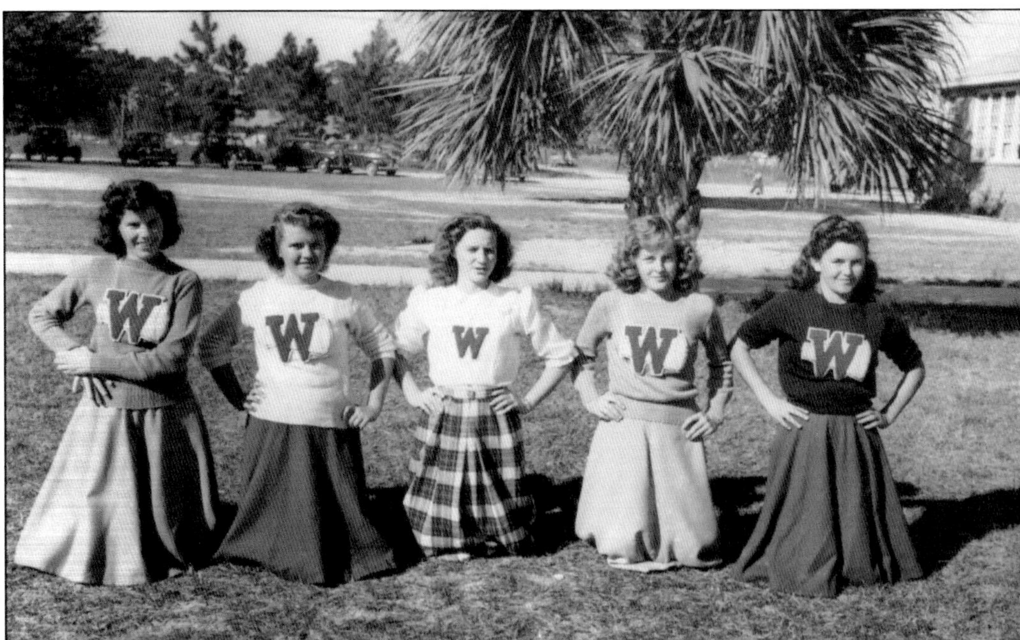

The Wewahitchka Gators junior and sophomore cheerleaders of 1948–1949 were, from left to right, Betty Ann Gaskin Owens, Betty Shirley Ganious, Joyce Daniels Strickland, Betty Ann Parramore, and Betty Dorsey Gaskin. (BBO.)

Graduation day at George Washington High School in May 1967 included, from left to right, Robert Wilson Sr., Lenora Peters Gant, Nathan Peters Jr., and Edwin Williams. Robert Wilson's wife, Lula, was the last principal at Washington High School, which closed in 1970. (NPJ.)

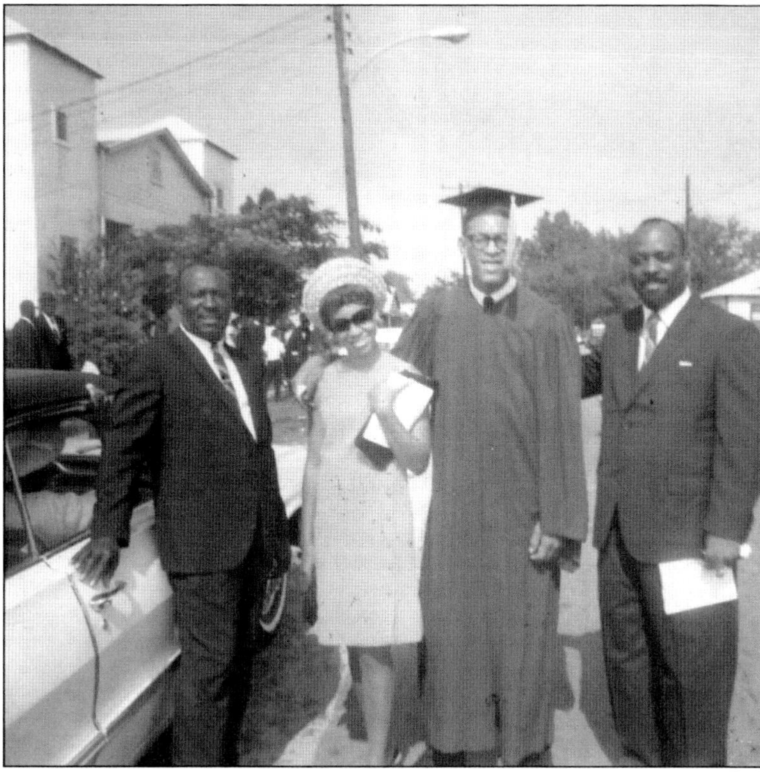

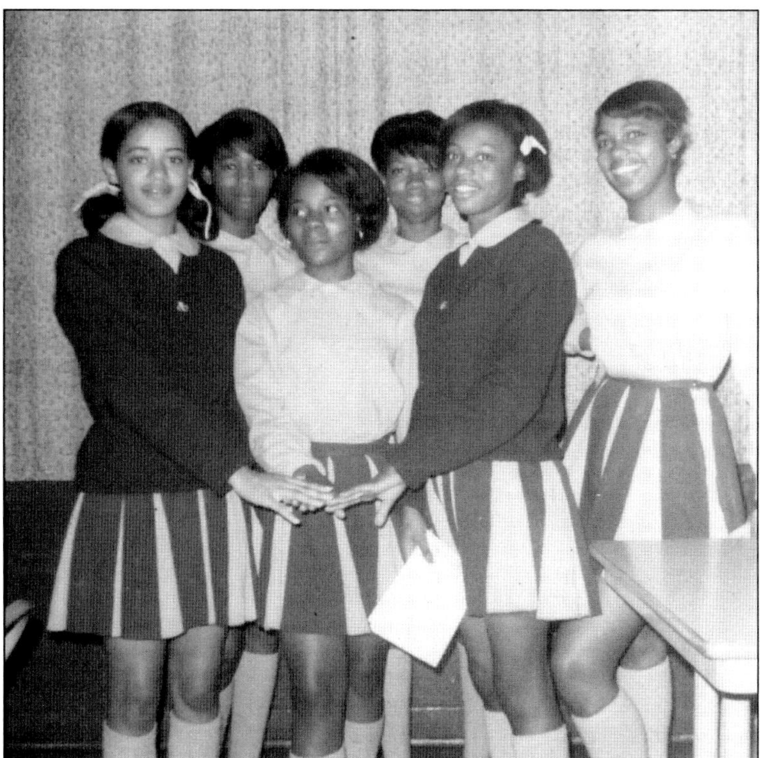

The Washington High School Tigers varsity cheerleaders are pictured in 1968–1969. From left to right are Joy Thompson, Delores Simmons, Debra Addison, Cherry Smith, Shirley Dawson, and Carolyn Dawson. (CM.)

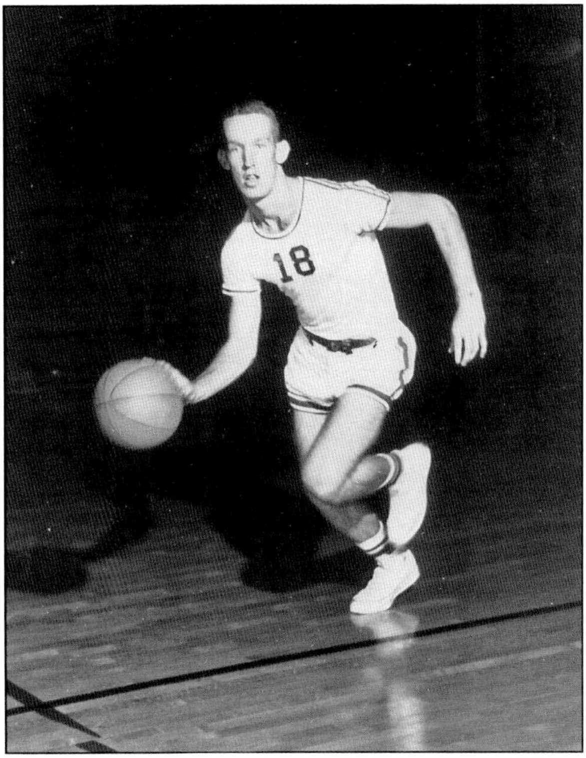

James Henry "Jimmy" Wilder was known to most as a sportsman of the river, woods, and the bay. He was also active in sports: he started very young playing Little League baseball, but what he loved best was playing basketball for the Sharks, which he did until graduation. He was a "good ole boy" and a friend to everyone he met. (PPL.)

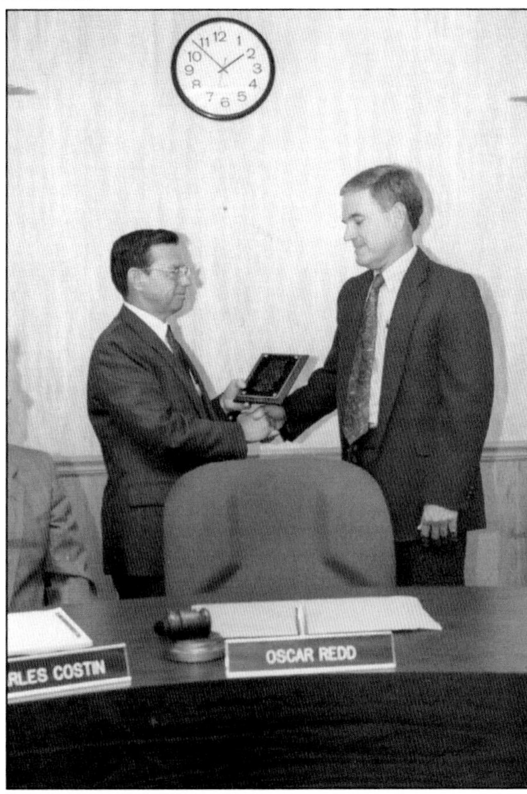

Former Gulf County School Board member Oscar Redd presents an award to Ted Whitfield for his services in the year 1994. Redd was with the school board until his death from cancer in 2005. The Wewahitchka Middle School's new wing was dedicated as the Oscar Redd Wing. (PSJHS.)

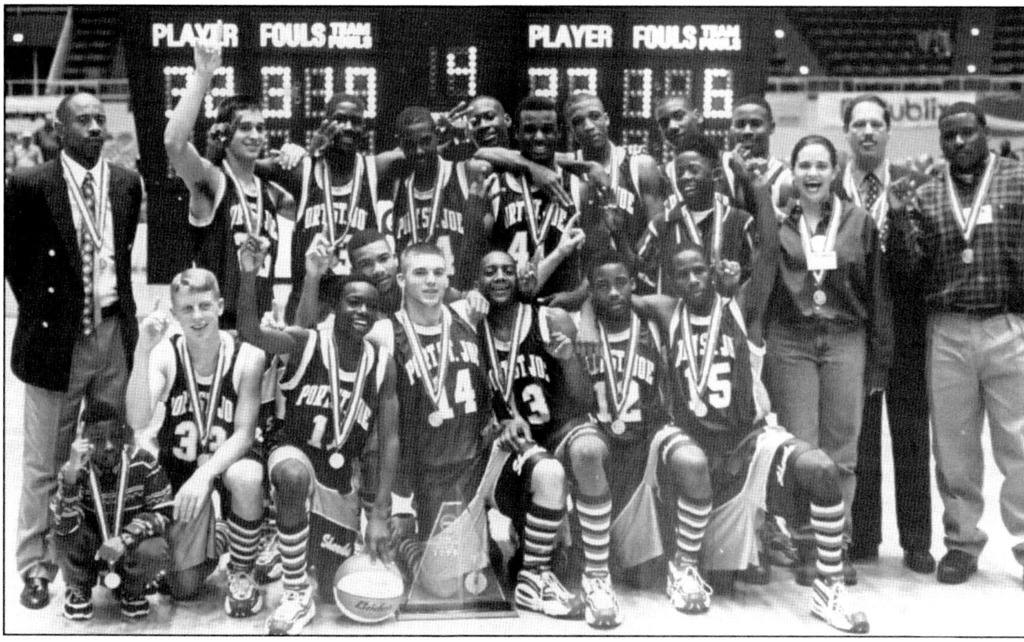

The Port St. Joe state championship basketball team of 1988 had a 29-3 season in the 3A Division. From left to right are (kneeling) Ahmad Skaggs, Clay Smallwood, Seneca Chambers, Lance Larry, Kyle Adkison, Rod Chambers, Mo Quinn, Keion McNair; (standing) coach Kenny Parker, Jeremy Dixon, Byron Bailey, Travis Jenkins, Tremaine Lewis, Tyson Pittman, James Daniels, Kedrick Larry, Darvis Chambers, Prince Jones, Jennifer Gaddis (videographer), head coach Vernon Eppinette, Jermaine Peterson (stats keeper). (PPL.)

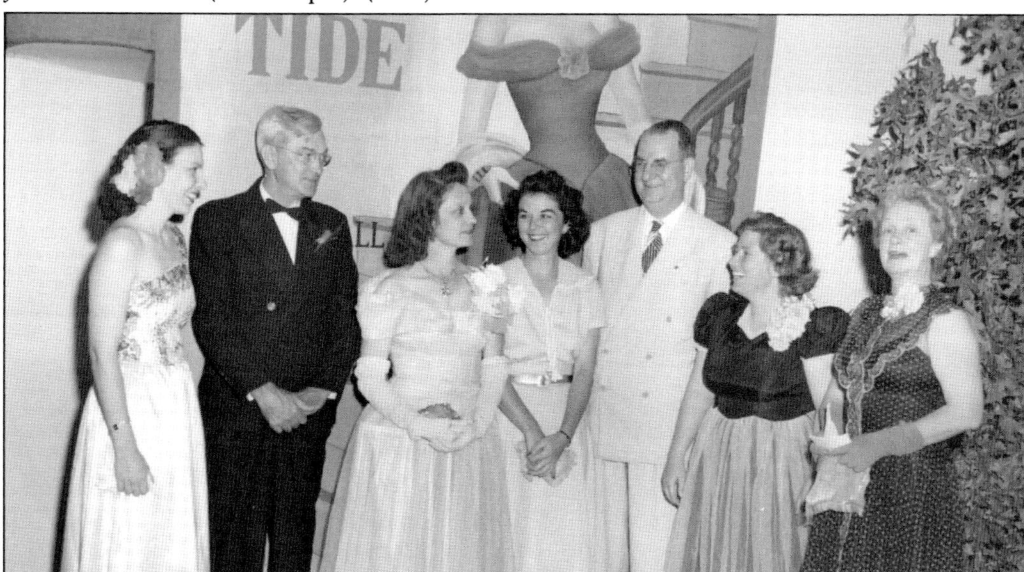

The theme of the 1947–1948 Port St. Joe High School prom was taken from *The Great Tide*, written by Mrs. Rubylea Hall, formerly of Jackson County, Florida. This book was a fiction story of how it was in Old St. Joseph before the fever. From left to right are Royce G. Dickens, Tom Alsobrook, Rubylea Hall, Karlene Owens, E. Clay Lewis Jr., Catherine Nix, and an unidentified teacher. (BBO.)

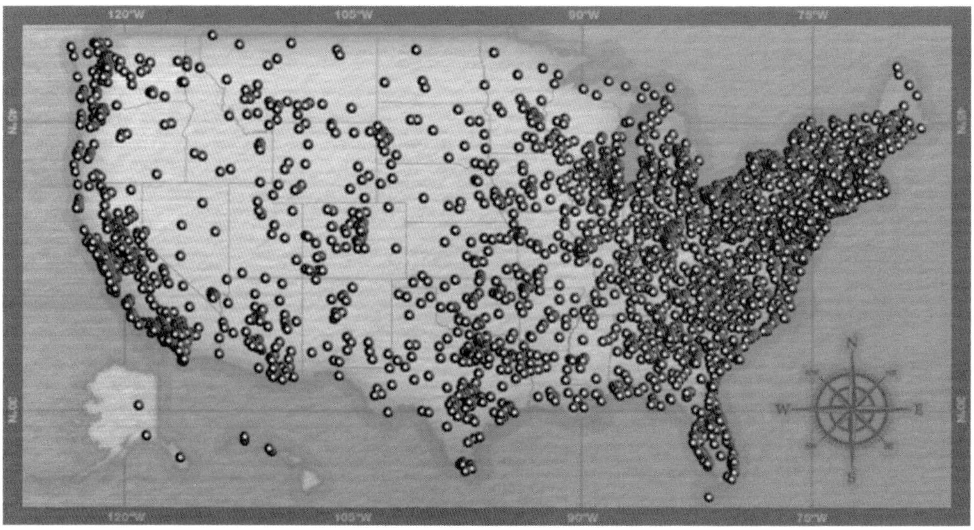